Vajolin

VAJOLIN

by MARIJAN
MEGLA Edited and
transposed
into ordinary
English by
REG SILVESTER

slipstream

an imprint of
The Books Collective
214 - 21 10405 Jasper Ave.,
Edmonton, Alberta, Canada T5J 3S2

Vajolin (Violin)

A Slipstream book
from River Books, an imprint of the Books Collective

River Books and the Books Collective acknowledge the support of the Canada Council for the Arts for our publishing programme.

Editor for the press: Candas Jane Dorsey Outside editor: Reg Silvester Front cover photograph copyright ©1990, 1998 by Evergon.
Cover design by Gerry Dotto.

Inside design and page set-up by Jason Bartlett. Printed at Houghton Boston, Saskatoon, on 50lb. Offset White with covers of Cornwall Cover.

Published in Canada by Slipstream (River) Books, an imprint of the Books Collective, 214-21, 10405 Jasper Avenue, Edmonton, Alberta, Canada T5J 3S2. Telephone (403) 448 0590.

2 4 6 8 10 9 7 5 3 1

Canadian Cataloguing in Publication Data

Megla, Marijan
  Vajolin (Violin)

  ISBN 1-895836-60-3

  I. Silvester, Reg, 1945- II. Title. III. Title: Violin.
PS8576.E34V34 1998   C813'.54   C98-911119-9
PR9199.3.M4285V34 1998

Vajolin

Shi kam in auer femili samtaim after Vorld Vor II. De old gipsi Janoshi Bachi left her van dei ven hi kud not pei for a pcr of nju butc det mai grenfader vos meking for him. Shi vos put an de master bedrum closet, goining der tu meni preshes dokjuments of auer femili histori and de big aples vich ver stored der for de vinter and promtli fergoten. In auer femili noubadi vas a musishen, so she vas never jused. Onli I visited her from taim tu taim, fascineted bai her smuth and fregail bodi.

Ven mai grenfader dai sun after det, de hol femili gedered to divaid ap his belongings. Shi vos olmost solt bek tu Janoshi Bachi den, bat mai fader menacht, vit a lat of lak and bai surending sam of properti, to bring her as hom for mi.

Old Janoshi Bachi vas a lital anhepi vit de autkom, bat hi akceptet dis dil. Not van of his kidc vanted tu lern tu plei de vajolin enihau. Vot mor cud a pur Nord-Croeshian gipsi vish for, den det his

---

She came into our family sometime after World War II. The old gypsy Janoshi Bachi left her one day when he could not pay for a pair of new boots that my grandfather was making for him. She was put in the master bedroom closet, joining there the many precious documents of our family history and the big apples which were stored there for the winter and promptly forgotten. In our family nobody was a musician, so she was never used. Only I visited her from time to time, fascinated by her smooth and fragile body.

When my grandfather died soon after that, the whole family gathered to divide up his belongings. She was almost sold back to Janoshi Bachi then, but my father managed, with a lot of luck and by surrendering some property, to bring her home for me.

Old Janoshi Bachi was a little unhappy with the outcome, but he accepted this deal. Not one of his kids wanted to learn to play the violin anyhow. What more could a poor North-Croatian gypsy wish for than that his

---

belaved vajolin have a kvaet, sekjur hom. Chens det shi, hu hed fed him and his famili for so meni jears, vold sorvaiv anader haf a senchuri, vere biger if I on her

Meni taims after det, venever hi cam tu taun, hi steyed et as ples. Pleing for as and old grenmader on vajolin vich vas stil part of his laif. A risen tu vok de ten mails betvin his taun and auers, no meter vat de veter vos laik.

In thos deis, televishen and redio praktikali dident egsist and vi vere gled ven ever hi kam. Samtaim vi denc vit auer grenmader in de kichen, samtaims vi vold lisen tu Janoshi Bachi storis ebaut his vajolin. I am teling ju, hi vas a gud stori teler! And mjusik det hi meid for as vos so bjutifol, no meter veder hi pleed a sed romens or a faeri chardash. I vos tu meni koncert sainc den, ver vajolinist performed hu vere mach mor haili regardet in de musikal vord den pur Janoshi Bachi. Bat, I hev never siing enibadi pleing de vajolin vit as mach filing for de instrument and de mjusik as him.

Van dei hi tol as hau his fader hed entrastet him vit de vajolin. It vos an fogi moning, gast befor de gandarms tuk

beloved violin had a quiet, secure home? The chance that she, who had fed him and his family for so many years, would survive another half century, were greater if I owned her.

Many times after that, whenever he came to town, he stayed at our place. He played for us and old Grandmother on the violin which was still part of his life. It was a reason to walk the ten miles between his town and ours, no matter what the weather was like.

In those days, television and radio practically didn't exist and we were glad whenever he came. Sometimes we danced with our grandmother in the kitchen, and sometimes we would listen to Janoshi Bachi's stories about his violin. I am telling you, he was a good story-teller! And the music that he made for us was so beautiful, no matter whether he played a sad romance or a fiery chardash. I've been to many concerts since then, where violinists performed who were much more highly regarded in the musical world than poor Janoshi Bachi. But, I have never seen anybody play the violin with as much feeling for the instrument and the music as him.

One day he told us how his father had entrusted him with the violin. It was on a foggy morning, just before the gendarmes took him evei to Nochkaniza prisen. Des het hepen a long taim ego, ven him self vos gast a lital boj. His fader vos not van of de best musishens. Most of his short laif hi hed spendet gembling and faiting. In van of dos faits, hi hed kiled de Hangerian gandarm Istvan, hu hed chitet him at cards.

"Disciplin mast bi," Janoshi seed tu as kidc der vere gedert eraund him. "Nau vat vold de world came tu if evri drank, shebi gipsi hu vos chitet bai his magesti's gandarms desaidet tu kil de bladi chiters. Laik his blesed badi vere chiken for sandei paprikash. A gipsi is boren tu plei de vajolin, and shud stei der, on de podium, meking aders hepi."

His fader never retrnet hom, and noubodi eksplened tu his mader vot had hepen tu him. Janoshi lrn tu plei mjusik. Lonlinis and an emti stomak vere a gud and fast ticher. In de seim jer hi vos olredi invaited tu pley at taun vedings, vich dident bring him eny moni, bat a fol stomak for a dei or tu. Hi kud bring kichen skrab for his hangri femili of faiv broders and sisters, helping so his aging mader.

Pleing de vajolin vas de onli gop Janoshi ever hev. A taun

---

him away to Nochkaniza prison. This had happened a long time ago, when he himself was just a little boy. His father was not one of the best musicians. Most of his short life he spent gambling and fighting. In one of those fights, he'd killed the Hungarian gendarme Istvan, who had cheated him at cards.

"Discipline must be," Janoshi said to us kids that were gathered around him. "Now what would the world come to if every drunk, shabby gypsy who was cheated by His Majesty's gendarmes decided to kill the bloody cheaters. Like his body were chicken for Sunday paprikash. A gypsy is born to play the violin, and should stay there, on the podium, making others happy."

His father never returned home, and nobody explained to his mother what had happened to him. Janoshi learned to play music. Loneliness and an empty stomach were good and fast teachers. In the same year he was already invited to play at town weddings, which didn't bring him any money, but a full stomach for a day or two. He could take kitchen scraps to his hungry family of five brothers and sisters, that way helping his ageing mother.

Playing the violin was the only job Janoshi ever had. A town veding, an ivning in a citi bar, a Guish fest provaidet him vit de incom tu bring de femili truaut de winter. Erlau him tu soplai de pur nesesiti of deli laif. For sek of mjusik and sorvaivel, dei shrt vos vosht, drti anderver chenched, de hors klinet. Iven de butc vos brod tu shain vit speshel krim, an inkredibel laksheri in his haus. Bad, vans de mjusik started, most of dos pur gipsis sols did not nidet eni cocsing or pushing tu kip pleing. Dei vajolins onli staped ven de bajologikal nids of a hjumen biing overcam de musishen. Samtaims dei gast kolepset for an auer or so in a dip slip besaid de teibel, in mits of drank gest, dei tuket vel evri melodi det dei plei.

Ven Janoshi vos in veri gud mud, hi tol as ebaut his grenpa. "Hi vos a rili musishen! Ju no, kidc, evribadi hir is meid from flesh and blad. Bat, I tenk mai grenpa had van mor konponent ... mjusik."

Hi hed bin van of de best plejers in dos deis in auer distrikt. Hi vos kolt tu plei ven auer graf vas heving a big denc on de dei hi bajet auer distrikt, and citadel. Ol respektfol pipel of auer lital siti and de rich farmers of de

wedding, an evening in a city bar, a Jewish feast provided him with the income to bring the family through the winter. It allowed him to supply the poor necessities for daily life. For the sake of music and survival their shirts were washed, dirty underwear changed, the horse cleaned. Even their boots were brought to shine with a special cream, an incredible luxury in his house. But once the music started, most of those poor gypsy souls did not need any coaxing or pushing to keep playing. Their violins only stopped when the biological needs of a human being overcame the musicians. Sometimes they just collapsed for an hour or so in a deep sleep beside the table, in the midst of the drunken guests who'd enjoyed every melody that they played.

When Janoshi was in a very good mood, he told us about his grandpa. "He was a real musician! You know kids, everybody here is made of flesh and blood. But I think my grandpa had one more component ... music."

He had been one of the best players in those days in our district. He was called to play when our Graf was having a big dance on the day he bought our district and citadel. All the respectful people of our little city and the rich farmers of the erias had gedert tu vish him vel. Dei ol hopt for les taksis and a lital mor grein in as grein bins tu fid dei hangri femilis.

"Boj, det vas a denc!" old Janoshi vos rekoling. "Grenpa told mi evribadi vos terebal drank. And de vumen ... ha ha ha ... dei vere gast going kresi, dencing so fest det ju cold si de sveti long anderver ander de long skirts for special okeshens. Iven auer Pater Sigmund, de hed of auer chrch, vas drank, tugeder vit a hol dasent of his monks. Tei vere tising old and jang fimels, gast laik de bed bois at de taun vel joked vit de fat vasher vumen. Noubadi nju et det taim det veri sun de mjusik vold bi not so hepi eni mor. Not onli vold de gipsi bi caled tu help celebretet meriges, shauers, namen deis and partis. Sun dei ver askt tu plei at simenteris, tu moren de jang bois hu had lost der laivs faiting egens de Hangerian gandarms.

"Laif vos hard at de begining of senchuri. Drinking and mjusik vere an isi eskep, med as ferget as trobels. Pipel ver living auers sitis and tauns in hop of fiding a beter laif in de big sitis ol ekros de glob. Most of dem endet ap in slams and living a vorser laif den befor.

ⓔⓔⓔⓔⓔⓔⓔⓔⓔⓔⓔⓔⓔⓔⓔⓔⓔⓔⓔⓔⓔⓔⓔⓔⓔⓔⓔⓔⓔⓔⓔⓔⓔⓔ

area had gathered to wish him well. They all hoped for less taxes and a little more grain in our grain bins to feed their hungry families.

"Boy, that was a dance!" old Janoshi recalled. "Grandpa told me everybody was terribly drunk. And the women ... ha ha ha ... they were just going crazy, dancing so fast you could see their sweaty long underwear under their long skirts for special occasions. Even our Pater Sigmund, the head of our church, was drunk, together with a dozen of his monks. They were teasing old and young females, just like the bad boys at the town well joked with the fat washer women. Nobody knew at the time that very soon the music would not be so happy any more. Not only would the gypsies by called to help celebrate marriages, showers, naming days and parties. Soon they were asked to play at cemeteries, to mourn the young boys who had lost their lives fighting against the Hungarian police.

"Life was hard at the beginning of the century. Drinking and music were an easy escape, that made us forget our troubles. People were leaving our cities and towns in hope of finding a better life in the big cities all across the globe. Most of them ended up in slums and living a worse life that before.

ⓞⓞⓞⓞⓞⓞⓞⓞⓞⓞⓞⓞⓞⓞⓞⓞⓞⓞⓞⓞⓞⓞⓞⓞⓞⓞⓞⓞⓞⓞⓞⓞ

"Ven ju a living an open fletnis of de pleins betvin de Drava and Mura, soraundet bai Hangari, Austria, de slavik cantris, de Trks ... pis vos preshes, bad rerli kept," old Janoshi reminised, voching mai old grenmader egriing an evriting vot hi gast seied. "Sam of dos bed-tempered gost vere olveis on de muv and pipel kot betvin ver hrt. It vos normal, in de laif of evri generation, det suner or leter sam of der faders and san vold bi lodet intu treins tu fid de ever hangri batel fronts akros de Evrop. And vi vantet pis so bedli!" hi rekoled. Hi diden ekspekt as kidc ever tu andestand de hol mining of his vords.

Hi kontinju his stori. "Ven de foli-lodet treins vit deir preshes cargo sloli disapired in de grin fletnis, der vas nating beter den de mjusik of gipsis tu chir ap ol dos maders, fiances and jang vidos. Siing dei lav vanc most probebli for letc taim, dei ver nau tu liv an dei on. Fesing hevi vork in de filds and ansev fektoris. Meni kidc vere stil boren long taim after det dei fader vos oredi kilet an de front for koses det dei never andestud."

~~~~~~

"When you are living in the open flatness of the plains between the Drava and Mura, surrounded by Hungary, Austria, the Slavic countries, the Turks ... peace was precious but rarely kept," old Janoshi reminisced, watching my old grandmother agreeing with everything that he had just said. "Some of those bad-tempered ghosts were always on the move and people caught in between were hurt. It was normal, in the life of every generation, that sooner or later some of their fathers and sons would be loaded onto trains to feed the ever-hungry battle fronts across Europe. And we wanted peace so badly!" he recalled. He didn't expect us kids ever to understand the whole meaning of his words.

He continued his story. "When the fully-loaded trains with their precious cargo slowly disappeared in the green flatness, there was nothing better than the music of gypsies to cheer up all those mothers, fiancés and young widows. Seeing their loved ones most probably for the last time, they were now to live on their own, facing heavy work in the fields and unsafe factories. Many kids were still born a long time after their fathers were already killed on the front for causes that they never understood."

~~~~~~

Marijan Megla

Ven de vor eskaletet and leters from de front, iven dos blek vit censur, diden rich hom eni mor, it vos taim for de sed romanccs tu bi plejed. Tu remember de gud old taims, iven if dei had never rili egsisted. Tu plak kerich aut of de strings and fregail bodi of de vajolin for a fjucher det in dos deis did not luk promising et ol.

"At de end of de vor, de vajolin vas de frst tu grit de homkaming gais ... cripelt, broken, taerd of laif. Dei vos hangri, fol of lais. Luking for dei vaivs, grls, sketered femilis. Meni had chenched in dos long jers of absenc. Curich vos nidet for a nju start, tu ferget frends slotered at de front, tu plei daun de broken merich. Fridem bels ... dei ar ebel to bring de bois hom, bat dei dont end de tragedis of vor. In dos frst naits of pis, de soft mjusik of vajolin cold restor mor harmoni den eni vel intendent vords.

"So vi plejed for dem ol. For strenger, for auer foks, for as, for solgers hu hes van or los de vor. Vi never asked for vot kos dei fait. And vaij shud vi? In dos deis, it cud cost ju jor laif, and no vor vas vort det mach. Ju nou, I samtaims

When the war escalated and letters from the front, even those black with censorship, didn't reach home any more, it was time for the sad romances to be played. To remember the good old times, even if they had never really existed. To pluck courage out of the strings and fragile body of the violin for a future that in those days did not look promising at all.

"At the end of the war, the violin was the first to greet the guys coming home ... crippled, broken, tired of life. They were hungry, full of lice. Looking for their wives, girls, scattered families. Many had changed in those long years of absence. Courage was needed for a new start, to forget friends slaughtered at the front, to play down the broken marriage. Freedom bells ... they are able to bring the boys home, but they don't end the tragedies of war. In those first nights of peace, the soft music of the violin could restore more harmony than any well-intended words.

"So we played for them all. For strangers, for our folks, for us, for soldiers who had won or lost the war. We never asked for what cause they'd fought. And why should we? In those days it could cost you your life, and no war was worth that much. You know I sometimes vander hau I and det vajolin cud hev sorvaived ol dos cresi deis. In auer femili, vi lost tri ... in jors tu in van sandei boming. De simenteri ar fol of pipel det vos inosent baistender. Meibi gast a lital tu slo tu agast tu nju rulers and dei samtaim chenchet in a singel dei.

"Wen de last of de vors endet — mej de lord bles de pis — vi ver pleing in de siti, ver auer laiberi is tudei. It vos der det I soet jor ded for de frst taim dencing vit jor mader.

"Ha ha ha. Boi vos hi ever fani! Hmmm ... hi diden denc veri vel, so ven I started a fest chardash, hi olmos lost his fit traing tu muv as fest as de aders. I vas lafing so hard det I hed tu let de orkestra pleing alon for a moment or tu. After det, hi kam tu mi and giv mi a 50 dinar braib. 'Ju shud never plei a fest chardash ven I danc,' hi plidet. De jer after det jor grended cam tu mai pur shek and seid tu mi: 'I nid ju for de merig of mai san. Tek onli jor best musishen.' Sou, for de frst denc of de braid and grum, I started a slo valc, bat on mai comend vi chenget tu a fest chardash. Ha ha ha. Fergiv mi lord! I am spiking of de ded ... God kip him hepi!

⊚⊚⊚⊚⊚⊚⊚⊚⊚⊚⊚⊚⊚⊚⊚⊚⊚⊚⊚⊚⊚⊚⊚⊚⊚⊚⊚⊚⊚⊚⊚⊚⊚⊚⊚⊚⊚

wonder how I and that violin could have survived all those crazy days. In our family we lost three ... in yours, two, in one Sunday bombing. The cemeteries are full of people who were innocent bystanders. Maybe just a little too slow to adjust to new rulers, and they sometimes changed in a single day.

"When the last of the wars ended — may the Lord bless the peace — we were playing in the city, where our library is today. It was there that I saw your dad for the first time dancing with your mother.

"Ha ha. Boy, was he ever funny! Hmmm ... he didn't dance very well, so when I started a fast chardash, he almost lost his feet trying to move as fast as the others. I was laughing so hard that I had to let the orchestra play alone for a moment or two. After that, he came to me and gave me a 50-dinar bribe. 'You should never play a fast chardash when I dance,' he pleaded. The year after that your granddad came to my poor shack and said to me: 'I need you for the marriage of my son. Take only your best musicians.' So, for the first dance of the bride and groom, I started a slow waltz, but on my command we changed to a fast chardash. Ha ha ha. Forgive me Lord! I am speaking of the dead ... God keep him happy!

⊚⊚⊚⊚⊚⊚⊚⊚⊚⊚⊚⊚⊚⊚⊚⊚⊚⊚⊚⊚⊚⊚⊚⊚⊚⊚⊚⊚⊚⊚⊚⊚⊚⊚⊚⊚⊚

Marijan Megla

"It vos so fani det evribadi in de danc hal vas lafing. Jor mam lost her veil becos jor ded step on it. Dont ask mi hau and vai. Ven de frst shu vos plaung truaut de er, vi staped emidietli. Vot kaind of gipsi vold I bi if I alau mai musishen tu kil de braid and grum vit mai mjusik! Ven de hepi gest sloli rekaveret from des bladi gok and I vidniset de frst famili clesh, jor ded vas redi tu kil mi. It tuk tri gais tu cul him daun. If jor fet oncel Emilko — lord bles his hjuch stamak and strong arms! — vos not an mai sait, I vos shor I vud bi choped ap tugeder vit de oniens tu mek a gipsi gulash. And hu nous, des vajolin meit never hev bin jors."

I vos onli seven jers old ven mai fader daid and I never nju mach ebaud him. Laik evri lital boi, I vas hepi tu diskavere samting aut of de laif of mai fader, spesheli if det vos samting I hed never ekspektet. Det hi diden no tu denc chardash vas rili a sopreis for mi. Det nait, ven old Janoshi had gon hom and evribodi in de haus vos saund a slip, I tuk a vajolin from de cabbord intu mai bed.

Shi vos old, and benit her tin smud skin meni scars told

"It was so funny that everybody in the dance hall was laughing. Your mom lost her veil because your dad stepped on it. Don't ask me how and why. When the first shoe was plowing through the air, we stopped immediately. What kind of gypsy would I be if I allowed my musicians to kill the bride and groom with my music! When the happy guests slowly recovered from this bloody joke and I witnessed the first family clash, your dad was ready to kill me. It took three guys to cool him down. If your fat Uncle Emilko — Lord bless his huge stomach and strong arms! — was not on my side, I was sure I would be chopped up together with the onions to make a gypsy goulash. And who knows, this violin might not have been yours."

I was only seven years old when my father died and I never knew much about him. Like every little boy, I was happy to discover something out of the life of my father, especially if it was something I had never expected. That he didn't know how to dance the chardash was really a surprise for me. That night, when old Janoshi had gone home and everybody in the house was sound asleep, I took the violin from the cupboard into my bed.

She was old, and beneath her thin smooth skin many scars told of raf naits in bars. Tu meni taim, glasis vere tron and chers vere nidet tu presju drinking braders tu end der fait. I tached her strings and emegin mai ded dencing de fani chardash. Shi smeled laik a open faer in pur gipsi homs, smoki bars, iven a tres of shafran from sam jidish fest. Shi vos vorm, laik de meni monings det shi hed grited vit her magik mjusik. Shi luked so sed as romanc det shi samtaims plejed, vich med mi crai ven I lisened. Vi toked, mi and mai vajolin, dip in de nait. Abaut laif hepenis, mai fader det I so miset. Shi vos laik an old mader hu nju tu kol daun her kidc, iven den if shi dont no de rait encer an ol dei problems.

I vas in mai tins ven, let van ivning in de spring, faiv sed gipsis shod ab in auer dark dorvei. Dei brodet reder sed njus, det old Janoshi Bachi vos redi tu giv his sol tu as gud lord. "I bi sun der," I sed, puting on mai clos and peking de vajolin for de long trip tu de pur litel vileg of de gipsis. An old bed in a rum filed vit pipel I diden not nou, old Janoshi Bachi vos geting redi tu his gernei tu heven. Ven I put de vajolin on his chest and plesed his olmost blad los hends

---

of rough nights in bars. Too many times glasses were thrown and chairs were needed to persuade drinking brothers to end their fights. I touched her strings and imagined my dad dancing the funny chardash. She smelled like an open fire in poor gypsy homes, smoky bars, even a trace of saffron from some Yiddish feast. She was warm, like the many mornings that she had greeted with her magic music. She looked as sad as the romances that she sometimes played, which made me cry when I listened. We talked, me and my violin, deep into the night. About life's happiness, and my father that I so missed. She was like an old mother who knew how to cool down her kids, even if she didn't know the right answers to all their problems.

I was in my teens when, late one evening in spring, five sad gypsies showed up in our dark doorway. They brought rather sad news, that old Janoshi Bachi was ready to give his soul to our good Lord. "I'll soon be there," I said, putting on my clothes and packing the violin for the long trip to the poor little village of gypsies. On an old bed in a room filled with people I didn't know, old Janoshi Bachi was getting ready for his journey to heaven. When I put the violin on his chest and placed his almost bloodless hands

eraund her, tirs roled from his ais. His old vaif on her nis besaid his bed vas draing her ais as shi seid tu mi:

"Sr, I dont hev cniting tu giv ju for meking mai Janoshi so hepi, bat if jou ar ever in auer taun, ju ar volkom at eni taim. Ju ar nau van of as."

Let des nait, ven a big mun vas kising de rufs of de shebi hauses of Janoshi's taun, I left de moning femili alon. De men det hed brot mi and mai vajolin tugeder hed daid. Deis leter at his grev in de gipsi simenteri, his vajolin vos plejed for frst taim bai sambadi als.

Old Janoshi Bachi's det brot a mor kvaet laif tu mai vajolin. Shi spendet most of her taim invisebel on top of mai old cab bord. Ven I vos ebaut tu go merit, I introdjus her tu mai vaif and her larg femili, bat bekos noubadi cold plei de vajolin, interest in her vos short-liv.

I tuk her evei, far from hom, tu a streng cantri in de Nort vest of Evropa, ver I faund a gop. I hop old Janoshi Bachi vud fergiv mi for des. Shi engoet her nju hom, iven raf hendeling of mai bebi san. Shi lostet sam of hr smel of de open faer, and de

---

around her, tears rolled from his eyes. His old wife on her knees beside his bed was drying her eyes as she said to me:

"Sir, I don't have anything to give you for making my Janoshi so happy, but if you are ever in our town, you are welcome at any time. You are now one of us."

Late that night, when a big moon was kissing the roofs of the shabby houses of Janoshi's town, I left the mourning family alone. The man who had brought me and my violin together had died. Days later at his grave in the gypsy cemetery, his violin was played for the first time by somebody else.

Old Janoshi Bachi's death brought a quieter life to my violin. She spent most of her time invisible on top of my old cupboard. When I was about to get married, I introduced her to my wife and her large family, but because nobody could play the violin, interest in her was short-lived.

I took her away, far from home, to a strange country in the northwest of Europe, where I found a job. I hoped old Janoshi would forgive me for this. She enjoyed her new home, even the rough handling of my baby son. She lost some of her smell of the open fire and the

bed bret of smoki bars, bad shi remein olveis nating bad a gipsi vajolin. I laiked ven sambadi stabernli insist an his origens. Ol as laif, laiket or not, vi ar olveis luking bek an auer origens, hendeling diferent situeshen in laif onli in de vei non tu as.

After krosing de Atlantik vit as shi vos lost for a auer or so, living mi alon vit de eroport clerk hu cud andersten vaj an erd dis vajolin vos so speshel tu mi.

"Sr, if shi isent a Stradivari, auer inshuranc for shor vold mek no trobel at ol, pej ju des handert-sam dolars for jor vajolin."

"Shi is not a Stradivari, shi never bi Stradivari! Shi is a plein vajolin of pur Nord-Kroeshen gipsi Janoshi Bachi, vich dai long taim ego! His sol bi nau hanting mi for rest of mai laif if I dont faind his vajolin. Andesten!??"

His vaid open ais ver shoing mi det hi diden hev a clu vot I vos toking ebaut. Vai in hevens neim I vas going cresi laik det. It vos gast a chip vajolin. Hi diden noet if dei kavered dos demet gipsi gost, vich refjus tu dai and liv mi in pis.

After vail, ven mai pur transletor end de cru of lagich

ⓢⓢⓢⓢⓢⓢⓢⓢⓢⓢⓢⓢⓢⓢⓢⓢⓢⓢⓢⓢⓢⓢⓢⓢⓢⓢⓢⓢⓢⓢⓢⓢⓢⓢⓢⓢ

bad breath of smoky bars, but she remained always nothing but a gypsy violin. I like it when somebody stubbornly insists on his origins. All our life, like it or not, we are always looking back on our origins, handling different situations in life only in the way known to us.

After crossing the Atlantic with us she was lost for an hour or so, leaving me alone with the airport clerk who couldn't understand why on earth this violin was so special to me.

"Sir, if she isn't a Stradivarius, our insurance for sure would make no trouble at all, pay you a hundred-some dollars for your violin."

"She is not a Stradivarius, she'll never be a Stradivarius! She is a plain violin of the poor North-Croatian gypsy Janoshi Bachi, who died a long time ago! His soul will now be haunting me for the rest of my life if I don't find his violin. Understand!??"

His wide-open eyes showed me that he didn't have a clue what I was talking about. Why in heaven's name I was going crazy like that. It was just a cheap violin. He didn't know if they covered those damn gypsy ghosts which refused to die and leave me in peace.

After a while, when my poor translator and the crew of luggage

ⓢⓢⓢⓢⓢⓢⓢⓢⓢⓢⓢⓢⓢⓢⓢⓢⓢⓢⓢⓢⓢⓢⓢⓢⓢⓢⓢⓢⓢⓢⓢⓢⓢⓢⓢ

Marijan Megla

hendlers hu hed gederd bekos of mai vajolent autbrst desperatli trajed tu get de clerk aut of mai fet hends, sambadi shautet from de holovei:

"Hir is de dem gost vajolin!"

It tuk meni jers befor I forget de shok det I hed gedet in aeroport. Shi is henging in mai apartment nau, praudli shoing her self tu auer gest. Shi is laik an old mader tu mi. Meni taims shi desagri vit mi, and samtaims shi kuls mi daun. In auer femili stil noubadi pleis de vajolin. Bad hu nos? Preheps vi hev a grendsan sam dei, a lital musishen. Boj I bi praud ven hi plei his frst concert tu de pipel of des cantri. Emegin ven I mit as old Janoshi Bachi egen, hau meni tings I hev tu tel him ebaut belavet vajolin.

---

handlers who had gathered because of my violent outburst desperately tried to get the clerk out of my fat hands, somebody shouted from the hallway:

"Here is the damn ghost's violin!"

It took many years before I forgot the shock that I had gotten in the airport. She is hanging in my apartment now, proudly showing herself to our guests. She is like an old mother to me. Many times she disagrees with me, and sometimes she cools me down. In our family, still, nobody plays the violin. But who knows? Perhaps we'll have a grandson some day, a little musician. Boy, I'll be proud when he plays his first concert for the people of this country. Imagine when I meet our old Janoshi Bachi again, how many things I have to tell him about the beloved violin.

It vos bjutifol somer moning. Mai slo kau tim rich as destination in boring tri auer march. Smeling vota and gud long rest, dei olmos ran daun de hil tu vel non vater mil. It vos old mil, and flotete an auer sait of a river an tu vuden barches. Chens and vait plenk vos it onli konekchen vit de bich. For mosli of a dei, an it lital pechi ruf, rested de shedo of a big brig gast handert meter evei.

Auer sait of a river, I kolet a lital overpopuletet poket of lend inbetvin tu river, Mura and Drava. It is frenli, pisfoli, grin, lodet vit tauns vich ar meni taim onli a fju kilometar evei from ichader. Der livet de pipel det, vit evri emigration vev, going tu ader kantris, selten retrning hom. It is lend haidet in fog, fladet olmos evri jer. Vi ar femos tu chench auer kaisers, kings, lords, cantris, vit aut eni meigar vajolenc. Tu sorvaiv ol det, vi develop a "gosop" det solving ol as deli problems. Dei lef over as vei of toking. Vi

---

It was a beautiful summer morning. My slow cow team reached our destination in a boring three-hour march. Smelling water and a good long rest, they almost ran down the hill to the well-known water mill. It was an old mill, and floated on our side of the river on two wooden barges. Chains and a wide plank were its only connections with the beach. For most of the day, over its little patched roof rested the shadow of a big bridge just a hundred meters away.

Our side of the river I call a little overpopulated pocket of land between two rivers, the Mura and the Drava. It is friendly, peaceful, green, full of towns which many times are only a few kilometres away from each other. The people who lived there, with every immigration wave, were going to other countries, seldom returning home. It is a land hidden in fog, flooded almost every year. We are famous for changing our kaisers, kings, lords, and countries, without any major violence. To survive all this, we developed a "gossip" that solved all our daily problems. They laugh over our way of talking. We

Vajolin

OLD LAICHI BACHI

olveis simstu bi in de midel, honoring as enimis laik as frends olmost de seim vei. It is sinpel logik behaind det. "Ju never no hu kud bi jor enimi and vich enimi kud bi jor frend." Vi dont hev tu mach feet in noubadi. Strenger mei kam and go, dei hev dei plezer, bad vi mek shor det dei no det onli vi belong der laik det vater mil.

Old brig vos hardli notesebel for his bjuti. Bildet from Croeshen tinber, det laik vi never giv ab. His prpes vos olveis mach mor inportant als des sols an vich lend hi vos bildet. Hi vos olveis de strenger, bekos Hangerians desain him. Tu bildet des strakcher dei tuket as hends, as blad, as laivs, bat iven so dei never krietet as brig. Dei protekt him vit hevi aern, smidet an his legs, so det river or vi pur sols kud not keri him evei.

Soet from brig, de lital mil vos so mach auers, iven vit des shit of veteri plaivud, vit "Faterland soldaten" an his demicht ruf. Nating kud rili provent it floting daun de river, and jet it stud der frili.

Old Laichi bachi spend mosli of his laif an des vel egt

always seem to be in the middle, honouring our enemies and our friends in almost the same way. There's a simple logic behind that. "You never know who could be your enemy and which enemy could be your friend." We don't have too much faith in anybody. Strangers may come and go, and they have their pleasure, but we make sure that they know that only we belong there, like that water mill.

The old bridge was hardly noticeable for its beauty. It was built from Croatian timber, the kind we never give up. Its purpose was always much more important than the people whose land it was built on. It was always foreign because the Hungarians designed it. To build this structure they took our hands, our blood, our lives, but even so they never created our bridge. They protected it with heavy iron, welded over its abutments so that neither the river nor we poor souls could carry it away.

Seen from the bridge, the little mill was very much ours, even with the sheet of weathered plywood with "Fatherland soldaten" on its damaged roof. Nothing could prevent it from floating down the river, and yet it stood there freely.

Old Laichi Bachi spent most of his life on this well aged

obgekt. Hi tuket des shop over ven his fader did not retrn from frst vorld vor. It vos onli opshen des hi hes, tu help de mader and for janger sisters.

An raf lital fes, dip vrinkals kauntet evri lital fait vit des cold triki river. Stak in big heri slads, his blu ais kud si evriting vot vota trai tu haidet from him. Laichi vos lital boni men, lost in his rumi vorking penc. His hevi blek shus aktet laik ankers, giving him enormes stabiliti an des vesel. Onli in bigeste somer dei hit, hi livet okeshenli de sefti of his larg gaket.

It tuk mi lital vail befor I friet mai bist from dei vuden harnis. After long sip from de river, dei hepili chuet dei hei in shedo of a big vilo. Laichi volkom mi laud and from ol hard. Bisaid de lital dasti vindo det overluk de river and de voter vil, stud a raf teibel vit kapel of cher. Det vos his ofis, and ples tu giv de kostimer drink akordingli tu his eg. De rest vos reservt for krainting stons, fenals, shekers, and a lital old veit indiketor.

Vi sedaun, muving laudli de chers. Hi vos hepi tu hev

---

object. He took the shop over when his father did not return from the First World War. It was the only option he had, to help his mother and four younger sisters.

On his rough little face, deep wrinkles counted every little fight with this cold tricky river. Stuck in big hairy slots, his blue eyes could see everything the water tried to hide from him. Laichi was a bony little man, lost in his roomy working pants. His heavy black shoes acted like anchors, giving him enormous stability on this vessel. Only at the hottest time in summer days would he occasionally leave the safety of his large jacket.

It took me a little while before I freed my beasts from their wooden harness. After a long sip from the river, they happily chewed their hay in the shadow of a big willow. Laichi welcomed me loudly and heartily. Beside the little dusty window that overlooked the river and the water wheel stood a rough table with a couple of chairs. That was his office, and the place to give the customer a drink according to his age. The rest was reserved for grinding stones, funnels, shakers, and a little old weight indicator.

We sat down, loudly moving the chairs. He was happy to have

sambadi tu tok tu. Veiding an letst njus from kostimer taun, hi goinet vit a lital glas of slivovic. Leter in de dei, ven vos nating mor left tu tel him, hi spreded de njus det hi hr from ader pipel. Meni of his njus hi repidet over and over, giving dem his vju, and nju imech. In vik or tu dei vos so hoplosli fertengelt vit nju minings and legends, det dei givet a gud stori. Iven ju njuet de autkom of det, der vos olveis veiding sam lital sopreis, fergoten tu bi telt et frst taim.

"Ja, ja, ja," justo sed de old Laichi. "Des old mil vos trocing de Drava, iven befor him!" Shol hi de big brig. "It luk nau so strong, bad ... ven hai spring voter rol daun from de Alps, his faif big legs heving trobels tu hold him in his ples," tok hi deliberatli, fergetinget de taim ven onli de brig help him tu sev his vater mil from floting daun de river. "Nating vos hir in dos deis. A old skviki feri, der ran gast ebaut ... der ... pest de brig. It vos big inaf tu setisfai lo trafik of hepi pilgrem tu Holi Vrgen Meri of Bistrica, during vorm mants of de jer."

somebody to talk to. Waiting for the latest news from the customer's town, he joined with a little glass of slivovica. Later in the day, when there was nothing left to tell him, he'd spread the news he'd heard from other people. Much of his news he repeated over and over, giving his view and a new image. In a week or two, it was so hopelessly tangled with new meanings and legends that it made a good story. Even if you knew the outcome, there was always some little surprise waiting, forgotten when he told it the first time.

"Ya, ya, ya," old Laichi used to say. "This mill was stroking the Drava even before him." And he points to the big bridge. "Now it looks so strong, but ... when high spring water rolls down from the Alps, his five big legs have trouble holding him in his place," he said deliberately, forgetting the time when only the bridge saved his water mill from floating down the river. "Nothing was here in those days. An old squeaky ferry, that ran just about ... there ... past the bridge. It was big enough to satisfy the low traffic of happy pilgrims to Holy Virgin Mary of Bistrica during the warm months of the year."

De mrchendais kam evri fol in des eria, ven de skini kesh vos evelebal from a harvost. Hi remember dos milki deis, ven de fog never liv de river. Taet skini horsis, oredi viks an de rod, hardli kud menagt overlodet vegens. Tu kvait dem daun, and preper for puling aut of des madhol, dei giv dem oc. An auer sait of a river, veidet onli nero madi rod slaist from tin aern vegen vils, biten tu pai vit horsis fit. It drai onli in hot samer.

"For long taim, des vos de onli vei tu rich des voter mil," tel de Laichi. "Samtam auer kostimer stak in des madi mes. Vit dei anerisht kaus dei gast diden meket des slaimi hil. Onli for des vi kipet a per of oksen. Dei vere slo, bad dei bring evrivan tu de top of a hil."

Laik kid I vos olveis laik tu kam tu his old mil. Des ples vos so fol of misteri, olmos skeri. It vos de ples an vich femilis from aper rivr kam frst if dei lostet dei lav van in de river. Badis of de sols de river keriet for tu long in hr chest, so det dei kud bi not rekognais, vere beri an de hil belo dos tris. Chip anmarkt kroses stud der for a vail, garding des pur sols.

⦿⦿⦿⦿⦿⦿⦿⦿⦿⦿⦿⦿⦿⦿⦿⦿⦿⦿⦿⦿⦿⦿⦿⦿⦿⦿⦿⦿⦿⦿⦿⦿⦿⦿⦿⦿

Merchandise came into this area every fall, when a bit of cash was available after the harvest. He remembered those milky days when the fog never left the river. Tired skinny horses, already weeks on the road, could hardly manage their overloaded wagons. To quiet them down and prepare for pulling out of this mudhole, they'd give them oats. On our side of the river was only a narrow muddy road sliced by thin iron wagon wheels and beaten to pie by the horses' feet. It dried only in the summer heat.

"For a long time, this was the only way to reach this water mill," Laichi would tell. "Sometimes our customers got stuck in this muddy mess. With their undernourished cows they just didn't make it up this slimy hill. Only for these did we keep a pair of oxen. They were slow, but they got everyone to the top of the hill."

As a kid I always liked to visit his old mill. The place was so full of mystery, almost scary. It was the place where families from up-river came first if they'd lost a loved one in the river. Bodies of those souls the river carried for too long in her breast, so that they could not be recognized, were buried on the hill below those trees. Cheap unmarked crosses stood there for a while, guarding these poor souls.

◉◉◉◉◉◉◉◉◉◉◉◉◉◉◉◉◉◉◉◉◉◉◉◉◉◉◉◉◉◉◉◉◉◉◉◉◉◉◉

Old Laichi hes olveis tu tel samting tu de lital boi, vich femili mens left him der tu veide an de flauer. His storis dependet an his mud and artraitis, det start tu deform his hends. Samtaim vos olmos inposebel tu lisen tu dos horor storis. Kruliti and anekspektet misteri kud kip ju evek in long vinter naits, ven dencing laits from krek in de oven kip muving an de vol. Ganping over pikcher of lavvans, ekonpaniet vit hauling of de taun dogs, dei koset olvei a gusbams. Ju kud si in kreking frosen vindos, gost pikcher of dos pur sols der endet dei laivs ganping from de brig tu de dark river. Iven if ju traet tu pul blanket over jor hed, ju kud olmos filet dei laiflos kold presents besaid jor bet. Emegint hau dei skrimet in de letct sekends of dei laifs.

I remember des sed stori of a rich jang taun vumen, Veronika, vich hes eniting vot shi vishes, onli not hr bjuti. Shi vos exidentali brnt vit de vota bai pleing eraund big maisnery stov. Shi vos given evri tritment tu sev hr, bad iven doktors and spas danet evriting posebel, dei kuden rekaver skin an hef of hr fes and badi. Pur

---

Old Laichi always had something to tell a little boy whose family's men left him there to wait for the flour. His stories depended on his mood and the arthritis that was starting to deform his hands. Sometimes it was almost impossible to listen to those horror stories. Cruelty and unexpected mystery could keep you awake in long winter nights, when dancing lights from the crack in the oven kept moving on the wall. Jumping over pictures of loved ones, accompanied by the howling of the town dogs, they always caused goosebumps. You could see in the cracking frozen windows the ghost pictures of those poor souls that ended their lives jumping from the bridge into the dark river. Even if you tried to pull the blanket over your head, you could almost feel their lifeless cold presence beside your bed. Imagine how they screamed in the last seconds of their lives.

I remember the sad story of a rich young town woman, Veronica, who had anything she wished for, but not her beauty. She was accidentally scalded with water when playing around a big masonry stove. She was given every treatment to save her, but even when the doctors and spas had done everything possible, they couldn't restore the skin on half of her face and body. Her poor

Marijan Megla

perenc trai tu sev hr from realiti of a laif, bad nesti taun gosop kol hr enivei de vich. Als onli chaild in femili, shi nuet det shi mas meri sambadi, tu inshur hr fader prosperiti on de farm. Bad, hu kud meri hr and liv vit hr onli for hr gut hart and tot? After de perenc pei hevili a taun mech mekers, dei faund de gai in ader kaunti. Zoltan vos older gai, pest his merich eg, dei spend his jang jers in Hangari. Sun gosop faund aut det hi vos in de gel for not obeing de los of auer gud lord. An big merich det pur perenc put tugeder, hoping for de best, hi vos ekting a gud jangved, bat in de seim nait hi vanet tu slip vit jang gipsi grl det vos der tu piked ab skrabs from de kichen.

Zoltan vos gud for nating, and from farm hi diden andesten nating, veiding delibretli det ol shors bi dan from old fader. His onli interes vos a big vainceler, in vich hi spendet mosli of his taim. Ven de perenc varn him tu bi litel mor interested in dei big farm and doter Veronika, hi chench for dei or tu. In sted tu drink hom, hi start tu vest his taim in taun bar. Auer blesed Pater Malek atakt him vans der,

---

parents tried to save her from the reality of life, but nasty town gossips called her a witch anyway. As the only child in her family, she knew she must marry somebody to insure her father prosperity on the farm. But who could marry her and live with her only for her good heart and thoughts? After her parents paid a high price to a matchmaker, they found a guy in another county. Zoltan was an older guy, past his marriageable age, that spent his young years in Hungary. Soon the gossips found out that he had been in jail for not obeying the laws of our good lord. At the big marriage the poor parents put together, hoping for the best, he was acting like a good newlywed, but on the same night he wanted to sleep with a young gypsy girl who was there to pick up scraps from the kitchen.

Zoltan was good for nothing, and didn't understand anything about the farm, waiting deliberately so that the chores would be done by the old father. His only interest was the big wine cellar, in which he spent most of his time. When the parents warned him to be a little more interested in their big farm and their daughter Veronica, he'd change for a day or two. Instead of drinking at home, he started to waste his time in the town bar. Our blessed Pater Malek once attacked him there, teling him befor hol sosaeti det hi dont laik det vot hi vos herin for him. Insted tu chench a lital, hi brod hom for frst taim his mistres. Des nait and meni dei folo, Veronika spend voking an auskrts of auer taun, inbetvin krset vilos, toking tu hr slf. Meni taims pipel dei kaming hom from let shift in de siti tek hr hom and kulet hr daun. Vit nju hop and aidias shi bi retrning hom tu fait for hr rait.

It pest a jer, and nating chenchet. Sik end taet tu voch hr perenc vorking evri dei, anebel tu solvt problem in hr laif, shi desapir. In hr lital leter tu auer belavet Pater Malek, shi giv him ol hr poseshen. Foloving nait, as Laichi godet a visit from brnet vumen. Shi vos taet and sed. Hi volkom hr, laik evri taim, vandering vai is shi hir. Tu pinch hr moral, hi giv hr sam old sosich dei hi hes, and lital vain. Det vork, end veri sun shi start iven lefing. So, pur old Laichi bringet his badel of slivovica. Dei finished de ol badel, dei goket.

Shi iven giv him a kis et van point, an his chik. Bad, old Laichi probebli drank mor als hi kud keri, and fol tu slip. A

ⓢⓢⓢⓢⓢⓢⓢⓢⓢⓢⓢⓢⓢⓢⓢⓢⓢⓢⓢⓢⓢⓢⓢⓢⓢⓢⓢⓢⓢⓢⓢⓢⓢⓢⓢⓢⓢⓢ

telling him before the whole society that he didn't like what he was hearing about him. Instead of changing a little, he took home his mistress for the first time. This night and many that followed, Veronica spent walking on the outskirts of our town, between the cursed willows, talking to herself. Many times people coming home from the late shift in the city would take her home and cool her down. With new hope and ideas, she would return home to fight for her rights.

A year passed and nothing changed. Sick and tired of watching her parents working every day, unable to solve the problems in her life, she disappeared. In a little letter to our Pater Malek, she left him all her possessions. The following night, Laichi got a visit from the burned woman. She was tired and sad. He welcomed her, as always, wondering why she had come. To pick up her morale, he gave her some old sausages and a little wine. That worked, and very soon she even started laughing. So, poor old Laichi brought out his bottle of slivovica. They finished the whole bottle. They joked.

She even gave him a kiss at one point, on his cheek. But old Laichi had probably drunk more than he could carry and fell asleep. A

ⓢⓢⓢⓢⓢⓢⓢⓢⓢⓢⓢⓢⓢⓢⓢⓢⓢⓢⓢⓢⓢⓢⓢⓢⓢⓢⓢⓢⓢⓢⓢⓢⓢⓢⓢⓢ

28 *Old Laichi Bachi*   **Marijan Megla**

skrim and splesh of a badi vok him ab. Ven hi soet des hi vos alon, hi ran aut an de barch. It vos tu let. Fest river tuket oredi de badi. Onli kold silver srfes vos left, and stum present of de dark brig. Bodi of des vumen vos never faundet. Sun after verds, old tutlos taun viches startet a nju gosop. "De river vos eshemt tu shol des vumen badi, so shi kip hr in hr kold chest for ever."

Jer after, hr nau rich hasbend, folot from his mistreses, draun bai beding in de seim river. Skeri vidnises tel in de taun des nait des dei soet tu hends, puling him in his det.

Samtaim Laichi remembering mor hepier hepenings from de river. For istanc ebaut gipsi Ivan, de vud karver. Hi vos drinking hol his laif, spreding miseri and trobels for his big femili. Tu stap des hi disaidet tu kil him self an his feveret spat, bisaid de brig overluking de mil. In his pur laif, mosli de taim hi veidet an des ples an his vaif tu fil his big stamak. For gudbai hi drenk hol bdel strong slivovica, and ledaun tu bi redi for auer gud lord kort. Old Laichi faund him an de vei hom, hepili sliping his bus aut. So laik evri respektfol men,

---

scream and splash of a body woke him up. When he saw that he was alone he ran out on the barge. It was too late. The fast river had already taken the body. Only the cold silver surface was left, and the silent presence of the dark bridge. The body of this woman was never found. Soon after, the old toothless town witches started a new gossip. "The river was ashamed to show this woman's body, so she kept her in her cold chest for ever."

The next year her now rich husband, followed by his mistresses, drowned while bathing in the same river. Scared witnesses told in the town that night they'd seen two hands pulling him to his death.

Sometimes Laichi would remember happier events from the river. For instance, about Ivan the gypsy wood carver. He was drinking all his life, spreading misery and troubles for his big family. To stop this, he decided to kill himself at his favourite spot, beside the bridge overlooking the mill. In his poor life, most of the time he'd wait in this place for his wife to fill his big stomach. As a good-bye, he drank a whole bottle of strong slivovica and lay down to be ready for our good lord's court. Old Laichi found him on his way home, happily sleeping his booze out. So, like every respectful man, hi danet evriting tu konfort him, not noing de rili prpes of his pig snoring. It vos fol and nait kud bi rili kold, so hi boro him his long ship skin gaket. Tu meket isier tu Ivans vaif tu faund him in de nait, hi putet bisaid an hasti emtet pamkin vit brning kendel. Tu enshur flo of fresh er, hi chopt tu long slads. Hepi vit his ekonplishing, hi left for his lital haus an de hil.

Ivans vaif vos strong vumen, bat iven shi kud not keri de bladi drank. Taet from dei long hasel vit de eit kidc, dei olveis hev in main onli de fud, shi mek de kemp bisaid. Samtaim des nait, pur drank raist his ais vait open. Tenking hi is in de heven, and des shaini obgek bisaid his hed is auer gud lord stimen med an him, veiding an his konfeshen, hi tel hol trut.

"Ha, ha, ha! Des nait, hi tel lital tu mach tu onest," left old Laichi. "Oooou, hi pei for det. Ivan shud no det no vaif kan lisening tolt de storis ebaut dei mens mistres."

Vans I remember Laichi vos in de bed mud. It vos poring hol dei. Mai onli interest vos hau tu liv des ples erli inaf vit mai tim of kaus. Hi vos nervesli voking ab end daun,

---

he did everything to comfort him, not knowing the real purpose of his piggish snoring. It was fall, and night could be really cold, so he lent him his long sheepskin jacket. To make it easier for Ivan's wife to find him in the night, he put beside him a hastily-emptied pumpkin with a burning candle in it. To insure a flow of fresh air, he chopped two long slits. Happy with his accomplishment, he left for his little house on the hill.

Ivan's wife was a strong woman, but even she could not carry the bloody drunk. Tired from a long hassle with her eight kids, who always had only food on their mind, she made camp beside Ivan. Sometime that night, the poor drunk opened his eyes wide. Thinking he was in heaven and the shiny object beside his head was our good lord steaming mad at him and awaiting his confession, he told the whole truth.

"Ha, ha, ha! That night he told a little too much too honestly," laughed old Laichi. "Oooo, he paid for that. Ivan should know that no wife can listen to stories about their man's mistress."

Once I remember Laichi was in a bad mood. It was pouring all day. My only interest was in how to leave the place early enough with my team of cows. He was nervously walking up and down, cheking from taim tu taim an his shekers. Noing det I vos tudei not in de mud tu tok, hi vochet de trafik an de brig sailend mamcling in his chin.

"Tja ... de brig. Vum, vum, evrivan pesing des river, not iven luk daun. Et sims tu mi det noubadi ker for des river eni mor." Den, skvising his hrting hends, hi edet, "Vum, vum, dei pesing from van sait tu ader, living dei problems redar bihaind, als fiksing dem. Dei living sols, hepinis, gast tu rich ader sait in de hri. Never luking bek, an de maunten of sednis dei gron after dei left. Sed. Sed." Den hi trn tu mi. "Ju no, mai boj, det brig der kil oredi so meni pipels laif, and vi stil peing for det litel konvinienc, tu pes des river," sed hi filosofikali, giving him self avord vit a glas of slivovica.

Let des nait, hi storet mai flauer benit of leder blanket so shi stei drai an de vei hom. Ven I finisht mai lind ti, vit big shat of slivovica, de sturm gst teket sekend ran. Lisening of klipklaping of hufs from mai kau tim, I vos glad tu hev a brig in bekgraund. His entering laits vos strong inaf tu hep mi tu menuvering aut aut des lital kanjon. A jang led, dei no

checking from time to time on his shakers. Knowing that I wasn't in the mood to talk that day, he watched the traffic on the bridge and silently mumbled into his chin.

"Tcha ... the bridge. Zoom, zoom, everyone crossing the river, not even looking down. It seems to me that nobody cares for this river any more." Then, squeezing his hurting hands, he added, "Zoom, zoom, they're passing from one side to the other, leaving their problems behind rather than solving them. Never looking back on the mountain of sadness that grows after they leave. Sad. Sad." Then he turned to me. "You know, my boy, that bridge there has already taken so many people's lives, and we're still paying for that little convenience, crossing the river," he said philosophically, rewarding himself with a glass of slivovica.

Late that night he stored my flour beneath a leather blanket to keep it dry on the way home. When I finished my lind tea, with a big shot of slivovica, the storm took a second run. Listening to the clip-clopping of hooves from my cow team I was glad to have the bridge in the background. Its entrance lights were strong enough to help me to manoeuvre out of this little canyon. A young lad that knows

hi bi veri sun vet tu his skin, vich is in komend of tu sker bist, gast kuden andestan vai des Laichi hetet des brig, der gast nau hep him.

Preheps hi hetetet ven auer pipel living de taun, luking for mor isia laif in vest. I egri vit him, det sacha masen emigration kos meni trobels det vi diden hev bifor. Iven I vos onli de tinaiger, et des point, I kud menchenet tu or tri neims of femili vich trobel lei in des emigration. Vi hr ebaut jang vidos, vich men vos kilt in mains or ansev fektoris, pregnet grls left alon, or iven perenc det diden andestan dei on kidc.

Living brig behain onli de sturm blek beli vos mai konpanien, gaiding mi in betvin kornfilds. I vos koncentreting an mai draiving. Skeri bister, der bai evri lital blo of vind or tander roring, hev tendensi tu ran, ver samtaims olmos inposible tu kontrol. Tri auer or so after, I vos glad tu si autskrts of auer lital taun. Reni nait vos seting tu rest, spreding hr darknis. In hefen auer or so I bi siting bisaid de big maisneri stov. Auer belavet grenmamichka bi raibing mai bek and frosen fit. Probebli

ⓢⓢⓢⓢⓢⓢⓢⓢⓢⓢⓢⓢⓢⓢⓢⓢⓢⓢⓢⓢⓢⓢⓢⓢⓢⓢⓢⓢⓢⓢⓢⓢⓢⓢⓢⓢⓢⓢ

he'll soon be wet to his skin, who is in command of two scared beasts, just couldn't understand why Laichi hated the bridge that just now helped him.

Perhaps he hated it when our people left town, looking for an easier life in the west. I agree with him that such a mass emigration causes many troubles we didn't have before. Even if I was only a teenager at this time I could mention the names of two or three families whose troubles lay in this emigration. We heard about young widows whose men were killed in mines or unsafe factories, pregnant girls left alone, or even parents who didn't understand their own kids.

Leaving the bridge behind, the storm's black belly was my companion, guiding me between cornfields. I was concentrating on my driving. The scared beasts, that with every little gust of wind or roar of thunder had a tendency to run, were sometimes almost impossible to control. Three hours or so after, I was glad to see the outskirts of our little town. The rainy night was setting to rest, spreading her darkness. In half an hour or so I would be sitting beside the big masonry stove. Our beloved grandmamichka would be rubbing my back and frozen feet. Probably

ⓢⓢⓢⓢⓢⓢⓢⓢⓢⓢⓢⓢⓢⓢⓢⓢⓢⓢⓢⓢⓢⓢⓢⓢⓢⓢⓢⓢⓢⓢⓢⓢⓢⓢⓢⓢⓢⓢ

big pot of mai feveret vaingulash bi spreding his aroma kros de haus. Sun, ol onkels and antis bi tugeder bai big teibel tising as belavet haus grendedushkin. Laf and hevi farmer goks tu let in de nait, ven kidc and grenma faineli go tu slip.

Hau fest jers pesing bai, and from lital boi olmost over nait I vos a gron jang men. Jestudei I kud folo Laichi onli, tu dei I keri for him hevi seks of korn and vit. Go tu de old mil, vos mor de hebetc. Hiden ples for drink, filing det ju ar men, and sam men veid an ju. It is de taim ven grls and vumen dond hev de dominent posishen. Ven ju mas meket klir tu ju self det no meder vot ju ekomplishet in laif, ju bi living and dai laik a men. It is de taim ven simstu bi inportent hau meni glasis of vain or slivovica ju ken drink, or tu hau meni grls yu kud giv de lav in van nait. Kvaliti? Rili lav, for det ju tu jang.

Van samer ivning, ven vi drenk tugeder and Laichi vos dranker den juzuli, hi sed tu mi: "Mai doter vos seim eg laik ju, ven des hepen tu hr, der in de mitel of a river. Jes bai

a big pot of my favourite wine goulash would be spreading its aroma through the house. Soon, all my uncles and aunts would be together at the big table teasing our beloved house grandedushkin. Laughter and loud farmer jokes would go late into the night, when the kids and grandma would finally go to sleep.

How fast the years passed by, and from a little boy overnight I became a grown young man. While yesterday I could only follow Laichi around, today I carry heavy sacks of corn and wheat for him. Going to the old mill became more of a habit. A hidden place for a drink, feeling that you are a man, and some men wait on you. It is the time when girls and women don't have the dominant position. When you must make clear to yourself that no matter what you accomplish in life, you will live and die like a man. It is the time when it seems to be important how many glasses of wine or slivovica you can drink, or how many girls you can make love to in one night. Quality? Real love - you're too young for that.

One summer evening, when we were drinking together and Laichi was drunker than usual, he said to me: "My daughter was your age when this happened to her there, in the middle of the river. Just by des send benk." Hi sardenli andestending det hi toking samting det mei hrt him.

In auer femili, meni taim vos menshenet de doter of old Laichi, bat ven ever sambadi of as kidc asket mor kveshchen, tema vos polaitli desmist. Vi vander vot kud hepen tu des grl vich grev vos olveis so klin and fol of kandels. Dei vos tok det after his doter dai, his vaif vos developing hevi depreshen. Shi spended mosli of de taim bisaid de vindo overluking de brig an de river, never kuking or shaping. Taun gosop vos teling det dos tu never hes a veri gud merig tugeder. Shi vanet tu go in de vorld, and liv des mini egsistenc from des old mil, bad hi never egri. Dei fait meni naits. Iven dei lital haus vos bjutifol and an prfekt ples, shi vos never dei heven. Auer Pater Malek justu sed, hel is not olveis vit de flem delivert, and if des vos ever tru, den in des kes for shor.

Dos deis pipel so hr samtaim voking bisaid de river, koling in fogi naits Ljubas neim. Mosli de taim, old Laichi bi bringing hr hom, bat samtaim ven hi vos tu taet, hi mist hr eskep. Ven sambadi brod hr hom, hi vos veri

꧁꧁꧁꧁꧁꧁꧁꧁꧁꧁꧁꧁꧁꧁꧁꧁꧁꧁꧁꧁꧁꧁꧁꧁꧁꧁꧁꧁꧁꧁

that sand bank." He suddenly understood that he was talking about something that might hurt him.

In our family the daughter of old Laichi was mentioned many times, but whenever one of us kids asked more questions the theme was politely dismissed. We wondered what could have happened to this girl whose grave was always so clean and covered with candles. There was always talk that after his daughter died his wife developed a deep depression. She spent most of her time beside the window overlooking the bridge and the river, never cooking or shopping. The town gossips told that those two never had a good marriage. She wanted to go into the world and leave this minimal existence from the old mill, but he never agreed. They fought many nights. Even if their little house was beautiful and a perfect place, it was never heaven. Our Pater Malek use to say that hell is not always delivered in flames, and if that was ever true, it was in this case for sure.

Those days people saw her sometimes walking beside the river calling Luba's name into the foggy night. Most times Laichi would take her home, but sometimes when he was too tired he'd miss her escape. When somebody brought her home he was very

Marijan Megla

tenkfol, and olveis giv fud and drink in big kvantiti. I mas edmitet, I never so hr. Preheps is det gud so. Meni taim I ask mai self, vot shud I du vit hr it des ever ekr. Des vos shedo an as frendship, and I vos glad det hi start tu tok ebaudet.

"Ljuba vos onli sikstin. Als ol jang pipel in des eg, shi vanet tu go samver, in big siti, hev fan. Shi vanet a beter taim. Shi belivt in des nonsens, det der samver in de streng vorld bi a ples det ju kud kol hom. In vich ju dont vork so hart laik hir for deli bred. Hau de hel shud I no, der never liv des kaunti, vot shi vanet. De vor vos noking an auer dors. Hol vorld simstu protest, provok, protekt, fait for sam bladi risen. Hr mader and shi vos veving from de brig. Den dei kiset ichader, and shi ran after sam jang gai. I diden stap hr.

"Tri jers pest, and onli de pipel det hev kam hom from big siti tel as det dei stil liv tugeder. Dei diden raid, and vi diden hev adres. De vor start and Adolf vos pushing his solger kros de vorld. Hangari putet vans egen border in midel of a river. Dedlivan - elektrikvan."

@@

thankful and always gave food and drink in big quantities. I must admit that I never saw her. Perhaps that is good. Many times I ask myself what I would do with her if it ever occurred. This was a shadow on our friendship, and I was glad that he had started to talk about it.

"Luba was only sixteen. Like all young people in this age, she wanted to go somewhere, see the big city, have fun. She wanted a better time. She believed in the nonsense that somewhere in the strange world was a place you could call home. In which you don't work as hard as she did for the daily bread. How the hell should I know, who never left this county, what she wanted? The war was knocking on our doors. The whole world seemed to protest, provoke, protect, fight for some bloody reason. Her mother and she were waving from the bridge. They kissed each other and she ran after some young guy. I didn't stop her.

"Three years passed and only the people who had come home from the big city told us that they were still living together. They didn't write, and we didn't have their address. The war started and Adolf was pushing his soldiers across the world. Hungary once again put a border in the middle of the river. A deadly one - electric one."

@@

Hi tuk a sigaret from mi. His hends vos shekin. In his ais gederet tirs. Reliving his on tragedi tuket evri nrv from him. Den, after long brek and big pafs, hi start egen.

"I vos bisi krainting de vit for a farmer aut jor taun. Hi slep an his vegen autsait, vit his dog and horsis, belo des ok. It vos pisfol nait. It vos vor and evrivan trai tu sorvaiv him. So meni taim vi soet korps vit shrapnels vunds, bat ju kud not rekaver de badis. Hm ... dei vere so jang. Meni taim I vos tenkig, de vor mas bi sun over, der is gast not so meni jang sols left.

"De dog start tu bark, and horsis vos nervos. So I kam aut tu si vot hepening. Sardenli a jang vumen start tu kol from ader sait of a river. 'Dedi... dedi...' I kuden si hu is es, and vot shi van, bat I nuet det sambadi van tu kros de river, going tu vords dedli vaer."

Hi stap for a vail, klining his dasti fes, an vich tirs livet lital strims, vit de old reg from his poket.

"'Stap! O plis stap! Dont go over de river, jus de brig,' jal I in de darknis. Traet tu loket de koler vit de lait der

---

He took a cigarette from me. His hands were shaking. Tears gathered in his eyes. Reliving his tragedy took all his nerve. Then, after a long break and big puffs, he started again.

"I was busy grinding wheat for a farmer from your town. He was sleeping on his wagon outside, with his dog and horses, below this oak. It was a peaceful night. It was war and everyone tried to survive it. So many times we saw corpses with shrapnel wounds, but you could not recover the bodies. Hmmm ... they were so young. Many times I would think the war would soon have to be over, there were just not very many young souls left.

"The dog started to bark and the horses were nervous. So I came out to see what was happening. Suddenly a young woman started to call from the other side of the river. 'Daddy... Daddy... ' I couldn't see who it was, and what she wanted, but I know that somebody wanted to cross the river, going towards the deadly wire."

He stopped for a while, cleaning his dusty face where tears left little streams, with an old rag from his pocket.

"'Stop! Oh please stop! Don't go over the river, use the bridge,' I yelled into the darkness. I tried to locate the caller with the light

---

brod mi hasti vekt farmer. Dei stap. Den kolerin kol vans egen. 'It is mi dedi, jor Ljuba. Dont yu no mi eni mor?' In taim ven I start tu skreping for vords in mai trot dei start tu vok egen. Plis Ljuba, jus de brig. I iven kros him for jor seg, plis...

"'Dedi, vi kan not jus de brig. Vi ar partisans!' Den, an ader sait of a river open de laits, flading ol river and brig. For sekend or so I soet a jang bjutifol skeri vumen and hr not vedet hasbent. Mai doter... Den de mashingang from brig endet hr and his laif," sed old pel gai, sailend kraing.

It pest auer or so, ven vi vos siting besaid ichadar. Taim of ankonchens, aut vich vi delibratli forespon auer exit. De Drava kontinju tu trn de vater vil. Chek ... chek ... chek ... chek. In dark plesis of a brash dei kaver lital slops besaid de river, fog vos gedering. Samver ab de river, stak vos retrning hom. Hepi hord of taun kids trotet behain de taet kaus. Skvising in betvin dei haim kvoters big pink odr, dei spletering from taim tu taim a hot palachinkas an dasti rod. Letct svimers peking laudli dei lanch bokses,

---

brought to me by the hastily-wakened farmer. They stopped. Then the one calling called again. 'It is me Daddy, your Luba. Don't you know me any more?' In the time I was scraping for words in my throat, they started to walk again. Please Luba, use the bridge. I'd even cross it for your sake, please ...

"'Daddy, we can not use the bridge. We are partisans!' Then, lights came on from the other side of the river, lighting all the river and the bridge. For a second or so I saw a young beautiful scared woman and her unwed husband. My daughter... Then the machine gun from the bridge ended her and his life," said the pale old guy, silently crying.

An hour or so passed with us sitting beside each other. It was a time of unconsciousness, from which we deliberately postponed our exit. The Drava continued to turn the water wheel. Chek ... chek ... chek ... chek. In dark places in the brush that covered the little slopes beside the river, fog was gathering. Somewhere upriver stock was returning home. A happy horde of town kids trotted behind the tired cows. Squeezing big pink udders between their hind legs, they splattered hot palachinkas from time to time on the dusty road. The last swimmers were loudly packing their lunch baskets,

living de biches tu moskitos. Samver daun de river taun chrch bels koling ol parish tu de ivning mes. Den a noisi emti mil stapet des pisfolnis.

"Dei faund hr nekst dei, tengelt in brig kold lek. His badi vos never faundet," sed old Laichi, stending ab tu fil de mil vit de nju korn.

Tri jers after det, as goverment disaidet tu bild a nju brig from ston. De lital mil vos muvt forder ab de river. Old Laichi bachi never sed a vort tu opos det. Hi never soet his konplishen. De gud lord tuk him from as shortli after dei blo ab a old brig. Hi vos a gud sol. His belavet vaif dei tuket in old foks speshal hom. De old mil vos et frst fergoten, bad den parkt olmos an seim ples tu bi a turist atrakchen.

---

leaving the beaches to mosquitoes. Somewhere down the river town church bells called the whole parish to evening mass. Then a noisy empty mill broke the peacefulness.

"They found her the next day tangled in the bridge's cold leg. His body was never found," said old Laichi, standing up to fill the mill with new corn.

Three years after that, our government decided to build a new stone bridge. The little mill was moved further upriver. Old Laichi Bachi never said a word of opposition. He never saw its completion. The good lord took him from us shortly after they blew up the old bridge. He was a good soul. His beloved wife was taken to a special old folks home. The old mill was at first forgotten, but then was parked in almost the same place to be a tourist attraction.

An anmarkt krosing of tu gravel rods der strech kros des vet flet stud de shebi krucefiks. Overgroen vit vic and grei mos, hi slud der moshenlos in shedo of a big ok. Hi vos letct marking an de vei tu old Julcha neni haus. From des point onli de svamp fol of sikrit ver tu pest and onli dei det truli nidet hr help marcht forder. Mosli de taim shi vos not sopreist, ekspekting visitor an de steps of hr lital haus. Det vos de ples ver dei, vit dei anshor voisis fol of hop, eksplening dei medikal trobels. Preheps ju kud not kam ansien or anhrt, from pek of dogs vich barking onli shi kud kvaet daun. Dei vos ol chep and saises — hef kripelt, hangri, dei cheset evriting itebal an det det end rod. Meibi ju kud not sopreist des old vumen Julcha bikos shi solt hr sol tu de devel. Pipel teling det in hr jang eig shi vos most bjutifol grinais grl in hol kantri.

For mostli de taim det I spendet vit mai old grenperenc an dei farm, I diden nju det shi egsistet.

At an unmarked crossing of two gravel roads that stretched across a wet flat stood a shabby crucifix. Overgrown with weeds and grey moss, it stood there motionless in the shadow of a big oak. It was the last landmark on the way to old Julcha Neni's house. From this point only the swamp full of secrets was to be passed, and only they that truly needed her help marched further. Most of the time she was not surprised, expecting visitors on the steps of her little house. That was the place where they, with their unsure voices full of hope, explained their medical troubles. Perhaps you could not arrive unseen or unheard because of the pack of dogs whose barking only she could quiet down. They were all shapes and sizes – half-crippled, hungry, they chased everything eatable on that dead-end road. Maybe you could not surprise this old woman Julcha because she sold her soul to the devil. People tell that in her younger days she was the most beautiful green-eyed girl in the whole country.

For most of the time that I spent with my old grandparents on their farm, I didn't know that she existed.

I vos lital and sik, anviling tu liv sefti of vorm kichen. Iven put in de properti tu kech fresh er ken not mek mi hepi. Vans, sorendet vit de flak of chiken, I start tu krai, luking for helping hends of mai greni. Noubadi rili njuet hau tu kjur mi, so evrivan trai tu bi polait, meking mi konfrtabel als posebel. Den van nait I vos rili bed, and auer taun prich vos kolt an mai sait. For frst taim I hr hr blesed neim.

"Pater Malek," sed mai grenmamichka, vich fes vos vet from tirs and voris, "preheps vi kud bring him tu old Julcha. Ju no, de taun vich. Bad kud det hrt auer blesed Jesus filing? Meibi vi godet sam help from 'dem' tu sev a lital krishchen," tok mai svit grenmamichka, trning hr vet skarf in de hends.

"Vel mai direst greni," tok hi, holding in his strong hends auer hef neket mesias an de krucefix, olmos breking his soft rips, "det vi living for letct resorc. Gud lord hlp as. Ju no auer jesus help ol krishchen, laif or det." Hi tachet mai hot forhet. "Bat auf ader hend, onli de laifvans reper chrch ruf and giv sakrament vain. Hmmm ... I tenk ju shud go, bad tek a chn of garlik and mai blesing. Gast in kes."

I was little and sick, unwilling to leave the safety of the warm kitchen. Even being put in the garden to catch the fresh air did not make me happy. Once, surrounded by the flock of chickens, I started to cry, looking for the helping hands of my granny. Nobody really knew how to cure me, so everyone tried to be polite, making me as comfortable as possible. Then one night I was really bad, and our town priest was called to my side. For the first time I heard her blessed name.

"Pater Malek," said my grandmamichka, whose face was wet from tears and worries, "perhaps we could bring him to old Julcha. You know, the town witch. But could that hurt our blessed Jesus' feelings? Maybe we can get some help from 'them' to save a little Christian," said my sweet grandmamichka, turning her wet scarf in her hands.

"Well, my dearest granny," he said, holding in his strong hands our half-naked messiah on the crucifix, almost breaking his soft ribs, "that we'll leave for the last resort. Good lord help us. You know our Jesus helps all Christians, alive or dead." He touched my hot forehead. "But on the other hand, only the live ones repair the church roof and give sacramental wine. Hmmm.... I think you should go, but take a chain of garlic and

Marijan Megla

Det shi sol hr sol tu de devel bi fergiven if shi samhau menagt tu kjur mi. After long trosting tu sekses of auer mishen, vi start tu pek. Mai belavet grenmader, lord giv hr best ples in heven, kuk egs, sosiches and tuket nju lof of bred in hr traveling basket.

It vos after vor, and meni anakauntet desises gast kuden bi hendelt from van old doktor, him self vos an end of his vorking kurier and seltan liv de opereting rum. I remember bi bedli il, bat iven so I kud not provaid de neim of des signis. So meibi I never nju if mai signis vos laif treten or not.

De vegen vos polsteret vit hevi matras of oc stro. An tape of det vos putet hevi dak daun plenket. Shi chench de anvelop of a big pilo, gast in kes det vi si sambadi from de taun. It bi a anfergibebal shem for mai grenmamichka if de gosop diskaver not vosht pilo. I vos putet in for long gons, tu per of penc, and tri hevi sveters benit of det hevenli soft blenket. After pater Malek blest as and auer tim of slipi kaus, vi start de grni. Lisening tu klip kloping of kau hufs, ebel tu si onli

my blessing, just in case"

That she sold her soul to the devil could be forgiven if she somehow managed to cure me. After a long toasting to the success of our mission, we started to pack. My beloved grandmother, lord give her the best place in heaven, cooked eggs, sausages, and took a new loaf of bread in her travelling basket.

It was after the war, and many uncounted diseases just couldn't be handled by one old doctor, himself at the end of his working career and seldom leaving the operating room. I remember being badly ill, but even so I could not provide the name of this sickness. So maybe I never knew if my sickness was life-threatening or not.

The wagon was upholstered with a heavy mattress of oat straw. On top of that was put a heavy duck down blanket. She changed the pillowcase on the big pillow just in case we saw somebody from town. It would be an unforgivable shame for my grandmamichka if the gossips discovered an unwashed pillow. I was put in four long-johns, two pair of pants, and three heavy sweaters beneath that heavenly soft blanket. After Pater Malek blessed us and our team of sleepy cows, we started the journey. Listening to the clip-clopping of

dark blu skai fol of star, I dosin. It mas bi a long grnei, bekos ven I vok ab vos dei, and hot. Mai tu grenperenc vos siting bisaid ichadar, komenting sambadis krop of korn. Julcha trobel start erli in hr laif. Shi vos deting van of de richeste and handsam boj in auer taun. For sam risen hi vant tu liv hr for sam anadervan. De old taun vidos stil chuing de stori. Vit evri pesing generation vird samting nju edet. Des terebel dei vos van bjutifol sandei, and auer chrch vos totali fol. Evrivan vos hepili singing ven shi start tu skrim and sver. Stending belo de mader virgen Meri shi kol de satan tu help hr panish det gai. "If ju meri anadervan, det shud strak ju sun! I prei for det an hr fit," jal shi tu him. Pur pater Malek, him self nju in de taun, trai hard tu ignor hr. Ven hr kraing and svering never stap hi ran in de chrch tu stop det. Shi left de chrch kraing, and meni pur sols in dilema hu tu blem. Hr ex boifrend vos lefing and holding ader grl for hend.

Hi chok tu det bai sapar des nait lefing over Julchas scin in de chrch.

⊚⊚⊚⊚⊚⊚⊚⊚⊚⊚⊚⊚⊚⊚⊚⊚⊚⊚⊚⊚⊚⊚⊚⊚⊚⊚⊚⊚⊚⊚⊚⊚⊚⊚⊚⊚⊚

the cow hooves, able to see only the dark blue sky full of stars, I dozed. It must have been a long journey, because when I woke up it was day, and hot. My two grandparents were sitting beside each other, commenting on somebody's crop of corn.

Julcha's trouble started early in her life. She was dating one of the richest and handsomest boys in our town. For some reason he wanted to leave her for some other one. The old town widows are still chewing the story. With every passing generation something new is added. This terrible day was one beautiful Sunday, and our church was totally full. Everyone was happily singing when she started to scream and swear. Standing below the mother Virgin Mary she called on Satan to help her punish the guy. "If you marry another one, death should strike you soon! I pray for this at her feet," she yelled to him. Poor Pater Malek, himself new in the town, tried hard to ignore her. When her crying and swearing didn't stop, he ran into the church to stop it. She left the church crying, and many poor souls were in a dilemma who to blame. Her ex-boyfriend laughed and held the other girl by the hand.

He choked to death that night at supper laughing over Julcha's

Old gosop kud hardli veiding det bed njus rich evri sol in de taun. "Shi is a vich! Shi sol hr sol tu de satan, and onli de bed tings ken hepen tu as if she stei in de taun! Preheps auer Pater Malek shud never liv hr in tu de chrch."

Lusing a jang felo in de taun brod olveis laca tirs. Evribadi hu kud vok ofer his sinpati tu de famili. Safering mader lostet hr konchens meni taim an de vei tu simenteri. Ol proseshen bi staping, peshentli veiding, befor dasent helping hends brod from samver de fresh vota. Vans shi regein hr konchens dei start tu vok. Rumers hau shi pul hr her, or drom an kofing vit hr hends, kip siping tru. Meni of hr helping hends givet ab resling vit hr, and vok nau in mor pisfol tel of proseshen. Evrivan egri det det vos de devels vork, tu kil det jang led. Pater Malek faeri spich diden erchiv nating bad totali konfjuzen.

Ven vos over sed pipel sloli living in smol grups. Staping bai de grevs of der lavvans, dei toket ebaut nju problem in taun. Jang Julcha. An ader end of a taun noubadi notest det jang grl, deskai in old grenis klos, living in tirs.

@@@

scene in the church.

The old gossips could hardly wait for that bad news to reach every soul in the town. "She is a witch! She sold her soul to Satan, and only bad things can happen to us if she stays in town! Perhaps our Pater Malek should never let her into the church."

Losing a young fellow in the town always brought lots of tears. Everybody who could walk offered his sympathy to the family. The suffering mother lost consciousness many times on the way to the cemetery. The whole procession would stop, patiently waiting, before a dozen helping hands brought, from somewhere, fresh water. Once she regained consciousness, they would start to walk. Rumours of how she pulled her hair or drummed on the coffin with her hands kept seeping through. Many of her helping hands gave up wrestling with her, and walked at the more peaceful tail of the procession. Everyone agreed that it was the devil's work, to kill that young lad. Pater Malek's fiery speech didn't achieve anything but total confusion.

When it was over, sad people slowly left in small groups. Stopping by the graves of their loved ones, they talked about the new problem in town. Young Julcha. At the other end of town nobody noticed the young girl, disguised in old granny's

@@@

Et frst shi vos siing in de svamps of a river Drava. Kemping vit de gipsis grup, shi help dei vaivs tu isi delivering dei bebis. Vit fol eproching, shi kjurt dei filti anerisht kidc of fiver. Bat sacha bjutifol jang vumen kud bi not veri long alon. Sun or leter det bi sam mens hart brok an hr.

Van let fol ivning tu gais kam in de totali vet gipsi kemp. Dei tok for long taim vit de lider. Julcha vos sliping vit ader vumen belo de old kar, onli drai ples in ol kemp. Den van of de men kam kloser tu de faer vich brnet besaid de vegen. "In gold vosher kamp, not veri far from hir, jang men nid jor help. Plis kam vit as." Noing det noubadi of gipsis bi rili sed if shi liv, shi egri. For meni deis dei diden hev mach tu it and van maut les tu fid bi helping. Bisaid, Drava kud start tu flading det eria eni dei nau, and dei liv hr behain. Der vos anader problem tu. For meni gipsi vumen, she vos revalin and dei van tu hev hr aut sun als posibel. Dei putet biger faer so she kud teket ol hr poseshen.

In denc fog, forest eraund de river is spuki. Vind brashed

clothes, leaving in tears.

At first she was seen in the swamps of the River Drava. Camping with a gypsy group, she helped the wives through an easy delivery of their babies. With fall approaching, she cured their filthy undernourished kids of fever. But such a beautiful young woman could not be alone for very long. Sooner or later some man's heart would be broken over her.

One late fall evening two guys came into the soaking gypsy camp. They talked for a long time with the leader. Julcha was sleeping with the other women below the old car, the only dry place in the whole camp. Then one of the men came closer to the fire, which burned beside the wagon. "In the gold washers' camp, not very far from here, a young man needs your help. Please come with us." Knowing that none of the gypsies would be really sad if she left, she agreed. For many days they hadn't had much to eat and one mouth less to feed would help. Besides, the Drava could start flooding that area any day now, and they would leave her behind. There was another problem too. For many gypsy women she was a rival, and they wanted to have her out as soon as possible. They made a bigger fire so she could gather all her possessions.

In dense fog, the forest around

de tris dei lusing dei livs. Evri muv, evri lital sneg an vet brash kud bi hrt far evei. Vet erd of a fores flor staket an hr samer shus, meket olmos inposible tu vok.

Onli in hr lait samer klos, shi vos totali vet and frosen an eraivel. De peshent vos bedli vundet vit de naif. Shi ordet a big faer. Shivering laik a lital flauer in de vind, shi koncetret an hr peshent vunds. Noing det onli a mirikal kud sev him, she preet laudli an hr nis. Auers peset, and his posishen diden chench. In erli moning auers, hi regein de konchens for a lital vail.

"If... I sorvaiv ... I meri ju."

She smailte onli tu him, noing det his chens ar rili slim. Bad ... laif is olveis fol of sopreis. De men rekaver egenc de od. De pur Julcha varn de jang felo det shi is krsed, bad hi never lisn. Dei fol in lav, and sun after dei start tu bild des lital haus. Dei vos a gud, hepi kapel. Hr noleg of helping vos respektet, and de pipel start tu kam tu hr lital haus. Evrivan vish dem long laif and hepinis. Iven auer taun gosop kuden faundet apsolutli nating vrong in des releshen.

ⓔⓔⓔⓔⓔⓔⓔⓔⓔⓔⓔⓔⓔⓔⓔⓔⓔⓔⓔⓔⓔⓔⓔⓔⓔⓔⓔⓔⓔⓔⓔⓔⓔⓔ

the river is spooky. Wind brushed the trees that were losing their leaves. Every move, every little snag in the wet brush could be heard far away. The wet earth of the forest floor stuck to her summer shoes, making it almost impossible to walk.

Only in her light summer clothes, she was totally wet and frozen on arrival. The patient was badly wounded with a knife. She ordered a big fire. Shivering like a little flower in the wind, she concentrated on her patient's wounds. Knowing that only a miracle could save him, she prayed loudly on her knees. Hours passed and his condition didn't change. In the early morning hours, he regained consciousness for a little while.

"If... I survive ... I will marry you."

She only smiled at him, knowing that his chances were really slim. But — life is always full of surprises. The man recovered against the odds. Poor Julcha warned the young fellow that she was cursed, but he never listened. They fell in love and soon after they started to build this little house. They were a good, happy couple. Her knowledge of helping was respected, and the people started to come to her little house. Everyone wished them long life and happiness. Even our town gossips could find absolutely nothing wrong

ⓔⓔⓔⓔⓔⓔⓔⓔⓔⓔⓔⓔⓔⓔⓔⓔⓔⓔⓔⓔⓔⓔⓔⓔⓔⓔⓔⓔⓔⓔⓔⓔⓔⓔ

Spring kam and triki Drava fladet vans egen. Meni gold vosher traet dei lak an nju benks. So de Julchas men, ignoring hr varnings det hi is stil not tu strong for des gop. "I van tu finish des haus, and vi nidet de mani," sed hi, pushing his long river bot in vota. Hi never retrn. Let des samer dei faund his bot. Litalbet leter in jer, njus kam elang det hi vos berit in sam lital taun daun de river.

After det, Julcha never meri enibadi in sker det hr grin ais bring de men sam harm. From des taim, mosli de pipel hev a sker tu si hr bjutifol ais. Sam of dem vuden iven tok tu hr, gast in kes, living tu sabadi als tu tel hr vot is dei problem, for a big chank of mani.

She, der vos pusht aut of taun, never refjus enibadi belo hr lital ruf. Helping evribadi hau she kud. Samhau she mengt tu hev medicin for evribadi and evriting. Meni taims det vos jang grls, hai in hop. Vaivs der despretli van tu fix dei meriches. Maders dei kud not fergiv dem self pushing dei doters in meriches dei diden vork aut. Julcha vos lisening and traet hr best. Noubadi expektet

with this relationship.

Spring came and the tricky Drava flooded once again. Many gold washers tried their luck on the new banks. So did Julcha's man, ignoring her warnings that he was not strong enough for the job. "I want to finish this house, and we need the money," he said, pushing his long river boat into the water. He never returned. Late that summer they found his boat. A little bit later in the year, news came along that he was buried in some little town down the river.

After that, Julcha didn't marry anybody, scared that her green eyes would bring the man some harm. From this time on, most people were scared to look at her beautiful eyes. Some of them wouldn't even talk to her, just in case, leaving it to somebody else to tell her their problem, for a big chunk of money.

She, who was pushed out of town, never refused to allow anybody under her little roof. She helped everybody as best she could. Somehow she managed to have medicine for everybody and everything. Many times it was young girls high in hope. Wives that desperately wanted to fix their marriages. Mothers who could not forgive themselves for pushing their daughters into marriages that didn't work out. Julcha would listen

Marijan Megla

mirikal, bikos tu fiks sambadis laif is rili hard gop.

Vans livt in auer neibar taun a vumen vit a krsed lek, justu tok old gosop. Pur ting merit sam felo det, veri sun after de kidc vos boren, lost evri interest in hr. Hi spendet mor and mor taim in taun bar, fiding de taun gosop. Meni taims, neibars hrt hau shi krai over hr krsed lek det simstu bring ol anhepinis. An edvais of old tutlos grenis, she vent tu si Julcha. Dei tok ebaudet and kraet in long ivning. Julcha njuet det she dont hev de medicin for hr, bad tu liv hr so desperatli vit hr trobels vere not fer. So, she giv hr betc der shi paundet for auer or so in fain blak dast.

Et frst de medicin sims tu vork. Anekspektetli tu enibadi, de men stei hom. Helping hr samtaim in de haus, hi bi goking vit hr and dei lef vans egen. Overhepi jang vumen prei meni taim for Julcha in aur taun chrch benit de vrgen Meri. Dei iven vent tu pilgremich tu pre for gut forchen tu holi mader Meri of Bistrica. Tu setisfai hr on promis, she brnet dasent of kandels for Julcha.

ⓔⓔⓔⓔⓔⓔⓔⓔⓔⓔⓔⓔⓔⓔⓔⓔⓔⓔⓔⓔⓔⓔⓔⓔⓔⓔⓔⓔⓔⓔⓔⓔⓔⓔⓔⓔⓔⓔⓔ

and try her best. Nobody expected a miracle, because to fix somebody's life is a really hard job.

There once lived in a neighbouring town a woman with a cursed leg, the old gossips used to say. The poor thing married some fellow who, very soon after the kids were born, lost every interest in her. He spent more and more time in the town bar, feeding the town gossip. Many times, neighbours heard how she cried over her cursed leg that seemed to bring all her unhappiness. On the advice of the old toothless grannies, she went to see Julcha. They talked about it and cried in the long evening.

Julcha knew she didn't have medicine for her, but to leave her so desperate with her troubles was not fair. So, she gave her bats that she'd pounded for an hour or so into fine black dust.

At first the medicine seemed to work. Unexpectedly to everybody, the man stayed home. Helping her in the house sometimes, he'd joke with her and they'd laugh once again. The overjoyed young woman prayed many times for Julcha in our town church beneath the Virgin Mary. They even went on a pilgrimage to pray for good fortune to Holy Mother Mary of Bastrica. To satisfy her own promise, she burned dozens of

ⓔⓔⓔⓔⓔⓔⓔⓔⓔⓔⓔⓔⓔⓔⓔⓔⓔⓔⓔⓔⓔⓔⓔⓔⓔⓔⓔⓔⓔⓔⓔⓔⓔⓔⓔⓔⓔⓔⓔ

Bat, kaming hom van dei from vork hi deskaver sam blek pauder in his fud. After she vos sevirli biten she edmet evriting. De hel brok aut and pur vumen vos bedli triten for rest of hr short laif. Frst ven kidc vit him retrn tu dei haus he andestud his big mistek. Ader vumen in taun diden van tu meri him, in sker det dei bi tritet laik his frst vaif. Ven his gron children diden van tu fergiv him hi start tu prei in de chrch. Bejond his gud eg tu muv and start a nju laif, hi spend meni naits bisaid hr grev preing for fergivnis.

Seltan, bat iven de men vos luking for ol kainc of remidis. Det brod van dei tu hr steps as baterflai Ishtvan. If eni mel in auer taun vos ever driming tu bi Suleiman pasha, supervaising his hjuch harem of pridi vumen, den him. I am positivli shor det auer taun polisman spend evri nait anet. Hi gast kuden bi setisfai vit van fimel in his haus, laik rest of pesents. Fergiv mi lord, I toking from van det sol. Hi lostet in Ferike hevi farmers hends his mens blesing. It vos his fold. Na vot a taun polismen hes tu luk in Ferikes bet, spesheli den ven

candles for Julcha.

But, coming home one day from work he discovered some black powder in his food. After she was severely beaten she admitted everything. Hell broke out and the poor woman was badly treated for the rest of her short life. When his kids first returned with him to his house he understood his big mistake. Other women in town didn't want to marry him, in fear that they would be treated like his first wife. When his grown children didn't want to forgive him he started to pray in the church. Too old to move and start a new life, he spent many nights beside his wife's grave praying for forgiveness.

It was seldom, but even men would look for all kinds of remedies. That brought our Butterfly Istvan to her steps one day. If any male in our town ever dreamt of being the Suleiman Pasha, supervising his huge harem of pretty women, then it was him. I am positively sure that our town policeman spent every night at it. He just couldn't be satisfied with one female in his house like the rest of the peasants. Forgive me lord, I'm talking about one dead soul. He lost his men's blessing in Ferike's huge farmer's hands. It was his fault. Now what business has the town policeman looking

Marijan Megla

his blesed vaif vos neket sliping inet. Shi is not de armi setl so det evrivan hu is plis raid onet.

Bisaid his kvik seks laif, der brod him des shemfol neim, he vos a gud felo. Vel it bi anfer tu put evriting onli in his buc. Evri vumen, vit vich he hes his henki penki vos involvt vit ol hr energi. I tenk it bi fer tu divaidet his bed hebec vit vumen and pesets. Dei vori mach mor ebaut dei krops als nid of dei svit vaivs.

Flaing from van taun ros tu ader, hi gast kuden meket vrong. Sam of dem vere kot so vit Baterflai Ishtvan apirenc det dei fergot vot sacha hepi taim hes in stor. If is taun gosop tu trast, den meni of baterflai children raning eraund in auer taun. Preheps vi kud andestan det at des taim, bikos his Marishka never giv him van on.

An his letct dei of sekshuel cheriti, ven his mens blesing vos rearencht from a bul tu oks in Ferikes bedrum, gipsis vos kolt. Dei shud delivert nau vorm ruster tu his blesed vaif. In sted tu krai vit him, his lavli Marishka put garlk an evri vindo and panch him in his devels skrambelt blesing. Ven

---

in Ferike's bed, especially when his blessed wife was sleeping naked in it? She is not an army saddle that everyone who pleases may ride.

Aside from his fast sex life, that brought him this shameful name, he was a good fellow. It would be unfair to put all the blame in his boots. Every woman with whom he had his hanky-panky was involved with all her energy. I think it would be fair to divide his bad habits between the women and the peasants. They worried much more about their crops than the needs of their sweet wives.

Flying from one town's rose to the other's, he could do no wrong. Some of them were so taken by Butterfly Istvan's appearance that they forgot what such a happy time has in store. If you trust the town gossips, then many of Butterfly's children were running around in our town. Perhaps we could understand that at the time, because his Marishka never gave him one of his own.

On his last day of sexual charity, when his men's blessing was rearranged from a bull to an ox in Ferike's bedroom, the gypsies were called. They delivered the now warm rooster to his blessed wife. Instead of crying with him, his lovely Marishka put garlic in every window and punched him in his

his perenc got de mesich, dei brot him emidiatli tu Julcha. Bat ... vot kan du de pur vumen tu is de pein and smesht blesing? Iven if det hes tu bi de veri inpotant pis of auer kaiser polisman, det kud not kontrol himself? Hi spendet rest of his deis laik a oks, drinking him self tu det. Sun after det, as lavli Marishka meri sekend taim. Vai not? Shi vos stil tu jang tu bi vido. An evrivan sopreis, shi giv a brt tu helti tvins. Preheps if as baterflai Ishtvan vos spending de seim emaunt of taim in his on bet als ol over de taun, vi kud si his and Marishka kids dos deis. De pur Ferike de meniak bi never in prisen, and his Julishka mei never brok de merich.

In ol dos jers, Julchas medicin trai tu kjur artraitis, epilepsi, shisofremi, bed bek, astma and hu nos vot not. Shi seltan push enibadi evei, never asking for big mani. Shi kjur as, as enimals, gost ... eniting. Onli bai hr haus kud a farmer get de medicin for overitet kau, bloen hors, sirup for on kof. Onli der vos dog tritet for broken bon in his leg. Meni of des enimal stil ran eraund hr haus, long taim fergoten from der ex oner. Sam of hr medicin vos

devil's scrambled blessing. When his parents got the message, they took him immediately to Julcha. But ... what could the poor woman do to ease the pain of a smashed blessing? Even if it happens to be a very important part of our kaiser policeman that could not control himself? He spent the rest of his days as an ox, drinking himself to death. Soon after that, our lovely Marishka married a second time. Why not? She was still too young to be a widow. To everyone's surprise, she gave birth to healthy twins. Perhaps if our Butterfly Istvan had spent as much time in his own bed as all over town, we could have seen his and Marishka's kids in those days. Poor Ferike the maniac never went to prison, and his Julishka may never break off the marriage.

In all those years, Julcha's medicine tried to cure arthritis, epilepsy, schizophrenia, bad back, asthma, and who knows what not. She seldom pushed anybody away, never asking for much money. She cured us, our animals, just ... anything. Only at her house could a farmer get medicine for an overfed cow, a bloated horse, and syrup for his own cough. Only there was a dog treated for a broken bone in his leg. Many of those animals still ran around her house, long forgotten by their ex-

svolot, sam raibet an de skin of viktem. Meni of des vos hrbs, bat sam of hr medisin iven as strong gosop kud identifai. Sam of hr medicin diden iven tach de badis for vich vos konstraklet. It vos henging eraund an de properti, or putet in de hol in de erd ver de enimal vos sliping. Tu meni of dos pekiches vorket onli in fol munlait. Adervan nidet a dark nait tu bi seksesual. Hau ever det fil fani for sam of ju, der belivet onli in klin hospitals, mosli de taim she danet a gud gop.

Sun after vi pest det lonli krucefiks, a hrd of dog volkom as vit dei beling. Ven auer vegen stap an lital forest plein, Julcha vos oredi veiding an hr steps. Kvaeting daun hr dogs, komending gipsis not tu muv kloser, si kam tu as. Hr blek hommeid klos vos sinpel and praktikal. She haidet hr long grei her an de nit of hr dark skarf. Shi voch mi vit big interes.

I kuden helpet. Iven I vos vornt nat tu luk in hr ais I never soet mor vorm, bjutifol ais als hr. Hr elegant strong hends tachet mai stamak det an det dei olmost eksplodet. In tirs, bot of mai grenperenc promis tu deliver tu begs of best

owners. Some of her medicine was swallowed, some was rubbed on the skin of the victim. Many of them were herbs, but some of her medicines even our strong gossips couldn't identify. Some of her medicines didn't even touch the bodies for which they were constructed. It was hung around the property, or put in a hole in the earth where the animal was sleeping. Too many of those packages worked only in full moonlight. Other ones needed a dark night to be successful. However that might feel funny to some of you who believe only in clean hospitals, she did a good job.

Soon after we passed that lonely crucifix, a pack of dogs welcomed us with their bellowing. When our wagon stopped on a little forest plain, Julcha was already waiting on her steps. Quieting down her dogs, commanding the gypsies not to move closer, she came to us. Her black home-made clothes were simple and practical. She hid her long grey hair underneath her dark scarf. She watched me with great interest.

I couldn't help it. Even though I was warned not to look into them, I never saw more warm and beautiful eyes than hers. Her elegant strong hands touched my stomach that on that day almost exploded. In tears, both of my grandparents promised

korn, an iven sakrament if she vishes, gast tu sev mi. Tu mek des dil ofishel, mai belavet grenmamichka giv hr dasent fresh egs det shi kipet an hr nis olovei from auer taun.

"O vel, grenmamichka, dont vori. Hi bi kering ju eraund for his merich," sei she, taching mai fiver straken hed.

I tenk noubadi hu kud si mi in mai miseri kud onesli beliv hr vorts. Stil rosting benit des hot plenket, I veidet an hr retrn. Keriing a lital pot vit sam bedli smeling ti, shi apir bisaid as vegen. De test of des ti vos so ofol det I regretet ever tu si hr. I drinket det bru bikos I kuden ran evei. Dei put mi tu svet vans egen, vich felt isi an des hot dei.

I vos vornt never tu tach mai badi no meter hau ich et bi. Sun after, excem, vich insait vos rapidli muving, apirt an mai stamak. I vos kvikli brot in de haus, stripet of ol mai klos, sopt and sun after shevt. If I bi not so skeri of grendedushkin sharp naif and eshemt from ol dos vimen det voch mi, I bi lefing. Vans des vos over dei rab mi vit strong dobelbrnet slivovic. It vos brning ven evar dei

---

to deliver two bags of the best corn, and even a sacrament if she wished, just to save me. To make the deal official, my beloved grandmamichka gave her a dozen fresh eggs she'd carried on her knees all the way from our town.

"Oh well, grandmamichka, don't worry. He'll be carrying you around at his marriage," she said, touching my fever-stricken head.

I think nobody who could see me in my misery would honestly believe her words. Still roasting beneath the hot blanket, I waited for her return. Carrying a little pot with some bad-smelling tea, she appeared beside our wagon. The taste of this tea was so awful that I regretted ever seeing her. I drank that brew because I couldn't run away. They put me to sweat once again, which felt easy on this hot day.

I was warned not to touch my body no matter how itchy it became. Soon after, eczema, which moved rapidly under the skin, appeared on my stomach. I was quickly brought into the house, stripped of all my clothes, soaped and soon after shaved. If I was not so afraid of the grandeduchkin sharp knife and ashamed that all those women watched me, I'd have laughed. Once this was over, they rubbed me with strong double-burned

tachet katet exscem. Mai kraing sims tu onli enkirich dos gais. Anadar bru vos given mi, and I entnoleg det hr kuking erpruvt.

Dei put mi tu slip in hr big dark bet. Veiding an mai slip I vochet ol dos diferent bandels henging an raf siling fol of smok. Bisaid of big blek kabert, strong teibel end chers, der vos onli de big stov. Kros de tu dasti vindos, gardet from big spinen net, brait laits foling an grob vuden flor. In des haus evri spes vos fol vit sam flauers. Sam of dem iven I njuet and vander vot dei hev insih det dei ar kipet hir.

Tja ... as gud Julcha neni vos vans egen rait. After mai long slip I rili vok tu as vegen. Shor, I nid mai greni tu help mi, bat adervais I filet fain. Pein vos gon and for frst taim I filet samting laik hanger. Vi kam let hom. Mosli de taun vos oredi sliping, bat mai grenmamichka stil faund de energi tu ran in de chrch for lital prei. It vos so mach given hr for tu begs of korn and holi sekrament.

Nekst dei mai grendedushkin chek evri korn him self, gast tu mek shor det evriting bi onli de best. Ven hi hes his tu begs

slivovica. It would burn whenever it touched the cut-open eczema. My crying only seemed to encourage those guys. Another brew was given to me, and I acknowledged that her cooking had improved.

They put me to sleep in her big dark bed. Waiting for sleep, I watched all those different bundles hanging from the rough smoky ceiling. Besides a big black cupboard, strong table and chairs, there was only the big stove. Across the two dusty windows, guarded by a big woven net, bright lights fell on a rough wooden floor. In this house every space was filled with flowers. Some of them I knew, and I wondered what they had inside that they are kept here.

Well, our good Julcha Neni was right once again. After my long sleep I really walked to our wagon. Sure, I needed my granny to help me, but otherwise I felt fine. The pain was gone and for the first time I felt something like hunger. We got home late. Most of the town was already sleeping, but my grandmamichka still found the energy to run to the church for a little prayer. So much was given to her for two bags of corn and a holy sacrament.

The next day my grandfather checked every grain of corn himself, just to make sure that everything was only the best.

pekt, and dasent of egs, sosiches and hu nos vot not, hi kol auer pater Malek. Dei vent hepi drinking from a big badel. Samtaim des dei auer Julcha neni resiv long eveidet holi sakrament.

Njus spredet kvikli over de taun. "Auer prich is gon tu devels haus! Wot shud vi du nau?" Meni of auer pipel expektet tu si Malek armt vit tu lital horns an his forhed ven hi eraivt bek. Sam of dem cheket his hevenli klos for pis of red tel. Taun gosop preper garlik chens tu sev as chrch dor if det ekr. In sted of tu devels, dei vartetet for tu terebel hepi dranks.

Julcha dai jr or so after, riching onli sixti faif. Hr fineral proseshen vos biger den ever rekordet. Entlest de taun det shi olveis so lavet and help peet hr long taim overdu honor. Sait den in auer taun vos boren meni grls vit grin ais, bat noubadi der kol dem vich.

─────────────────────────────────────

When he had packed his two bags and a dozen eggs, sausages and who knows what, he called our Pater Malek. They went off happily, drinking from a big bottle. Sometime that day our Julcha Neni received a long-awaited holy sacrament.

News spread quickly over the town. "Our priest is going to the devil's house! What should we do now?" Many of our people expected to see Malek armed with little horns on his forehead when he arrived back. Some of them checked his heavenly clothes for a piece of red tail. The town gossips prepared garlic chains to save our church door if that occurred.

Instead of two devils, they waited for two terribly happy drunks.

Julcha died a year or so after, reaching only 65. Her funeral procession was the biggest ever recorded. At least the town that she always so loved and helped paid her a long-overdue honour. Since then, many girls with green eyes were born in our town, but nobody dared call them witch.

It vos sandei. Bjutifol septenbar koloret ol livs in auer lital taun. Fogi monings lodet de moister an rufs, and grin gras fol vit shafrans.

Eraund auer blesed chrch entrens vos gedert ol kids in de taun, in dei gud klos and vilo baskets. As belavet mader oversierin vos siting an hors driven vegen. Vit hai picht vois shi vos anauncing de neim of strit, and neim of dos det sopostu go der. Jang nan siting bisaid, putet der neims on a pepir and der dei vent. Emilko and mi vos olmost de letct, and de strit dei vi gedet vos far from chrch, bordering vit pablik pashcher. Emilko vos shor hi nju a shortkat, and vi bi not lusing auer hends keriing de frut.

Auer frst haus vos det from old Lovro and Ana. For mosli of his laif old Lovro vas a grauch. Hi endlodete his forstreshen vit aut vorning an his femili and gud neibers. Iven so dei akchili laik him, lefing over his anjuzuli lav tu his kaus. His kaus vos best fed, best tritet and olmost idiotikali

---

It was Sunday. Beautiful September coloured all the leaves in our little town. Foggy mornings loaded the roofs with moisture, and the green grass was full of saffron.

Around our blessed church entrance were gathered all the kids in town, with their good clothes and willow baskets. Our beloved Mother Superior was sitting on a horse-drawn wagon. With a high-pitched voice she would announce the name of a street and the name of those who were supposed to go there. A young nun sitting beside her put their names on paper, and there they went. Emilko and me were almost the last, and the street we got was far from the church, bordering on the public pasture. Emilko was sure he knew a shortcut, so our hands wouldn't get tired carrying the fruit.

Our first house was that of old Lovro and Anna. For most of his life Lovro was a grouch. He unloaded his frustrations without warning on his family and good neighbours. Even so, they actually liked him, laughing over his unusual love for his cows. His cattle were the best fed, best treated, and were almost idiotically

---

lavt. Old gosop vos toking det Lovro lav mor his kaus als his on old Ana. Shi akceptet des step an de sait, of hr men. Beter hi lav his on kaus als luking for sei ting in de taun, giving gosop nidet fid, sei Ana meni taim. Shi vos a veri gud vumen, det in hr eg developing sam kain of hamp, vich putet hr hepi fes klose tu erd.

Dei haus bordert an pablik pashcher, fol of krset vilos. In long samer deis, des vos de ples in vich jang taun vumen lisen an old gipsin predikument aut dei lavli pink pos. Dei avordet gipsis vumen for a gud njus vit laiv chikens, fresh egs, or iven vit pis of smoket mit. Belo Lovros vindos det vos not tu hai from de srfes enivei, gipsi fait, kraet, pleet dei vajolins. Lovro end Ana never konplen over des noisi neibers. An gut deis, ven Lovro vas setisfai vit luk of his overfetet superklin kaus, gipsi kud iven akspektet glas of vain or slivovica for dei goking. Bat, if eniting go vrong, and sanbadi sei samting vrong ebaut his bjutis, frendli grendedushkin kud trn in sekend in poisen skorpio.

───────────────────────────

loved. The old gossips said Lovro loved his cows more than his own Anna. She accepted this sidestep by her man. Better he love his own cows than look for the same thing in the town, giving the gossips needed feed, said Anna many times. She was a very good woman who, as she aged, developed some kind of hump which put her happy face close to the earth.

Their house bordered on the public pasture, full of cursed willows. In the long summer days, this was the place where the young town women listened to gypsies make predictions out of their lovely pink paws. They awarded the gypsy women for good news with live chickens, fresh eggs, or even with a piece of smoked meat. Below Lovro's windows, that weren't too high above the surface anyway, gypsies fought, cried, played their violins. Lovro and Anna never complained about these noisy neighbours. On good days, when Lovro was satisfied with the look of his overfed super-clean cows, gypsies could even expect a glass of wine or slivovica for their joking. But if anything went wrong, and somebody said something wrong about his beauties, this friendly grandeduchkin could turn in a second into a poisonous scorpion.

His lital haus vas vait, vich smol vindos vos overlodet vit red perangonian. In hr bek sait vos old big epels tris, lining over hr stro ruf. An de nit of des enchen ruf vos krset, laft, drinket, gosopt, daid, gest srvt, lesen for laif given. Lovros haus vos gast kopi of det seim haus, vich ripided it patern, cros de taun over and over, chenching onli de sais and kolor.

Bad, vot bi de laif vit aut problems. It simstu mi det problem laik a taun gosop liv noubadi in pis. Not iven Lovro and Ana ver sev of det. Dei big problem vos dei mauli doter. Shi vos oredi tventi faif, and stil not merit. For mosli of a taun shi vos konsider als old meid, and de rumers ebaut hr vos raising evri dei. Pur Lovro and Ana vos hontet vit aidija det dei mei never si dei gren children. Anas sednis vos bordering an gelosi, ven shi luket in de chrch an grenis vit dei children. Lovro samtaim diden iven vanet tu go tu de jer market, noing det is noubadi der tu hu hi kan giv for karusel rait.

Lovros doter vos a gud luking grl and normal fimel. Lord shud panish mi, if I kontribjutet tu rong konkluzen. Shi vos prfekt in de kichen, and an hr badi ju kud not skrepet a

His little house was white, with its small windows overloaded with red begonias. At the back, big old apple trees leaned over the straw roof. Underneath this ancient roof had been cursing, laughing, drinking, deaths, guests served, life's lessons given. Lovro's house was just a copy of the same house whose pattern repeated across the town over and over, differing only by size and colour.

But, what would life be without problems. It seems to me that problems, like town gossips, leave nobody in peace. Not even Lovro and Anna were safe. Their big problem was their mouthy daughter. She was already twenty-five and still wasn't married. Most of the town considered her an old maid, and rumours about her arose every day. Poor Lovro and Anna were haunted with the idea that they may never see their grandchildren. Anna's sadness bordered on jealousy when she saw grannies in church with their children. Lovro sometimes didn't even want to go to the big annual market, knowing that there was nobody he could take there to give a carousel ride.

Lovro's daughter was a good looking girl and a normal female. Lord punish me if I contributed to a wrong conclusion. She was perfect in the kitchen and you couldn't scrape a

singel spun of fet. So, vot vos vrong vit hr? Hr big maut, vit vich shi brok evri kurig in sinpl men dei ask hr for merich.
Des moning ven vi kam an dors of des lavli haus, dei ol grit as an de sters. Vi vos eskortet in de kichen and fidet vit kukis. Dei doter gok vit as, iven chencht as her stail. Mi and Emilko vere for shor not in gud eg tu meri hr, bad des moning shi simstu bi gast rait for fjucher mader. Ana brodet from samver dasent of best apel ever sin in de kaunti. An end of as short visit, shi vokt as aut tu de strit. "Plis, sei tu as mader oversiarin, meibi vi hev a hepi vinter befor as." Shi krost hr self and den desapirt behain hai properti fens.
Auer nekst haus vos from divorsi Olga and hr laver strong Mishka. Shi ran from hr bed gipsi hasbent and as Mishka kuden faundet pis vit his belavet Tilchika. Dos deis det haus is veri pisfol, bat not veri long det vos de point of meger trobels. Vel, tu bi onest, meibi vi ol kontributet tu des big kresh. Vi njuet for des romens for long taim. Bad vot shud vi du? So vi vos veiding peshentli ven auer svit Tilchika endet det suspenc.

singel spun of fat from her body. So, what was wrong with her? Her big mouth, with which she broke all the courage of simple men who might ask her for marriage.

This morning when we came to the doors of this lovely house they all greeted us at the stairs. We were escorted to the kitchen and fed cookies. Their daughter joked with us, even changed her style for us. Me and Emilko were certainly not old enough to marry her, but on this morning she seemed to be just right for a future mother. From somewhere, Anna brought a dozen of the best apples ever seen in the county. At the end of our short visit she walked us out to the street.

"Please, tell our Mother Superior that maybe we'd like a happy winter ahead." She crossed herself and then disappeared behind the high fence.

Our next house was home of the divorcee Olga and her lover strong Mishka. She had run from her bad gypsy husband, and Mishka had never found peace with his beloved Tilchika. In those days that house was very peaceful, but not much later it was the point of major troubles. Well, to be honest, maybe we all contributed to this big crash. We'd known about this romance for a long time. But what should we do? So we were patiently waiting when our sweet Tilchika ended the suspense.

Marijan Megla

Van bjutifol ivning, ven hol neibarhud kuket de saper, inkluding Olga, Tilchika strak vit revench. An inkredibal jauling of a vundct men fris evrivan hart. Des tu vimen skrimet, puling ichader for long her and tering de klos from dei lavli badis. Bai eraiving of frst helpers, Mishka vos teken emidietli tu hospital, vit his penc henging daun from his nis. Tu kul daun det tu vaild chiken vos nidet ten strong gais. De hol ausmas of des Tilchika panishment serfest ven gais, vich brodet Mishka tu de doktor vit Baterflai Istvan kerich, retrnet hom. Dei teling de veiding gosop over terebel brns an his barom and det vos not ol. Ven dei tuket a vuden span from his mens blesing, hol hospital personal vos nidet tu kip him daun an doktor teibel.

Insted tu tenk de doktor for de trobel, Mishka nokt im daun med over peinfol operation. Ven he kud pul his penc ab and stap advertaising his brnet barom kros de stritc of auer kaunti, Baterflai Istvan and tu helper tuket stil in shok Mishka.

Ol pipel in taun egri, det Mishka shud bi panisht for his sekshuel cheritis. Bad, for mosli sol vos Tilchikas panishment

One beautiful evening, when the whole neighbourhood was cooking supper, including Olga, Tilchika struck for revenge. The incredible howling of a wounded man froze everyone's heart. Those two women screamed, pulling each other by their long hair and tearing the clothes from their lovely bodies. By the time the first helpers arrived, Mishka had to be taken immediately to hospital with his pants hanging down from his knees. Ten strong guys were needed to cool down those two wild chickens. The whole outcome of Tilchika's punishment surfaced when the guys who'd taken Mishka to the doctor in Butterfly Istvan's carriage returned home.

They told the waiting gossips about the terrible burns on his bottom and that wasn't all. When they took a wooden sliver from his men's blessing, the whole hospital personnel was needed to keep him down on the doctor's table.

Instead of thanking the doctor for his trouble, Mishka knocked him down, mad over the painful operation. When he could pull his pants up and stop advertising his burnt bottom across our county, Butterfly Istvan and two helpers took the still in shock Mishka.

All the people in town agreed that Mishka should be punished for his sexual charities. But, to most of us, Tilchika's punishment

tu harsh. Vel, a brnet barom vos fer inaf vit as, stafet mens blesing tu mach. Iven vit auer lords help, vi kuden emegin hau kud svit Tilchika vunding hr hasbent an tu plesis. Es tuk mor den a jer befor as lavli Orel bachika revil his ofserving in a taun bar.

"He-he-he," lef old Orel bachika. "Des ivning ven evrivan vos jaling laik a bist in sloter haus, i vok in tu de haus."

"So vot vos der?" asket de gais, puting dei heds tugeder.

"Vel, belivet or not, I soet de vumens barom prest in de soft vorm shishkerli do, spredet an raf teibel," sed de old gai.

"I never hr det ju mek shishkerli vit vumens barom," sed a naiv lisener.

"Ju idiot. Ven lav strak strak. Enivei if ju kuking de gulash or meking de shishkerli an raf teibel."

"A..a..a..a. Vel I diden andestand et frst," toking inosent lisener.

"Des mek senc nau?" tok ekseidinli old Orel bachika. "Ven de Tilchika kam tu piket ab hr ruster, shi faund him meking shishkerli vit de Olga an de kichen teibel."

ⓢⓢⓢⓢⓢⓢⓢⓢⓢⓢⓢⓢⓢⓢⓢⓢⓢⓢⓢⓢⓢⓢⓢⓢⓢⓢⓢⓢⓢⓢⓢⓢ

was too harsh. A burned bottom was fair enough with us, but a stuffed men's blessing was too much. Even with our lord's help we couldn't imagine how sweet Tilchika could wound her husband in two places. It took more than a year before our lovely Orel Bachika revealed in the town bar what he'd observed.

"He-he-he," laughed old Orel Bachika. "That evening, when everyone was yelling like a beast in the slaughterhouse, I walked into the house."

"So what was there?" asked the guys, putting their heads together.

"Well, believe it or not, I saw a woman's bottom pressed into the soft warm shishkerli dough spread on the rough table," said the old guy.

"I never heard you could make shishkerli with a woman's bottom," said a naive listener.

"You idiot. When love strikes it strikes, even if you are cooking goulash or making shishkerli on a rough table."

"Aaaahh. Well, I didn't understand at first," said the innocent listener.

"Does this make sense now?" old Orel Bachika said excitedly. "When Tilchika came to pick up her rooster, she found him making shishkerli with Olga on the kitchen table."

ⓢⓢⓢⓢⓢⓢⓢⓢⓢⓢⓢⓢⓢⓢⓢⓢⓢⓢⓢⓢⓢⓢⓢⓢⓢⓢⓢⓢⓢⓢⓢⓢ

Marijan Megla

"So, shi troet a pot of boiling vota an his neket barom, tu mek a prodakshen rili hot," se de old blek shmit.

"Samhau, in des frst pein, hi godet his stafet mens blesing," sed de old Orel bachika.

"O..o..o..o. Nau I andestan vai i mas smudet de bladi teibel," sed de taun karpenter. "Olga vos prsonli supervasing de gop. Ha..ha..ha."

After des dei Mishka and Olga livet pisfol, and no merich vos mor preist from old gosop laik deis. Ven vi kam in de haus, der vos oredi veiding. Olga vos in hop, and hardli muving in de kichen. Dei giv as apels, and vi shud prei det pater Malek disaidet tu bles dei kaming chaild.

Nekst haus belong tu old Marishka, dei ol sols in taun kolet Pepi neni. Vi kidc never faund aut vai is det bat vi ol egri shi vos de best hjumen bin eraund. In long hot samer deis, ven vi vos voching an auer gresing enimals, det vos de onli ples ver vi godet votar from de glas. Ol aders bi gast pointet an de voter vel tu stil as drst. Vi lavet sam of des glasis mor den aders, and olmos fait tu hev a drink.

⊚⊚⊚⊚⊚⊚⊚⊚⊚⊚⊚⊚⊚⊚⊚⊚⊚⊚⊚⊚⊚⊚⊚⊚⊚⊚⊚⊚⊚⊚⊚⊚⊚⊚⊚⊚

"So, she threw a pot of boiling water on his naked bottom to make the production really hot," said the old blacksmith.

"Somehow, suffering this first pain, he got his men's blessing stuffed," said old Orel Bachika.

"Oooo..oh. Now I understand why I had to smooth the bloody table," said the town carpenter. "Olga personally supervised the job. Ha-ha-ha."

After those days Mishka and Olga lived in peace, and no marriage was more praised by the old gossips. When we came to their house they were already waiting. Olga was pregnant and hardly moving in the kitchen. They gave us apples, and we should pray that Pater Malek will decide to bless the coming child.

The next house belonged to old Marishka, who all souls in town called Pepi Neni. We kids never found out why that was, but we all agreed she was the best human being around. In long hot summer days, when we were watching our grazing animals, hers was the only place where we got water from a glass. All the others would just point us to their water well to still our thirst. We loved some of those glasses more than others, and almost fought to have a drink.

Hr haus vos rili smol, vich shi kip in prfekt kondishen. Ven evar vi singing for de falentin dei et hr ples as atenchen vos dron an a streng frnach and lemps. Shi godet det from hr bos in Wijena long taim ego. Bed tong teling det shi hes mach mor als det properti from fild marshal Muler. Hr san. I olveis vanet tu no, vai is de Pepi neni san sacha misteri. Bad, auer groen abs in a femili vuden diskastet.

Van taim I vos safering from astma atek. Onli mi and mai lavli grenmamichka vos hom. Shi vos an hr nis preing tu as belavet gesus, voriing hr tu det. Det vos mai onli chens tu get an de barom of des misteri. I promis hr tu bi vans egen helti if shi tel mi det. O vel, grenmamichkas ar sacha isi prei in hends of dei grenchildren. Shi sedaun in hr big hevi cher, chek vans egen if noubadi als is lisening, and start teling.

Marishka vos hepi jang grl, der in hr fortin jer of eg godet a gop in Wijena. It vos gast tu prfekt tu bi tru and dei stap toking frst ven shi vos gon, end de postmen brod de mani hom from Wijena det shi giv hr mader tu help res de rest of femili.

Her house was really small and she kept it in perfect condition. Whenever we sang for Valentine's Day at her place our attention was drawn to the strange furniture and lamps. She got those from her boss in Vienna a long time ago. Bad tongues said she had much more than that property from Field Marshal Muler. Her son. I always wanted to know why Pepi Neni's son was such a mystery. But the grownups in our family wouldn't discuss it.

One time I was suffering from an asthma attack. Only me and my lovely grandmamichka were home. She was on her knees praying to our beloved Jesus, worried to death. That was my only chance to get to the bottom of this mystery. I promised her I'd get healthy if she told me that. Oh well, grandmamichkas are such easy prey in the hands of their grandchildren. She sat down in her big heavy chair, checked again to make sure nobody else was listening, and started to tell.

Marishka was a happy young girl who in her fourteenth year of age got a job in Vienna. It was just too perfect to be true, and they first stopped talking when she was gone and the postman brought money from Vienna that she'd given her mother to help raise the rest of the family.

Marijan Megla

Evri jer shi vos vans visiting hom, giving evrivan of hr braders and sisters big present. Vit eitin shi vos luking laik rili miledi.

Marishka vos onli grl in hol taun, der in samer nidet hot voter and a smeling sop tu vosh hr self, sed mai lavli grenmamichka. Is gast nachurali det sacha bjuti diden go veri long vit aut a men redi tu dai for hr. Auer taun bojs njuet det dei mei laiket Marishka, bad dei kud not erforder hr. Na hu in lords neim kud hev a vaif det nidet hitet vota ven ever shi vosh hr pridi fes? Sacha ekspencis kud keri onli de Eprahim auer taun jidish. Plis dont hev mi rong, dei ol lav him, and noubadi akcheli nuet eni beter gai for as Marishka ... bad ... jidish? Des taim ven Marishka vos retrning tu hr gop in Wijena, shi livet a taun divaidet. Dei vos der dei belivet in des merig, ignoring det dei kam from tu diferent religen, and aders. Bot of de front faitet biterli for dei kos.

Auer pater Malek stud in betvin, kiping pis and kuling daun farmers sol. "Luket des laik mi, mai belavet pipel. I bi invaitet, or bikos I danet de mekremoni or bikos dei sker sam bed

@@

Every year she visited home once, giving every one of her brothers and sisters a big present. By eighteen she was looking like a real milady.

Marishka was the only girl in the whole town who needed hot water and scented soap to wash herself in summer, said my lovely grandmamichka. It was just natural that such a beauty didn't go very long without a man ready to die for her. Our town boys knew they could like Marishka, but they could not afford her. Now who in the lord's name could have a wife who needed heated water whenever she washed her pretty face? Such an expense could be carried only by

Abraham, the town Jew. Please don't take me wrong, they all loved him and nobody actually knew a better guy for our Marishka ... but ... Jewish? This time when she returned to her job in Vienna she left the town divided. There were those who believed in this marriage, ignoring that they came from two different religions, and the others. Both fronts fought bitterly for their cause.

Our Pater Malek stood between them, keeping peace and cooling down the farmers' souls. "Look at this like me, my beloved people. I've been invited, either because I'm doing the matrimony or because they're scared of some bad

@@

spel from mai chrch. So, vai shud I bi med?" Bad insted tu kam hom vit frst tren, keriing hr sevings, she never retrn.

Faif jer letar. Auer lavli Eprahim het faineli fergoten his belavet Marishka and vos hepili merit vit Golda. She vos svit jang ledi, preheps lital tu skini for as men det simstu lavet soft plesis ven in lav. Auer taun gosop fergedet ebaut Marishka and det krost merich det never hepen enivei, Marishka kam hom. Shi hes in hr hends a bebi boy, a lital Pepi. She hes mani for a properti and de benk. Marishka stei bai as, bikos hr femili obendet hr and des chaild vit aut fader. Sun after dei giv hr de neim Pepi neni, bikos shi vos anved.

Vot hepen in Wijena is gast evrivans gest, bat shi tol mai grenmamichka det Muler merig vos oredi broken ven shi kam tu vork der. His vaif vos spending hr deis in spas, kjuring hr depreshen and sednis for lusing hr jang laver. So de Muler relai an de bjutifol Marishka tu res his kidc. Marishka vos toren in betvin Vijena and Muler, and auer Eprahim in auer taun. Mulers kidc dei kol hr "Mutti." Shi

spell from my church. So why should I be mad?" But instead of coming home on the first train, carrying her savings, Marishka didn't return.

Five years later. Our lovely Abraham had finally forgotten his beloved Marishka and was happily married to Golda. She was a sweet young lady, perhaps a little too skinny for our men who seemed to love soft places when in love. Our town gossips had forgotten about Marishka and that crossed marriage that never happened anyway, when Marishka came home. She had in her hands a baby boy, a little Pepi. She had money to buy property and to put in the bank. Marishka stayed with us because her family abandoned her and this fatherless child. Soon after they gave her the name Pepi Neni because she was unwed.

What happened in Vienna was anyone's guess, but she told my grandmamichka that Muler's marriage was already broken down when she went to work there. His wife was spending her days in spas, curing her depression and sadness over losing her young lover. So Muler relied on the beautiful Marishka to raise his kids. Marishka was torn between Vienna and Muler, and our Abraham in our town. Muler's kids called her "Mutti." She

dont belong eni mor tu as sosaeti and dei diden van hr der. Muler lav hr, bat his femili not. For jer pest and dei livet tugeder, kidc vere aut de haus and sun after she vos pregnet. Den ven bebi vos gast boren, Muler perenc smeling big skendal kol his vaif hom, and Marishka vos put an de trein vit inaf mani tu start a nju laif.

Pepi vos veri ambishes boy, de best in auer skul. Marishka giv him in gimnasium in nekst siti, and den on juniversiti. Veri sun after det, hi develop sam jentelmen signis det sloli destroi his brein. Pur Pepi vos stil living in des hospital, hoping tu rekaver, endet mai grenmamichka hr stori.

Old Marishka vos given as dasent of bjutifol piches for as nans, and after vi finisht apelgus, shi sed: "Tu mai san go evriting oreit after ol. Sei tu mader oversierin, if vi ol prei hard auer gud lord mei fri him from his safering." Vi hag de old greni and vok evei.

Vi diden no vot tu tenk ebaut nekst haus. It vos inhebitet from rili old Ivan and Verona, vich hardli liv dei lital rum ... and as ticherin. Vi diden vanet tu put dos old gais in bed

ⓔⓔⓔⓔⓔⓔⓔⓔⓔⓔⓔⓔⓔⓔⓔⓔⓔⓔⓔⓔⓔⓔⓔⓔⓔⓔⓔⓔⓔⓔⓔⓔ

didn't belong to our society any more, and they didn't want her there. Muler loved her but his family didn't. Four years passed and they lived together, the kids left the house and soon after she was pregnant. Then when the baby was just born, Muler's parents, smelling a scandal, called his wife home and Marishka was put on the train with enough money to start a new life.

Pepi was a very ambitious boy, the best in our school. Marishka sent him to the gymnasium school in the next city, and then on to university. Very soon after that he developed some kind of gentleman's sickness that slowly destroyed his brain. Poor Pepi was still alive in the hospital, hoping to recover, said my grandmamichka to end her story.

Old Marishka gave us a dozen beautiful peaches for the nuns, and after we finished our apple juice she said: "Everything will go all right with my son after all. Tell Mother Superior that if we all pray hard the good lord may free him from his suffering." We hugged the old granny and walked away.

We didn't know what to think about the next house. It was inhabited by the very old Ivan and Verona, who hardly left their little room ... and our teacher. We didn't want to put those old guys in a bad

ⓖⓖⓖⓖⓖⓖⓖⓖⓖⓖⓖⓖⓖⓖⓖⓖⓖⓖⓖⓖⓖⓖⓖⓖⓖⓖⓖⓖⓖⓖⓖⓖ

spat if dei dont hev a frut for as basket. End den vos ticherin, femes for fiksing as bladi heds, bat onli vi kidc nju samting aut hr praivat laif. Jusing vans shortkat vi diskavert hr kising as jang dikan. Vi njuet shi is a komjunist, and lav kud bi veri pauerfol, bad bring des tu tugeder ... iven spiking in lav trms mas bi a pjur mirikel.

"Vel," sed Emilko, skraching his short her, "so votju tenk? Shud vi go in or not?"

"Ju hev isi tu sei, it is mai klas ticherin!" jal I vandering vot shud I du. "Hau ebaut vi gast peset des haus?"

"Du ju remembar vot mader oversiarin tol as?" ask hi puting his gogels klos tu mai nos. "Evri singel haus. No chiting!" sed hi, stretening his nju shrt.

"Bat, auer ticherin is in de parti, iven shi kis holi dikan," sed I, pointing tu hr vindos.

"It is not aponas tu opos nans vish," sed filosofikli mai old pal end enter de properti.

Old Ivan vos laudli kofing, fiding a lital oven in de korner of a rum. An de nit of hevi feder bet, suportet vit tri

---

spot of they didn't have fruit for our basket. And then there was the teacher, famous for fixing our bloody heads. But only we kids knew something about her private life. Once, using a shortcut, we discovered her kissing our young deacon. We knew she was a communist and love could be very powerful, but to bring these two together ... even speaking in terms of love it must be a pure miracle.

"Well," said Emilko, scratching his short hair, "so what do you think? Should we go in or not?"

"It's easy for you to say, but it is my class teacher!" I yelled, wondering what I should do. "How about we just pass this house?"

"Do you remember what Mother Superior told us?" he asked, putting his goggles close to my nose. "Every single house. No cheating!" he said, straightening his new shirt.

"But our teacher is in the party, even if she did kiss the holy deacon," I said, pointing to her windows.

"It isn't up to us to oppose the nun's wish," my old pal said philosophically and entered the property.

Old Ivan was coughing loudly, feeding a little oven in the corner of the room. Underneath a heavy feather bed, supported by three big pilos, old Verona vos mor det den a laiv. In midel of a rum der vos a hjuch kolonial teibel. In litel basked der vos apels for a nan, and bisaid pleit fol vit kukis. Old Verona neiberin beket for hr des kukis, so det shi hes for kidc dei geder frut for a nans. Vi bod kis grenmamichka, tenks for frut and kukis and help old Ivan rich his bed. Dei diden hev nating tu vish, so vi left.

Ven vi vos stanbeling kros de dark koridor, as jang ticherin open de dor. Mai vois desapir in dip of mai badi. Hef ankonchens I lisening charming Emilko eksplening tu hr prpes of auer kaming. Shi lef, haging mi and Emilko.

"Religen kud not stap as tu bild des kantri, so vai not?" sei shi, giving as a pers.

Mai juzuli strang spich diden van tu rekavcr, and Emilko vos teking ker of a bisnis. Laik sam prich, hi bi tenking for pleg and giving promis tu bring mesiches tu as nans.

In letct haus det vi visiting des dei vi tok vit old mader of taun shumeker, der in his trtis stil diden van tu meri. Shi giv as per and faif dinar tu ich. Ven shi vos kising as gudbai shi

---

big pillows, old Verona was more dead than alive. In the middle of the room was a huge colonial table. In a little basket there were apples for our nuns, and beside it a plate filled with cookies. Old Verona's neighbours baked those cookies for her so she would have them for the kids who gather fruit for the nuns. We both kissed grandmamichka, thanked her for the fruit and cookies and helped old Ivan reach his bed. They didn't have anything to wish, so we left.

When we were stumbling across the dark corridor, our young teacher opened the door. My voice disappeared in the depths of my body. Half unconscious I listened to charming Emilko explaining to her the purpose of our coming. She laughed, hugging me and Emilko.

"Religion couldn't stop us from building this country, so why not?" she said, giving us a pear.

My usually strong voice didn't want to recover, and Emilko was taking care of business. Like some preacher, he thanked her for her pledge and promised to take messages to our nuns.

In the last house we visited that day we talked with the old mother of the town shoemaker, who in his thirties still didn't want to marry. She gave us a pear and five dinar each. When she was kissing us good-bye she sed: "Tel as mader hi is in lav, preheps if vi help a lital meibi hi meri des vinter."

Emilko and mi vos glad ven vi finisht auer strit. Auer vilo basket vos fol and kvait hevi. For as der never ver mach gud klos, spesheli bai vork, vos difikalt tu hendle des basket in des sandei klos. Emilko shortkat trn tu bi desaster. For mor den hefen auer vi vochet as ticherin kising as dikan an sikrit spat. Vi diden andestand mach ebaut kising bisnis den, bad dei shor danet gut gop for a komjunist and a katolik.

Vi kam de letct, as juzuli. Taet, overfed vit svits and kukis, vi iven remember ol dos mesiches. Mader oversiarin and hr helperin lisening peshentli and blest as.

Let des vinter, auer stro or shingel rufs muv tugeder, smoking hevili kros big chimnis. In long ivnings, siting bisaid ichader, dei toket ebaut let njus in de taun. I vos not sopreis, ven I hr det old Lovro vos luking for gipsis, tu meri his lavli doter. Vot hi vos not teling eraund, bat de old gosop faund aut enivei, is det hi giv van of his kaus for det tu jang shumeker. Dei vos faiting and deskasing des metar,

said: "Tell our Mother that he is in love, and perhaps if we help a little maybe he'll marry this winter."

Emilko and me were glad when we finished our street. Our willow basket was full and quite heavy. For us who never wore many good clothes, especially for working, it was difficult to handle the basket in our Sunday clothes. Emilko's shortcut turned out to be a disaster. For more than half an hour we watched our teacher kissing our deacon in their secret spot. We didn't understand much about this kissing business, but they sure did a good job for a Communist and a Catholic.

We came back last, as usual. Tired, overfed with sweets and cookies, we even remembered all those messages. Mother Superior and her helper listened patiently and blessed us.

Late that winter our straw or shingle roofs huddled together, smoking heavily across the big chimneys. In the long evenings, sitting beside each other, they talked about the latest news in town. I was not surprised when I heard that old Lovro was looking for gypsies to play at the marriage of his lovely daughter. What he wasn't telling, but the old gossips found out anyway, is that he gave one of his cows for that to the young shoemaker. They were fighting and discussing this matter

laik ten jidish befor open tora. Ven de dil vos strakt ten big gais vos nidet tu provent Lovro from susaid in his kaushed. Vel, after ol a kau is les vortet als de grend children and hepinis of his onli doter. Tudei, olmost trti jers after, I am not shor if as Lovro evar egri an desvan. Bat, ju no self vot kud vi du ol for seg of auer kidc. An dei of merich, Lovro and Ana vos hepili goking vit de mader in lo.

Short befor nju jer old Pepi neni, lost hr sik san. It vos hart tu si hr kraing, bad iven shi edmitet det vos de best. Gipsis pleet vajolins an his grev, and no ais stud drei. Onli tu of Pepi neni bradars sho aban simenteri bat iven des mek hr mach mor hepier.

Old Ivan and Verona vos putet in old foks hom, ver dei akcheli rekaver for a jer or so. Mai grenmamichka and mi visitet dos gais meni taim, and dei simstu bi veri hepi.

Det as ticherin nid mor as auer lord help vos klir in let vinter. Shi tuk as noubadi als bat auer jang dikan. Old gosop vos so histerikal ebaudet, det pur pater Malek gard de haus tu provent blad shed. Bad, ven dei faineli

---

like ten worshippers before the open Torah. When the deal was struck, ten big guys were needed to prevent Lovro from suicide in his cow shed. Well, after all, a cow is worth less than grandchildren and the happiness of his only daughter. Today, almost thirty years after, I am not sure if our Lovro would ever agree on this one. But you know yourself what we all would do for the sake of our kids. On the day of the marriage, Lovro and Anna were happily joking with the mother-in-law.

Shortly before the new year old Pepi Neni lost her sick son. It was hard to see her crying, but even she admitted that this was best.

Gypsies played violins at his grave, and no eyes stayed dry. Only two of Pepi Neni's brothers showed up at the cemetery, but even that made her much happier.

Old Ivan and Verona were put in an old folks home, where they actually recovered for a year or so. My grandmamichka and me visited those guys many times, and they seemed to be very happy.

That our teacher needed more than our lord's help was clear in late winter. She took as husband no-one else but our young deacon. The old gossips were so hysterical about it that poor Pater Malek had to guard the house to prevent bloodshed. But, when they finally

apir an dor of auer belavet chrch, evrivan vos chiring. Vit lav kan noubadi bad lord komend and hi gast epruv des per.

In let spring auer belavet Olga and Mishka brodet dei tu bebis tu bi blest in de chrch. Taun gosop vos stil remembering Olgas teibel romans. Bed tongs sed det sam of de old viches akspektet tu si des tvins vit vuden lek, or barom. At frst as belavet pater Malek diden vant tu bles dem, bad den vuden or not dei vos auers enivei. Preheps, auer pater Malek vanet tu sho as vot kud bi enkomplisht bai solad lav bes.

═══════════════════════════

appeared at the door of our beloved church, everyone was cheering. With love, nobody but the lord can command, and he just approved of this pair.

In late spring our beloved Olga and Mishka brought their two babies to be blessed in the church. Town gossips still remembered Olga's table romance. Bad tongues said that some of the old witches expected those twins with a wooden leg, or bottom. At first our beloved Pater Malek didn't want to bless them, but then wooden or not, they were ours anyway. Perhaps our Pater Malek wanted to show us what could be best accomplished by solid love.

It vos not so det hi het hr. Bat faundet eni simpati for Rosi felt hevi for auer blesed pater Malek. She vos his meid, det vori ebaut his volbiing, klin haus and chrch. Hr domen vos soplaing de flauers for chrch oltar, from her chrch garden or from doneshens.

Pater Malek endherotet hr from as pater Florian, de lord srvent in St. Jelena befor long taim. Florian vos streng stabern katolik not veri populer in auer taun. Risen for det vos paushali his overdosis of festing in fud and drinks. His religes vju vos gast so hart tu mech in des grin gulash flet draun in vain and slivovica. Ven hi dai and pater Malek tuk over, lord fergiv as, noubadi vos rili sed.

Rosi vos a staki fimel, der gro tu des proporshen det she start tu luk laik a men. Hr heri chin end softli blak mustash belo hr zukini nos brod meni of as kidc in dilema — tu kol her mister Rosi or stei laik tolt hom bai mis Rosi — ven vi delivert samting an chrch

@@

It wasn't that he hated her. But to find any sympathy for Rosie was hard for our blessed Pater Malek. She was his maid, who worried about his well-being, cleaned the house and church. Her domain was supplying flowers for the church altar from her garden or from donations.

Pater Malek inherited her from our Pater Florian, the lord's servant for a long time before him. Florian was a strange stubborn Catholic not very popular in our town. The reason was partially his overdoses of fasting from food and drink. His religious views were so hard to meet in this green goulash flat drowned in wine and slivovica. When he died and Pater Malek took over, lord forgive us, nobody was really sad.

Rosie was a stocky female who'd grown to such great proportions that she started to look like a man. Her hairy chin and soft black moustache below her zucchini nose put many of us kids in a dilemma — whether to call her Mister Rosie or, as we were told at home, Miss Rosie — when we delivered something to the church

haus sters. Hr kuking vos veri femos and meni of as diden resistet tu sei jes ven shi giv as hr kukis. Bad iven ol dos gudis dei kam vit hr big badi, she kuden bi a nais kadli fimel ... teking ker for as pater Malek.

Ist gast nachurali dat auer prist from St. Jelena spendet mor taim in taun bar als in betvin hevenli vols of auer chrch. De men akcheli lavet det. Dei vos eprishietet drainis of his blesed trot, peshenli veiding an his bed konchens tu emrg.

"So mai belavet braders, (hik) hir I am. A holi gost vich soposto protekt as chrch (hik) from satan. Drank laik mader erd, anebel tu stend ab. Nau, I ask ju mai dir braders, hau ken I protekt as taun chrch? Hik!" pater Malek bi toking tu his liseners, vich brein hes de seim destrbenc laik hi ekspirients.

"O dir pater Malek. De vor vich kud sev as from satan is lost oredi from as pater Florian det in dos deis releksing an siti cimenteri," sed de Orel bachi, teping him an bek.

"Ju si, van alon kud not vin de vor, speshali not de holi vor. Vot ju van? Vi ar gud pipel hir, vi lavja," tok old Sablanich. "Dont vori so mach, if de bishop dont tenk

○○○○○○○○○○○○○○○○○○○○○○○○○○○○○○○○○○○○

house stairs. Her cooking was very famous and many of us didn't resist saying yes when she gave us her cookies. But even with all those goodies that came with her big body, she couldn't be a nice cuddly female ... taking care of our Pater Malek.

It was just natural that our priest from St. Helena spent more time in the town bar than between the heavenly walls of our church. The men actually loved that. They appreciated the dryness of his blessed throat, and patiently waited for his bad conscience to emerge.

"So, my beloved brothers, (hik) here I am. A holy ghost which is supposed to protect our church (hik) from Satan. Drunk as mother earth and unable to stand up. Now, I ask you my dear brothers, how can I protect our town church? Hik!" Pater Malek asked his listeners, whose brains had the same disturbance as he was experiencing.

"Oh dear Pater Malek. The war to save us from Satan was lost already by that Pater Florian who is relaxing these days in the city cemetery," said Orel Bachi, patting him on the back.

"You see, one alone could not win the war, especially not the holy war. What do you want? We are good people here, we love you," said old Sablanich. "Don't worry so much that the bishop doesn't think

○○○○○○○○○○○○○○○○○○○○○○○○○○○○○○○○○○○○

ju gud ... hi tro ju aut aut de chrch ... and den vi tro him from his posten. Vi lavja, ju are gud prist."

"Ju tenk so?" ask de jang Malek des older gais. "Ju tenk I am rili duing gut?" ask hi, puting his hed kloser tu dos tu hef bolt drank baluns. "Bartender! Tri krug of vain. Ask vot ol aders drink. Hik! Shud noubadi sei det Malek is bed, gast if hi drink a lital. Mai chrch is sev so long ven de big Rosi der slip. Hik! I van tu si de satans fes ven shi open de dor. ... Ha ha ha."

"Hi mei for ever liv det erd," lef Orel.

"And if hi disaidet tu kam, vi are an jor sait," sed old Sablanich. "Dont vi van fait for as Malek?" ask de Sablanich de mens kraud det gast start tu resiv from Malek peit vain.

"Shor vi du. Dont ju vori Malek. Ven mai vaif sit hefor chrch, no satan bi ever traing der tu kam," jaling de kraut bek, tosting tu pater Malek.

Sun ader krugs of vain bi den folo and gipsis peit tu plei de chardash for ol drank sosaeti. Meni taim a nju don kech ol of dem stil toking, and hevili lafing.

⊚⊚⊚⊚⊚⊚⊚⊚⊚⊚⊚⊚⊚⊚⊚⊚⊚⊚⊚⊚⊚⊚⊚⊚⊚⊚⊚⊚⊚⊚⊚⊚⊚⊚⊚

you're good ... that he'll throw you out of the church ... or we'll throw him from his position. We love you, you're a good priest."

"You think so?" young Malek asked the older guys. "Do you think I'm really doing good?" he asked, putting his head closer to those two half-bald drunk balloons. "Bartender! Three jugs of wine. Ask what the others are drinking. Hik! Nobody should say that Malek is bad just because he drinks a little. My church is safe so long as big Rosie sleeps there. Hik! I want to see Satan's face when she opens the door. ... Ha ha ha."

"He may leave this earth forever," laughed Orel.

"And if he decides to come, we are on your side," said old Sablanich. "Don't we want to fight for our Malek?" asked Sablanich of the crowd of men who were just starting to receive the wine Malek had paid for.

"Sure we do. Don't you worry Malek. When my wife sits in front of the church no Satan will every try to come there," the crowd yelled back, toasting Pater Malek.

Soon more jugs of wine followed, and gypsies were paid to play the chardash for the whole drunk society. Many times the new dawn caught all of them still talking and laughing loudly.

ⓞⓞⓞⓞⓞⓞⓞⓞⓞⓞⓞⓞⓞⓞⓞⓞⓞⓞⓞⓞⓞⓞⓞⓞⓞⓞⓞ

"Ju no mai dir belavet pater Malek," toking de bar oner, "bar is veri inportant in det taun."

"Hau ju min?" ask de Malek naiv.

"Luk, if evri men bi spending his ol laif hom in vorm bet, ver ju godet der fani aidijas, spesheli ven a hot vumen slip bisaid ju. Na preheps ju du not hev det trobel, bad I teling ju, if vi bi not heving det bar, vi bi heving populeshen of Nyu Jork."

"Hi is rait mai dir Malek. Jor hends bi taet of blesing de fresh baroms. Preheps jor apetait bi daun smeling ol dos lital baroms?" tok de Orel.

"Is nating rong tu hev samtaim a chaild, bad evri jer? Na, det is tumach," tok de Sablanich. "Tu mach vork."

Auer gosop, and sam fimels det oredi fergoten vich plesher kud hev de laif, soet det hevenli problem laik a retrning of Lucifer taim. Tu protekt auer taun of sacha ivel, dei push pater Malek tu enlos prei seshen. Old gosop iven gan so far tu pushan an his bek evri mishep det hepen in auer taun in Malek taim. So prest from auer gosop, hi vos veri klos tu resain et van point.

⊛⊛⊛⊛⊛⊛⊛⊛⊛⊛⊛⊛⊛⊛⊛⊛⊛⊛⊛⊛⊛⊛⊛⊛⊛⊛⊛⊛⊛⊛⊛⊛⊛⊛⊛⊛

"You know, my dear beloved Pater Malek," said the bar owner, "the bar is very important in this town."

"How do you mean?" asked Malek naively.

"Look, if every man spent his whole life at home in a warm bed, you get funny ideas there, especially when a hot woman is sleeping beside you. Now perhaps you do not have that trouble, but I'm telling you, if we didn't have this bar we'd have the population of New York."

"He's right, my dear Malek. Your hands would be tired of blessing fresh bottoms. Perhaps you'd lose your appetite smelling all those little bottoms?" said Orel.

"There's nothing wrong with having a child sometimes, but every year? Now that's too much," said Sablanich. "Too much work."

Our gossips, and some females who'd already forgotten life's pleasures, saw this heavenly problem as a return to Lucifer's time. To protect our town from such evil, they pushed Pater Malek to endless prayer sessions. The old gossips even went so far as to lay blame on his back for all the mishaps in our town in Malek's time. Under such pressure from our gossips, he was very close to resigning at one point.

꧁꧁꧁꧁꧁꧁꧁꧁꧁꧁꧁꧁꧁꧁꧁꧁꧁꧁꧁꧁꧁꧁꧁꧁꧁꧁꧁꧁꧁꧁꧁

"Mens," sed de Orel in bar, "I tenk as Malek van tu resain from his holi gop! Vi mas du samting. Ju vanet det vi godet sam kain of Florian bek? If not vi mas ekt nau."

"Ja, as bleset vaivs mek im kresi vit det preing evri dei. I am shor Malek nis ar oredi fol of artraitis, from kold chrch flor," sed de Sablanich. "I tenk vi shud du samting. Hi is dem gut felo and vi shud kip him."

"Ja. Ju rait. Mai vaif bi no mor going tu chrch for a vail," teling de gais an des miting.

"I tenk vi shud mek a parti for him. Preheps hi stei. Hu is for det?" ask Orel bachi.

"Mi mi mi, dont ferget mi," sed de kraut.

De big parti, vit faeri gipsis mjusik, tron for him from ol mel in auer taun chench his main. Na vot hi des for taun in vich sacha lavli prist laik pater Malek resain. Vot ju tenk vot for skandal? Gosop bi spreding kros as kaunti, over as heds.

Nachurli, det diden min det hi kud faer Rosi, vit aut risking a anpresidentet revolushen inbetvin as vimen. "Na vat bi des for a taun, det erlau as lord srvent tu faer a fimel,

---

"Men," said Orel in the bar, "I think our Malek wants to resign from his holy job! We must do something. Do you want us to get some kind of Florian back? If not, we must act now."

"Yeah, our blessed wives make him crazy with that praying every day. I'm sure Malek's knees are already full of arthritis from the cold church floor," said Sablanich. "I think we should do something. He's a damn good fellow and we should keep him."

"Yeah. You're right. My wife won't be going to church any more for a while," said the guys at this meeting.

"I think we should make a party for him. Perhaps he'll stay. Who is for that?" asked Orel Bachi.

"Me me me, don't forget me," said the crowd.

The big party — with fiery gypsy music — that was thrown for him by all the men in our town changed his mind. Now, what would you say about a town in which such a lovely priest as Malek resigned. What do you think would be the scandal? Gossip would be spreading across the country over our heads.

Naturally, that didn't mean that he could fire Rosie without risking an unprecedented revolution among our women. "Now what would you say about a town that allowed our lord's servant to fire a female,

dislaiking hr overgron figjur."
Malek tuket his safering laik lords panishment.
Probeishen, if hi is vrdigt in des taun tu kondakt hevenli
bisnis. Sloli bat shorli, his hop tu hev sam beter luking meid
fedet. Meni taim hi kudn slip, torchert vit dos ankrishchen
aidija tu kil his Rosi. Preing for fergivnis in his soft bet, in
vich iven skeleton kudn faund eni hard ples, hi faitet vit his
naitmers. Bed drims start tu ruin his jang laif. Van vorm
nait, he iven soet as vuden stachu of blesed vrgen Meri. Shi
develop a mustash and goc bird. Hr stamak vos big laik shi
gast svolo vit hr blesed maut hol chrch. Sheking laik a vilo
in de vind, hi ran intu kold dark chrch, tu chek if des is a
bed drim or trut. Laik a skeri fet gost hi ran from korner tu
korner tu inshur him self det nating hes hepen tu his lavli
chrch. His vait rumi pigama flait laik a pis fleg behaid him,
keching samtaim an rovs of hevi vuden benches. Des
cheking stap vit bret teking skrim of pater Malek ven ader
mach mor biger gost enter de dark chrch. Nemli de svit Rosi,
in her vait pigama and hasti putet vorking buc. Laik a

disliking her overgrown figure?"
    Malek took his suffering as the lord's punishment. It was probation, to see if he belonged in this town to conduct heavenly business. Slowly but surely his hopes of having a better looking maid faded. Many times he couldn't sleep, tortured by the un-Christian urge to kill Rosie. Praying for forgiveness in his soft bed, in which even a skeleton couldn't find any hard places, he fought with his nightmares. Bad dreams started to ruin his young life. One warm night he even saw our wooden statue of the blessed Virgin Mary. She developed a moustache and goatee. Her stomach was as big as if she'd just swallowed the whole church through her blessed mouth. Shaking like a willow in the wind, he ran into the cold dark church to check if it was a bad dream or the truth. Like a fat frightened ghost he ran from corner to corner to assure himself that nothing had happened to his lovely church. His roomy white pyjamas flew like a peace flag behind him, catching sometimes on the rows of heavy wooden benches. The checking stopped with the breath-taking scream of Pater Malek when another much bigger ghost entered the dark church. Namely, sweet Rosie, in her white pyjamas and hastily put on working boots. Like a

stanpid of vaild kaus shi trai tu kech de prist vich eskep loking de dor of a chrch behaind.

"Oh-oooo mai svit lord, I nju ju ask mi tu srv ju vel, bad kud ju not sev mi from des monster vumen? I teling ju mai dir lord, van dei she bring mi tu ganp from as chrch tauer. Plis lord, du samting," tok Malek, keching his bred bihain de loket chrch dor, an vich vos Rosi paunding from insait de chrch.

"Pater Malek ... Pater Malek... a ju orait der?" jal shi vit hr dip vois.

"Jes Rosi, I am fain," encer he.

"Kan I du samting for ju?"

"Jes mai dir. Go end prei for mi and ju. Trti Auer Fader, and never du des egen," sed hi releksing.

Sun from de emti dark chrch vos kaming laut Rosis preing. "Auer fader, det ju in de heven..." Hi vos sev vans egen.

Safering so bedli, Malek bi meni taim veking ab in midel of a nait vit satans skrim. Hevili briding, hi bi draing his lavli forhed presing his fet leks an kold flor of his chenber tu kul daun. Auer Rosi, lord tikelet hr fid, juzuli slep laik a log

ⓔⓔⓔⓔⓔⓔⓔⓔⓔⓔⓔⓔⓔⓔⓔⓔⓔⓔⓔⓔⓔⓔⓔⓔⓔⓔⓔⓔⓔⓔⓔⓔ

stampede of wild cows she tried to catch the priest, who escaped and locked the church door behind him.

"Oh-oooo, my sweet lord, I know you asked me to serve you well, but could you not save me from this monster woman? I'm telling you my dear lord, one day she will bring me to jumping from our church tower. Please lord, do something," said Malek, catching his breath behind the locked door, on which Rosie was pounding from inside the locked church.

"Pater Malek ... Pater Malek ... are you all right there?" she yelled with her deep voice.

"Yes Rosie, I am fine," he answered.

"Can I do something for you?"

"Yes my dear. Go and pray for me and you. Thirty Our Fathers, and never do this again," he said, relaxing.

Soon Rosie's loud praying came from the empty dark church. "Our father who art in heaven..." He was safe once again.

Suffering so badly, Malek woke up many times in the middle of the night with a Satanic scream. Breathing heavily he would dry his lovely forehead and press his fat legs on the cold floor of his chamber to cool down. Our Rosie, lord tickle her feet, usually slept like a log

ⓔⓔⓔⓔⓔⓔⓔⓔⓔⓔⓔⓔⓔⓔⓔⓔⓔⓔⓔⓔⓔⓔⓔⓔⓔⓔⓔⓔⓔⓔⓔ

hepili snoring tu vords moning. Bat ven ever pater Malek vos in nid of hr, she samhau menagt tu vek ab. Mosli de taim she sturm de hevi ok dor of Malek chenber, faunding him chenging his rumi pigama. Iven he vos a lord srvent and praktikli nating ken hepen tu him hi vos shokt evri taim. Hi bi med ven she menagt tu si glims of his pink blesed barom.

"Rooosiii! Mast ju olveis du sacha ting. I min mai barom is blest lital harder, bat is a stil a barom," sed hi kavering his preshes part of a bodi.

"I am so gled tu si eni mens barom, and jors is so kjut. Hev a lital baterflai brt mark an de left chik," sed Rosi romantikli.

"Barom is a barom ... plein or vit baterflai. It is main and I dont van tu sho ju mai bodi enker. Kjut or not, klir?" sed hi bek, releksing ven shi klos de dor behain hr.

Bisaid, siing Rosi in de short naitgan, sholing her hevi platfus fit and flet chest, never help him tu de svit drims afteverc. Tu kul him self daun, hi prei for a vail bisaid his bet, tu eskep his bed laif besaid des monster fimel.

---

happily snoring towards morning. But whenever Pater Malek needed her she somehow managed to wake up. Most of the time she would storm the heavy oak door of Malek's chamber, finding him changing his roomy pyjamas. Even though he was the lord's servant and practically nothing could happen to him, he was shocked every time. He'd be mad when she managed to see a glimpse of his pink blessed bottom.

"Rooosiiie! Must you always do such a thing. I mean my bottom is a little more blessed, but it's still a bottom," he said, covering the precious part of his body.

"I am so glad to see any man's bottom, and yours is so cute. It has a little butterfly birth mark on the right cheek," said Rosie romantically.

"A bottom is a bottom ... plain or with a butterfly. It is mine and I don't want to show you my body's anchor. Cute or not, clear," he replied, relaxing when she closed the door behind her.

Besides, seeing Rosie in a short nightgown, showing her heavy platypus feet and flat chest, never helped him into sweet dreams afterward. To cool himself down, he prayed for a while beside his bed for an escape from his bad life beside this monster female.

Marijan Megla

Den van nait, ven hi vos voshing his miseri daun de trot in de olmos emti taun bar, hi mit Josef. Josefs trot vos drai laik a Sinai, and noleg ebaut vumen minimal. Ist gast normal det frst ting det pest kros de pater Malek brein vos: "Det is de mech for mai Rosi." Hi andestud det sacha chens dont kam tvais in a mens laif, and hi meket shor det Josef dont eskep. Gipsi vos kolt tu plei, and vainkrug vere never emti. Vans de hol gipsi orkestra koleps from hevi vain and dei mjusik simstu bi tu konpliketet for normal lisener, barmen tro evrivan aut an fresh er. Josef vos drank inaf for transport.

"Qvik Orel bachi! Ju tu, old Sablanich. Det is mai mech for Rosi. Help mi tu bring him in mai vain celer," tok hi eksaidig tu his best frens. "Hi is dam inaf tu fri mi of mai manster."

"Vi du evriting vot ju van, yast don push so hart," tok de Orel bachi, keriing de drank felo, faiting vit his and his on legs. "Boj, ven ju not drank, tu fit is gud. Bad ven ju drank de lord shud tek kontrol of van."

"Vot ju tok?" ask de Malek in de dark strit.

⁂⁂⁂⁂⁂⁂⁂⁂⁂⁂⁂⁂⁂⁂⁂⁂⁂⁂⁂⁂⁂⁂⁂⁂⁂⁂⁂⁂

Then one night, when he was washing his misery down his throat in the almost empty town bar, he met Joseph. Joseph's throat was dry as the Sinai, and his knowledge of women minimal. It was normal that the first thing that passed across Pater Malek's brain was: "This is the match for my Rosie." He understood that such a chance doesn't come twice in a man's life, and he made sure that Joseph didn't escape. Gypsies were called to play and the wine jugs were never empty. After the whole gypsy orchestra collapsed from strong wine, and their music seemed to become too complicated for a normal listener, the barman threw everyone out into the fresh air. Joseph was drunk enough for transport.

"Quick Orel Bachi! You too, old Sablanich. That is my match for Rosie. Help me take him to my wine cellar," he said excitedly to his best friends. "He is dumb enough to free me of my monster."

"We'll do everything that you want, just don't push so hard," said Orel Bachi, carrying the drunk fellow, fighting with his and his own legs. "Boy, when you're not drunk, two feet is good. But when you're drunk the lord should take control of one."

"What are you talking about?" asked Malek in the dark street.

"Never main. Hi hes trobel tu komand an de seim taim tu his and (hik) Josef leks," ancer laut old Sablanich.

"Ven vi kam tu chrch haus bi kvaet gais. Rosi shud not bi vekt ab," tok de Malek, supervaising tri totali drank. De gipsis folo for sam blaks, pleing mjusik, bad den dei koleps an dei soft leks. Rosi diden vek ab des nait so long ven Orel and Sablanich ver gon. Drank Josef vos hepili sliping besaid de berls of vain, onli Malek grob hendeling de haus kis vek hr ab. For frst taim, hi diden skrim ven hr hends helping him in bet.

De stupid drank Josef engoet des taim of his laif mor den ever. End vai not? Evri lital vish vot he hes vos epruvt. Hi gedet de ki for chrch vainseler, vich he liv enivei onli for bajologikal nids. If eni drank drimet ebaut heven an de erd, Josef vos inen and detrment tu jus his posishen best vot he kud. Shor, der vos sam hjumen bin, kaming evri dei daun de stip sters vit fud, demiching de prfekt lak, bad dos deis is nating mor prfekt. Vit ader vorts hu kers, so long ven hi dont nid tu tach hr. Bisaid she simstu not hev eni interest an him, endlis not ven hi is evek.

◉◉◉◉◉◉◉◉◉◉◉◉◉◉◉◉◉◉◉◉◉◉◉◉◉◉◉◉◉◉◉◉◉◉◉◉

"Never mind. He's having trouble commanding both his and (hik) Joseph's legs at the same time," Sablanich answered loudly.

"When we come to the church house, be quiet guys. Rosie should not be woken up," said Malek, supervising three total drunks. The gypsies followed for some blocks, playing music, but then they collapsed on their soft legs. Rosie didn't wake up this night until Orel and Sablanich were gone. Drunk Joseph was happily sleeping beside the barrels of wine when Malek's rough handling of the house keys woke her up. For the first time he didn't scream when her hands helped him into bed.

Stupid drunk Joseph enjoyed this time of his life more than any other. And why not? Every little wish he had was approved. He got the key to the church wine cellar, which he left only for biological needs. If any drunk dreamt about heaven on earth, Joseph was in it and determined to use his position the best he could. Sure, there was some human being coming down the steep stairs with food, damaging the perfect luck, but nothing could be more perfect than these days. In other words, why care about her as long as he didn't have to touch her. Besides, she didn't seem to have any interest in him, at least not when he was awake.

◉◉◉◉◉◉◉◉◉◉◉◉◉◉◉◉◉◉◉◉◉◉◉◉◉◉◉◉◉◉◉◉◉◉◉◉

Marijan Megla

A mant pest and ol hops of auer pater Malek det in betvin dos godlos kricher sprang ever eni romans. Malek nju det his slim chens bi olmost nan if he klos de celer. Josef bi probebli gan and he bi left alon vit Rosi. If hi veidet for long, taun gosop bi puting his fingers in des metar and det bi end of gud forchen. Older Orel and de old Sablanich diden hev a klu hau tu help.

"Vi mas du samting. Det godlos drank kud not drink ol sakrament vain," sed de old Sablanich.

"Vot a vest, hi kud drink de veniger and not noing de sauer test," sed de sed Orel bachi.

"Vel, I dont no vot I bi duing, bad samting mas bi dan," tok konsrn pater Malek.

After long prei tu auer lord he desaidet tu help a lital an des metar. Van let ivning, ven de Rosi vos oredi in hr chember hepili snoring, and Josef vos sliping his bus aut, hi strakt. He vokt an his fingers in de vain celer. Openet berl of vain veniger and livet raning. Ven de hol flor vos kavert vit det red veniger, hi open de red vain berl and klos de veniger. Den hepi vit his ekonplishing, hi skrim laut. So laut det

ⓔⓔⓔⓔⓔⓔⓔⓔⓔⓔⓔⓔⓔⓔⓔⓔⓔⓔⓔⓔⓔⓔⓔⓔⓔⓔⓔⓔⓔⓔⓔ

A month passed and with it all of Pater Malek's hopes that romance would ever spring between those two godless creatures. Malek knew that his slim chance would be almost none if he closed the cellar. Joseph would probably be gone and he'd be left alone with Rosie. If he waited much longer, the town gossips would be putting their fingers in the matter and that would be the end of good fortune. Older Orel and old Sablanich didn't have a clue how to help.

"We must do something. That godless drunk can't drink all the sacramental wine," said old Sablanich.

"What a waste — he could drink vinegar and not notice the sour taste," said a concerned Pater Malek.

After a long prayer to our lord he decided to help this matter on a little. One late evening, when Rosie was already in her chamber happily snoring and Joseph was sleeping his booze out, he struck. He crept on his fingers into the wine cellar. Opened a barrel of wine vinegar, left it running. When the whole floor was covered with red vinegar, he opened the red wine barrel and closed the vinegar. Then, happy with his accomplishment, he screamed loudly. So loudly that

ⓥⓥⓥⓥⓥⓥⓥⓥⓥⓥⓥⓥⓥⓥⓥⓥⓥⓥⓥⓥⓥⓥⓥⓥⓥⓥⓥⓥⓥⓥⓥ

skolpcher of auer blesed gesus olmost fol from de big vuden krucefiks in dark chrch.

"Ro..o..o..o..s..s..i..i! Ju lesi meid. Vain is raning aut of berl. Ken I no mor relai an ju, not iven so mach det ju kontrol det bladi drank?" jal hi engoing komoshen det hi koset. Den hi help Josef tu pul his korpus delikti an lital berl for slivovic. Not iven hrd of vaild horsis kud meket sacha big nois det folo Rosi daun de stip sters. Faineli daun, she planch hr big flapi badi in des si of red vain jusing hr fet nis laik a anker. Laik sam overgron shepard she start laut preer.

"0..o..o, fergiv mi pater Malek. I diden no det des godlos bestie kud not iven klos de berl behain. Nau is ol mai folt. 0 fergiv mi ... plis!" mamelt de Rosi in tirs.

"I, de prist of des parishment bi panisht nau, and vai? Bikos ju tu godlos sols jused bedli mai frenship. Hu nos vot parishment if eni auer ekselenci bishof hev for mi. Nau after so meni jers..."

"0 plis fergiv mi as blesed pater Malek! Plis..."

"Mi tu," mamelt gast vekt drank Josef.

⊙⊙⊙⊙⊙⊙⊙⊙⊙⊙⊙⊙⊙⊙⊙⊙⊙⊙⊙⊙⊙⊙⊙⊙⊙⊙⊙⊙⊙⊙⊙⊙⊙⊙⊙

the sculpture of our blessed Jesus almost fell from the big wooden crucifix in the dark church.

"Ro..o..o..o..s..s..i..i! You lazy maid. Wine is running out of the barrel. Can I no more rely on you, not even so much that you control that bloody drunk?" he yelled, enjoying the commotion that he caused. Then he helped Joseph pull his corpus delecti on top of a little barrel of slivovica.

Not even a herd of wild horses could make a noise as big as what followed Rosie down the steep stairs. Finally down, she plopped her big floppy body in this sea of red wine, using her fat knees like anchors. Like some overgrown shepherd she started a loud prayer.

"0..o..o, forgive me Pater Malek. I didn't know that this godless beastie couldn't even shut the barrel behind him. Now it's all my fault. Oh forgive me ... please!" Rosie mumbled in tears.

"I the priest of the parish am being punished now, and why? Because you two godless souls used my friendship badly. Who knows what parish our excellency the bishop now has for me. Now after so many years..."

"Oh please forgive me blessed Pater Malek! Please..."

"Me too," mumbled the just-wakened drunk Joseph.

⊙⊙⊙⊙⊙⊙⊙⊙⊙⊙⊙⊙⊙⊙⊙⊙⊙⊙⊙⊙⊙⊙⊙⊙⊙⊙⊙⊙⊙⊙⊙⊙⊙⊙⊙

"Sori ... sori. Is det ol vot I ken hr in des chrch? Auer gesus kindem kud bi bildet tri or for taim vit ol dos sori," tok de pater Malek engoing his ofensive.

"Vot shud vi du nau? Hau vi ever ken meket gut an des demich? O plis tel as pater Malek," asking de Rosi stil niing in des red si.

"Vel mai children, ju tu hev latc tu pei bek, and I am not shor if ju kud du des," tok Malek.

"O tel as, plis tel as vi du evriting for ju. Is det not tru Josef?" ask de Rosi de sheki felo, panchin him an de sholder.

"O jes, jes!" jal hi bek.

"Vel kidc ju esket foret. Hauebaut det ju tu goinet in holi makremoni tumoro, and den peet bek lital bai lital?" ask Malek, skert tu hr de bed njus.

"Merich?" ask de big Rosi. "Is det not tumach for des lital vain?"

"I teling ju gast, hau bi isi tu pei mi bek. Bisaid, I diden meket des mes!" ancer Malek olmos shor de Rosi dont vanet des dil.

@@

"Sorry ... sorry. Is that all I can hear in this church? Our Jesus's kingdom could be built three or four times with all those sorries," said Malek, enjoying his offensive.

"What should we do now? How can we ever make good on this damage? Oh please tell us Pater Malek," asked Rosie, still kneeling in this red sea.

"Well my children, you have lots to pay back and I am not sure if you can do this," said Malek.

"Oh tell us, please tell us, we'll do everything for you. Is that not true Joseph?" Rosie asked the shaken fellow, punching him on the shoulder.

"Oh yes, yes!" he yelled back.

"Well kids, you asked for it. How about you two join in holy matrimony tomorrow and then pay it back little by little?" asked Malek, scared to hear the bad news.

"Marriage?" asked big Rosie. "Is that not too much for this little wine?"

"I'm just telling you how it would be easy to pay me back. Besides, I didn't make this mess!" answered Malek, almost sure that Rosie wouldn't want the deal.

Bat de pur Rosi teket det chens. Preheps ver hr klir det felos det shi kud tengelt in hr nec vere not in taun. So she tuket de chens vit Josef.

In laif of pater Malek, never vos a kvaet minit longer als in des krushel nait. Ven de Rosi faineli egri, hi vos so hepi det hi promis big veding pekich, veding dres and hu nos vot not. An nekst dei vos merich, and auer after hi hed faineli a nais lital Marishka. Lital slo an tenking bat mach mor nais tu luk anet, vortet tu stei hom and not spend evri minit in bar. Gosop vos frst shokt, bad ven auer pater Malek vos no mor sin in de bar pis retrnt tu St Jelena.

Vel, noubadi is shor vot auer Josef vos tenking ven hi vek ab aut his dranknis. Klemt vit tu big leks, vit aut his blesed anderver and snoring Rosi fes besaid his. Bed tongs teling det dei hr a long and skeri skrim from Josef. O vel, sambadi safer nau, sambadi safer after, bat evrivan hes his trn.

But poor Rosie took the chance. Perhaps it was clear to her that fellows she could tangle in her nets were not in town. So she took the chance with Joseph.

In the life of Pater Malek, never was a quiet minute longer than in this crucial night. When Rosie finally agreed, he was so happy that he promised a big wedding package, wedding dress and who knows what not. On the next day was the marriage, and one hour after he finally had nice little Marishka. She was a little slow at thinking but much nicer to look at, well worth staying home for and not spending every minute in the bar. The gossips were shocked at first, but when our Pater Malek was no longer seen in the bar peace returned to St. Helena.

Well, nobody is sure what our Joseph thought when he woke up from his drunkenness. Clamped between two big legs, without his blessed underwear, and snoring Rosie's face beside his. The bad tongues say they heard a long and frightened scream from Joseph. Oh well, somebody suffers now, somebody suffers after, but everyone has his turn.

It vos hot saterdei ivning, short befor vit harvest. Vi vos siting belo as krset vilo, an pablik pashcher. Dei vos meni of dem agli luking tris sketart in lo plesis dei filet vit vota bai evri flading. Dei soraundet auer taun laik a stum gard. Kids from auer blok chosen van not far evei from taun vater hol. Jang vans from ader bloks in de taun chosen sam ader krset vilo. Dei ver auer fortres, vich vi gardet vit hol pauer det vi hev. Mosli of broken heds in betvin as kidc kam aut sacha feroshes fait for des strategik inportent plesis an de pashcher.

Taet of pleing karts, or sviming in madi vota shert vit ol dos enimals, vi veidet for Toni. Hi soposto stil sam epels from neerbai garden. Des snek mas kip as hepi olmost tu darknis, ven vi kud retrn hom vit auer bists.

I vos olveis gelos an Toni. Hi vos biger den mi, and kud stilet most bjutifol tings and vos never kot. An auer taun fjesta, hi vos de gai hu provaid as vit mirors,

---

It was a hot Saturday evening shortly before the wheat harvest. We were sitting below our cursed willow in the public pasture. There were many of those ugly looking trees scattered in the low places that filled with water with every flood. They surrounded our town like a silent guard. Kids from our block chose one not far from the town water hole. Young ones from other blocks in town chose other cursed willows. They were our fortresses, which we guarded with all our power. Most of the broken heads between kids came out of ferocious fights for these strategically important places on the pasture.

Tired of playing cards or swimming in the muddy water shared with all those animals, we waited for Tony. He was supposed to steal some apples from a nearby garden. This snack would have to keep us happy almost until dark, when we could return with our beasts.

I was always jealous of Tony. He was bigger than me and could steal the most beautiful things and never was caught. At our town festival, he was the guy who provided us with mirrors, koms, and marcipan harts. Toni hat gac tu du olmost evriting and I hetet him for det. Bat der vos samting als vot hi ken hev and I faitet for det, never shor in mai viktori — Tanja, de most bjutifol grl an des erd. Des ivning shi vos der. If ever samting vos ekomplisht vitaut eni misteks from auer gud lord, den vos krieshen of Tanja. Hr blek bluish her vos long and soft, laik nating tu mi non. In samer mants, shi justu put vaild flauers in hr her. I teling ju, shi luk laik Ev in de hevenli garden befor apel fist. Bat hr grin ais an tin hends, vos det akshili stolet mai hart. Des ivning, ven Toni kam vit his stolen apels, hangri Tanja godet from him most bjutifol apel. An tape of det, she giv him a kis. Kud ju emegin vot min det for a jang gai det divotet his ol lav laif onli tu van vumen? Tanja.

"O vel, det is nating. Going in old tutlos grenmamichka garden, and stilet hend fol of apels. Shi ken not si ju and not kech ju," sed I gelosli, voching Toni emtiet his shrt fol of apels. "Emilko and I kud stil de apels iven from chrch garden ... if vi vanet tu."

⊙⊙

combs, and marzipan hearts. Tony had the guts to do almost everything and I hated him for it. But there was something else he could have and I fought for it, never sure I could win — Tanya, the most beautiful girl on this earth. That evening she was there.

If ever something was accomplished without any mistakes by our good lord, then it was the creation of Tanya. Her black bluish hair was long and soft, like nothing else known to me. In the summer months she used to put wild flowers in her hair. I'm telling you she looked like Eve in the heavenly garden before the first apple feast. But her green eyes and thin hands were what actually stole my heart. That evening, when Tony came with his stolen apples, the hungry Tanya got the most beautiful apple. On top of that, she gave him a kiss. Could you imagine what that meant to a young guy who devoted his whole love life to only one woman? Tanya.

"Oh well, that's nothing. Going into a toothless old grandmamichka's garden and stealing a handful of apples. She cannot see you or catch you," I said jealously, watching Tony empty his shirt full of apples. "Emilko and I could steal apples even from the church garden ... if we wanted to."

⊚⊚⊚⊚⊚⊚⊚⊚⊚⊚⊚⊚⊚⊚⊚⊚⊚⊚⊚⊚⊚⊚⊚⊚⊚⊚⊚⊚⊚⊚⊚⊚⊚⊚⊚⊚⊚⊚

Marijan Megla

If Tanja bi not der, Toni meibi gast ignor mi. Noing hau klamsi I am, filing det hi kud vans for ol heving Tanja for himself if I dont retrn, hi sed: "I van tu si det."

Emilko, mai frst neibar and best frend, kros him self trning vit his ais. Hi vos gut felo, lital klamsier den mi. Hi hes gast tu gut hart tu tel mi "mek jor gop alon," so hi egri.

Voking barfit after kaus des ivning, vi diden hev a klu hau ekonplisht auer mishen. Auer kaus vevet vit dei tels, spletering kau pais in vorm dasti strit sloli troting hom. As mishen vos mach mor konpliketet vid de bed njus det rich as short befor vi liv pashcher an de vei hom. Noubadi als bad de drank Josef vocht an det apels. Bisaid pater Malek, det vos de prson det vil desaidet if vi liv or dai if vi go kot an des sandei moning. Old tutlos vidos teling det hi akcheli kil a rashien solger vit de naif. If vi kud beliv tu de taun gosop, Josef lost sam of his marmels in de vor and is stil luking for dem.

"So," sed de Emilko, fiksing his hevi raund glasis an sveti nos. "Ju kuden bi kvaet egen. Nau, mi, a inosent taun

---

If Tanya hadn't been there, maybe Tony'd have just ignored me. Knowing how clumsy I am, feeling that he could once and for all have Tanya to himself if I didn't return, he said: "I want to see that."

Emilko, my next door neighbour and best friend, crossed himself and rolled his eyes. He was a good fellow, a little clumsier than me. He just had too good a heart to tell me "do your job alone," so he agreed.

Walking barefoot behind the cows that evening, we didn't have a clue how we would accomplish our mission. Our cows waved their tails, splattering cow pies in the warm dusty street as they slowly trotted home. Our mission was made more complicated by the news that reached us shortly before we left the pasture on the way home. Nobody but the drunk Joseph guarded those apples. Beside Pater Malek, that was the person who would decide if we lived or died if we got caught on that Sunday morning. Old toothless widows told that he'd actually killed a Russian soldier with a knife. If you could believe the town gossips, Joseph lost some of his marbles in the war and is still looking for them.

"So," said Emilko, adjusting his heavy round glasses on his sweaty nose. "You couldn't be quiet again. Now me, an innocent town

sol, mas dai tumoro. And ver? In as holi chrch garden."
Fiksing his rumi short penc an his skini badi, hi edet: "Det is
not ol! Preheps auer pater Malek bi so med an mi, det hi vil
nat permitet mai pur perenc tu dig mai lital grev in auer
simenteri. Mai grev bi probebli meid in sam dark korner of a
prisen simenteri in as siti. Evri singel rabar, det for his sins
klinet det rabar grevjard, bi pointing an mai grev. 'And det
is a grev of a lital Emilko, det stolet from holi chrch
garden'." Klining his bar fit from fresh kau pais, an soft grin
gras, hi olmos jal. "End for vat? Gast bikos his bladi frend
hes noubadi als tu lav, bad Tanja!"
"Ju dont andesten Emilko," I trai tu eksplen. "Tanja is
samting so bjutifol, so preshes. If shi bi living in holi Josef
taim, I am shor vi bi heving in de chrch holi vrgen Tanja,
insted of Meri."
Emilko diden enceret. His ais flotet over his lital taun,
der hi so lavet and vich hi probebli lus tumoro. Hi grit
chirfoli evri singel sol det pest as an de strit. De pipel shud
remember him for his gudnis.

---

soul, must die tomorrow. And where? In our holy church garden." Fixing his roomy short pants on his skinny body, he added: "That is not all! Perhaps our Pater Malek will be so mad at me that he will not permit my poor parents to dig my little grave in our cemetery. My grave will probably be made in some dark corner of the prison cemetery in the city. Every single robber, who for his sins has to clean that robber's graveyard, will point at my grave. 'And that is the grave of little Emilko, that stole from the holy church garden'." Cleaning his feet from the fresh pies on the soft green grass, he almost yelled. "And for what? Just because his bloody friend has nobody else to love but Tanya."

"You don't understand Emilko," I tried to explain. "Tanya is something so beautiful, so precious. If she was living in the time of holy Joseph I'm sure we'd have in church the holy Virgin Tanya, instead of Mary."

Emilko didn't answer. His gaze floated over his little town, which he loved so and which he would probably lose tomorrow. He cheerfully greeted every single soul who passed us on the street. The people should remember him for his goodness.

Marijan Megla

Duing mai shors an de farm, mai main vos preokupaid vit singel problem. Hau tu stil dasent hevenli apel aut of holi chrch garden? I kud emegin mai viktori. Hevenli Tanja kadelt eraund mi lisening of never ending oveshen of mai bojs, belo de krset vilo. Bat, ven ever I soet mai defid, it vos so bed det mai hart stap biting in midel of overhitet kau barn.

Hol nait des tema diden chenchet befor mai ais. Hm, sopost I kud teket mai on apels and tel de gais det ar from holi garden. Dei kuden tel de diferenc enivei. De apels are apels, auers or hevenli, or? Hm, Toni is not dam and sun or letar hi bi faunding aut de trut. Brrrrr, I gast kud not lus Tanja den. Preheps mai lital hart kud koleps and ol mai fjucher bi an sailend simenteri.

I kuden go tumoro tu de pater Malek and simpli sei him det I nidet a dasent of his apels. "Vel, vel, vel," hi probebli sed, voching mi bihain his sinpel glasis. "And for vot kain of prpes a jang gentelmen hir nidet nating als bat mai apels? If I kan ask."

"For sek of lav, for a vrgen Tanja! Shi promis mi a big kis," I bi encering red in nek and chiks. Kud hi als prist

@@

Doing my chores on the farm, my mind was preoccupied with a single problem. How do you steal a dozen heavenly apples out of the holy church garden? I could imagine my victory. Heavenly Tanya cuddled around me listening to the never ending ovation of my boys below the cursed willow. But, whenever I saw my defeat it was so bad that my heart stopped beating in the middle of the overheated cow barn.

The whole night this theme didn't change before my eyes. Hmmm, suppose I took my own apples and told the guys that they were from the holy garden. They couldn't tell the difference anyway. Apples are apples, ours or heavenly, or? Hmmm, Tony is not dumb and sooner or later he'd find out the truth. Brrrrr, I just could not lose Tanya then. Perhaps my little heart would collapse and my whole future would be in a silent cemetery.

I couldn't go to Pater Malek tomorrow and simply tell him that I needed a dozen of his apples. "Well, well, well," he'd probably say, watching me from behind his simple glasses. "And for what purpose would this young gentleman need nothing else but my apples? If I can ask."

"For the sake of love, for the Virgin Tanya! She promised me a big kiss," I'd be answering, red in the neck and cheeks. Could he as a priest

@@

andesten mai trobels? Probebli not. Hau kud hi? Hi never
vos siing Tanjas megik ais. Hi vos never merit, hau kud hi
posibel andesten vot going tru a men in lav?

Tu as anon, pater Malek hes dis deis his on problems —
mor religes nechur — auer mader oversierin, vich svit tang
vos vol respektet iven bai gron men. Dei bot vos lavet from
as and ven ever vos sam merich, pipel ensistet tu hev im bot
laik a gests. An sacha okeshen auer mader soet pater Malek
meni taim drank, and shi diden laiket. Nechurli des lital
eskaped vos part of de merich celebreshen. Vot kan pur
pater Malek du if dei giv him so meni tu drink. Stil hi hed
teken siriesli hr mislaiking of his behevju. Preheps shi bi
toking an rong ples and det kud bring him bishop an his
nek. Na, I dont vant tu bi andastend det Malek diden laik
his ekselenci, bat bishop shud bi bishop, and hi vanet tu kip
des vei. It vos his parishment and hi van tu kip him. So, in
hop det hi kud softenet mader oversierin hart hi dediketet ol
apels of des sisen tu nans. Tu meket shor det no devel sol
ever kam an aidija tu tach his apels, hi haert drnk Josef.

⊚⊚⊚⊚⊚⊚⊚⊚⊚⊚⊚⊚⊚⊚⊚⊚⊚⊚⊚⊚⊚⊚⊚⊚⊚⊚⊚⊚⊚⊚⊚⊚⊚⊚⊚⊚⊚⊚⊚

understand my troubles. Probably
not. How could he? He had never
seen Tanya's magic eyes. He was
never married, so how could he
possibly understand what a young
man in love was going through?

Unknown to us, Pater Malek
had his own problems these days
— more religious in nature —
our Mother Superior, whose sweet
tongue was well respected, even
by grown men. They were both
loved by us and whenever there
was a marriage, people insisted
on having them both as guests.
On such occasions our Mother
saw Pater Malek drunk many
times, and she didn't like it.
Naturally this little escapade was
part of the marriage celebration.
Still he has taken seriously her
dislike of his behaviour. Perhaps
she'd be talking in the wrong
place and that could bring the
bishop down on his neck. Now, I
don't want it thought that Malek
didn't like His Excellency, but a
bishop should be a bishop and he
wanted to keep it that way. It
was his parish and he wanted to
keep it. So, in hope that he
could soften Mother Superior's
heart he dedicated all the apples
of this season to the nuns. To
make sure that no devil's soul
ever came up with the idea of
touching his apples, he hired
drunk Joseph.

⊚⊚⊚⊚⊚⊚⊚⊚⊚⊚⊚⊚⊚⊚⊚⊚⊚⊚⊚⊚⊚⊚⊚⊚⊚⊚⊚⊚⊚⊚⊚⊚⊚⊚⊚⊚⊚⊚⊚

Emilko kam let an nekst moning. Tu bi shor det hi dont chench his main, I disaidet tu braib him vit a big sosich. Hi tuket, bad kuden it bikos nervis stamak. His glasis hi left hom, so his perenc kud chench dem for mani if hi dont retrn.

"Demet, vit aut jor gogels, ju kud not destingvisht hors from kau," tok I medli, not pushing mai lak tu far.

"Det is tru. Preheps I dont van tu si a big Josef naif kaming in mai pur lital chest!" sed Emilko apatik. "Hi vos not iven long inaf an des erd tu gro sam hers onet," tok hi, luking in his fresh shert.

From evri sait in de strit kam veri hepi mjusik. Skrim of a jang kidc, dei horsing eraund in dei pigamas, raning in dei pleis iven an de strit. Vi vos olmost der, ven sambadi an de properti klosest tu de chrch disaidet tu kil her fet ruster. Hi vos probebli no mor kepebal tu kip ol dos bladi chiken hepi. Nau an end his badi bi just for chiken paprikash and ver ivan bi konplening over his hart of ganping mit. Vot a vei tu go pel. Lisening his grgl, Emilko trn bek hom.

"O kaman, I sopos daing is no plezerhaft, bat vi nuet

Emilko came late on the next morning. To be sure that he didn't change his mind, I decided to bribe him with a big sausage. He took it, but couldn't eat it with his nervous stomach. He'd left his glasses at home so his parents could exchange them for money if he didn't return.

"Dammit, without your goggles you couldn't distinguish a horse from a cow," I said angrily, but not pushing my luck too far.

"That is true. Perhaps I don't want to see Joseph's big knife coming into my poor little chest!" said the pathetic Emilko. "He was not even on this earth long enough to grow hair on it," he said, looking under his fresh shirt.

From every side of the street came happy music. The screams of young kids, horsing around in their pygamas, running in their play even onto the street. We were almost there when somebody in the yard closest to the church decided to kill her fat rooster. He probably wasn't capable of keeping all those bloody chickens happy any more. Now at the end his body will be just for chicken paprikash and we'll even be complaining over his heart of jumping meat. What a way to go pal. Listening to his gurgle, Emilko turned back home.

"Oh, come on, I suppose dying is no great pleasure, but we know vot kam mas go samtaim. Det is de laif," tok I, raning bihain him.

"Jes, I no," sed de chok pel Emilko. "Det kiling gast kam in rong taim. If I hed mai gogels nau hir, I bi voking hom. Is det klir?" sed hi, viving belo mai nos vit his point finger.

"Jes, I no," anceret I.

Vi klaim de maisen vol det gaidet as belavet chrch from as devels sol in de taun. Siting for a moment an his tap, I soet drank Josef sliping his bus aut belo de hevenli apel. Tu tel det tu Emilko vos anveis. Vai destroi de pikcher of hevenli garden in his short sait ais. Amesing, evriting hir luk so hepi, kam, iven de taun bestie Josef luk mor laik sam anshevt engel.

After his retrn from Rashia, and drank him self olmos tu det, hi merit a fet Rosi. Shi vos a meid det auer pater Malek entherotet from pater Florian and vich brod him olmos tu de susait. I dont van tu gosoping, bad tu si in hr a ledi, a simpel men nidete evri emaginashen vot lord giv him. Shi vos fet, and gron tu des monsteres proporshen. If det semi heri fimel dont sker ju, shi olveis hes hr big maut, aut vich iven sinpel "amen"

⊙⊙⊙⊙⊙⊙⊙⊙⊙⊙⊙⊙⊙⊙⊙⊙⊙⊙⊙⊙⊙⊙⊙⊙⊙⊙⊙⊙⊙⊙⊙⊙⊙⊙⊙⊙⊙⊙

it must come some time. That's life," I said, running behind him.

"Yes, I know," said the chalk-pale Emilko. "That killing just came at the wrong time. If I had my glasses here now I'd be walking home. Is that clear?" he said, waving his pointing finger under my nose.

"Yes, I know," I answered.

We climbed the masonry wall that guarded our beloved church from our devil's souls in town. Sitting for a moment on top of it, I saw drunk Joseph sleeping his booze out below the heavenly apples. To tell that to Emilko would be unwise. Why destroy the picture of the heavenly garden in his short-sighted eyes. Amazing how everything here looked so happy, calm, even the town beast Joseph looking more like some unshaved angel.

After his return from Russia, when he drank himself almost to death, he married fat Rosie. She was a maid that our Pater Malek inherited from Pater Florian, and who almost drove him to suicide. I don't want to gossip, but to see a lady in her a simple man needed all the imagination the lord gave him. She was fat and grown to monstrous proportions. If that semi-hairy female doesn't scare you, there's always her big mouth, from which even a simple "amen"

⊙⊙⊙⊙⊙⊙⊙⊙⊙⊙⊙⊙⊙⊙⊙⊙⊙⊙⊙⊙⊙⊙⊙⊙⊙⊙⊙⊙⊙⊙⊙⊙⊙⊙⊙⊙⊙⊙⊙

vos dedli. Dei hev a big femili. Sam of dos gais konpidet for status of taun drank vit dei on fader. Noing det, I tenk evrivan kud andestan Josef, and his overtaims in taun bar and Malek vainseler. Tenking vot kud bi his laif vortet if hi diden hes sacha idiot Josef, Malek vos olveis mor den gladli helping dem aut. Bat, pater Malek never trastet mach auer drank Josef. Auer hop det his haus fol of nan, det gast eraivet vit kerich, kud help as vi slipet in tu de garden and an de hevenli tri. Tugeder vit his meid slo Marishka, dei diskaset his blesed anderver, laik der ver not kloding samting so inportent als his holi behain. Pleing gud host, he stil faundet de taim tu chek ab an his apels. His skviki vindo openet ven vi vos gast redi tu tek af vit auer stolen guts, from de tri.

Ven hi so as in de tri, and men der hi haer for protekchen sliping belo, hi jal.

"Ju dem batel, vit aut barom! Ju taun bist der dogs snifing, ven hi koleps on de strit! Ju det I keri eraund de vorld laik Gesus Craist his hevi crucefiks on maunt of Golgota! Vek ab! Te kidc ar stiling mai heven apels."

⊚⊚⊚⊚⊚⊚⊚⊚⊚⊚⊚⊚⊚⊚⊚⊚⊚⊚⊚⊚⊚⊚⊚⊚⊚⊚⊚⊚⊚⊚⊚⊚⊚⊚⊚⊚⊚⊚⊚

was deadly. They had a big family. Some of them competed for the status of town drunk with their own father. Knowing that, I think everyone could understand Joseph and his overtime in the town bar and Malek's wine cellar. Wondering what his life would be like if he didn't have such an idiot as Joseph, Malek was always more than glad to help them out.

But Pater Malek never trusted our drunk Joseph much. Our hope was that his house full of nuns, who'd just arrived by carriage, could help us slip into the garden and onto the heavenly tree. Together with his maid slow Marishka, they were discussing his blessed underwear as if it did not clothe something as important as his holy behind. Playing the good host, he still found time to check on his apples. His squeaky window opened when we were just ready to take off from the tree with our stolen goods.

When he saw us in the tree, and the man he'd hired to protect it sleeping below, he yelled.

"You dumb bottomless bottle! You town beast the dogs sniff when he collapses on the street! You who I carry around the world like Jesus Christ his heavy crucifix on Mount Golgotha! Wake up! The kids are stealing my heaven's apples."

⊚⊚⊚⊚⊚⊚⊚⊚⊚⊚⊚⊚⊚⊚⊚⊚⊚⊚⊚⊚⊚⊚⊚⊚⊚⊚⊚⊚⊚⊚⊚⊚⊚⊚⊚⊚⊚⊚⊚

Josef lipt ab laik hi vos strak from laitening. Vi lendet praktikli in his arms ven vi ganpet from de holi tri. As gast stolen apels spredet in dark gras. Det inposibel hepen, vi vos kot.

Olmost emidiatli, Josef start tu sver and tretening as. De faif heds of a skeri vumen apir an de vindos, asking vot an erd hepen hir. Ignoring dem, pater Malek ran in his garden tu finishet vit as. I remember siing pur Emilko olmos ankonchen, henging in Josef hend, ven ai vos traing tu fri mi. Bat laik in sam kult, ver vi bi sun lending an ofer pleit, vi vos hendet tu pater Malek vich holi hends vere nating softer.

I began tu emegin henging on the bel rop, vit mai hends tait behaind mai bek, in tauer besaid entrenc of de chrch. Evri singel sol det des moning atend de erli moning mes stafet in mai penc hend fol of ents. Ven ever I muv in deskanfert, de chrch bel vold ringing acros auer kaunti tu anonc de exekjushen of a taun tifs. Pipel bi gedering tugeder tu si as, det hev stolen a hevenli apels vich as pater Malek hes seving for nans, tu softenet dei holi mauls.

⦿⦿⦿⦿⦿⦿⦿⦿⦿⦿⦿⦿⦿⦿⦿⦿⦿⦿⦿⦿⦿⦿⦿⦿⦿⦿⦿⦿⦿⦿⦿⦿⦿⦿⦿⦿⦿

Joseph leaped up like he was struck by lightning. We landed practically in his arms when we jumped from the holy tree. Our just stolen apples spread in the dark grass. The impossible had happened, we were caught.

Almost immediately, Joseph started to swear and threaten us. Five heads of frightened women appeared in the window, asking what on earth happened here. Ignoring them, Pater Malek ran into his garden to finish with us. I remember seeing poor Emilko almost unconscious, hanging in Joseph's hand, when I was trying to free myself. But like some cult, where we would very soon be landing on the offering plate, we were handed to Pater Malek whose holy hands were not at all softer.

I began to imagine hanging by the bell rope with my hands tied behind my back in the tower beside the entrance to the church. Every single soul that attended mass that morning stuffed a handful of ants in my pants. Whenever I moved in discomfort, the church bell would ring across our county to announce the execution of town thieves. People would be gathering to see us, who had stolen the heavenly apples which Pater Malek was saving for the nuns to soften their holy mouths.

Never in as short laif mi and hef ankonches Emilko preet so dipli and so truli divotet tu de lord gesus, laik des moning. Meibi bikos in hel, ver vi going, de preing ist not erlaut. Preheps bikos vi sun bi lusing auer nek, des lavli konekchen in betvin as badi and dam brein.

Auer lord enceret as preers. Blesed mader oversierin pute hr vorts for as. In long intelekchuel tok det vi diden andesten in auer agoni, shi iven promises not tu bi so efektiv in cheking of pater Malek laif.

After des vords, Malek fes openet into big lefter. Hi iven giv as dasent of hevenli apels, aut his garden of iden. Hu nos, Emilko and mi mei stil kising mader oversiarin blek dasti shu, if pater Malek had not startet de sandei moning mes.

Vel, ven vi faeneli rich as gud old stinki krsed vilo, de ol grup ver der. Toni vos praudli shoing tu gais and Tanja hau vi desperatli preet for as laif in Josefs hends. Hau de pater Malek vos blesing as hed and videt as short her. Dei lefet laudli roling an de vet moning gras. Mai Tanja, lord

⚬⚬⚬⚬⚬⚬⚬⚬⚬⚬⚬⚬⚬⚬⚬⚬⚬⚬⚬⚬⚬⚬⚬⚬⚬⚬⚬⚬⚬⚬⚬⚬⚬⚬⚬⚬⚬

Never in our short life had me and half-unconscious Emilko prayed so deeply and with such true devotion to the lord Jesus as on that morning. Maybe it was because in hell, where we were going, praying was not allowed. Perhaps it was because we'd soon be losing our neck, that lovely connection between our body and the damn brain.

Our lord answered our prayers. The blessed Mother Superior put in words for us. In a long intellectual talk that we didn't understand in our agony, she even promised not to be so effective at checking Pater Malek's life.

After these words, Malek's face opened up with loud laughter. He even gave us a dozen heavenly apples out of his Garden of Eden. Who knows, Emilko and me might still be kissing Mother Superior's black dusty shoe if Pater Malek hadn't started the Sunday morning mass.

Well, when we finally reached our good old stinking cursed willow, the whole group was there. Tony was proudly showing two guys and Tanya how we desperately prayed for our lives in Joseph's hands. How Pater Malek blessed our heads and wetted (sprinkled) our short hair. They laughed loudly, rolling on the wet morning grass. My Tanya, lord shud never ferget det, ask Toni tu repid and hi danet. I svoloet laik a big shishkerl. Vot kud I du stil sheking and voching aders iting stolen hevens apel. Ju kan emegin det nider of as hes eni apetait, so I kud not tel ju if dos epels ver diferent.

Ju ges, mai Tanja, lords prfekshen in krieshen of an anfergedebel fimel, kuden lav mi laik a luser. Et frst I van tu dai, den de Emilko kasin from big siti kam tu vikeshen in auer taun of St. Jelena. I sun diskaveret det as gud lord hes meni aders prfekt fimels in stak.

⦿⦿⦿⦿⦿⦿⦿⦿⦿⦿⦿⦿⦿⦿⦿⦿⦿⦿⦿⦿⦿⦿⦿⦿⦿⦿⦿⦿⦿⦿⦿⦿⦿⦿⦿⦿⦿

never forget it, asked Tony to repeat it, and he did. I swallowed hard. What could I do, still shaking and watching the others eating stolen heaven's apples? You can imagine that neither of us had any appetite, so I couldn't tell you if those apples were different.

You guessed it, my Tanya, the lord's perfection in the creation of an unforgettable female, couldn't love me as a loser. At first I wanted to die, but then Emilko's cousin from the big city came to vacation in our town of St. Helena. I soon discovered that our good lord had many other perfect females in stock.

⦿⦿⦿⦿⦿⦿⦿⦿⦿⦿⦿⦿⦿⦿⦿⦿⦿⦿⦿⦿⦿⦿⦿⦿⦿⦿⦿⦿⦿⦿⦿⦿⦿⦿⦿⦿⦿

Des ivning auer pater Malek divaidet vit his strong hends de letct fisikal blesings an as bois devels heds. Puling as angels klos over heds, det vi ver in de mes, sambadi of as pul de big glas ves from enchen teibel. It vos Malek feveret obgekt in sakristai and so ver panishmant mach mor biger. After frst laut ekspresing of his tots, hi vos svinging eraund medli. Tu of as devels iven goinet de broken ves and flauers an vet flor. Dei det oredi resivet de nidet blesing vos in mic of klinab, ven sardenli hevi dor openet and kraing slo Marishka ran in tu de rum.

"Pater! Pater Malek, jor lavli mis Pigi is gon," sei she foling in a big cher reservt onli for as prist mediteshen, tu krai. If bi eni ader pig mist, hi bi prosu vit as blesing of as lital devels, bat his mis Pigi? Vi ol ran aut tu luk ver she haidet. Sam of as ver stil in angels klos det in dip mad eraund chrch barns geding drti in de hri. Vit red chiks det gast nau vos fresh

───────────────────────────────

This evening our Pater Malek divided his last physical blessings on us boys' devilish heads. While pulling the angel's clothes that we wear in the mass over our heads, somebody among us knocked the big glass vase off the ancient table. It was Malek's favourite object in the sacristy and so the punishment was much worse. After first expressing his thoughts loudly, he swung about madly. Two of us devils even joined the broken vase and flowers on the wet floor. Those who had already received their needed blessing were in the midst of cleanup when suddenly the heavy door opened and slow Marishka ran crying into the room.

"Pater! Pater Malek, your lovely Miss Piggy is gone," she said, falling into a big chair reserved only for our priest's meditation, to cry. If it had been any other pig missing, he'd have continued with his blessing of us little devils, but his Miss Piggy? We all ran out to see where she was hiding. Some of us were still in our angel clothes that, in the deep mud around the church barns, were getting dirty in a hurry. With our red cheeks which were just freshly blest Emilko and mi traet tu plis as lavli pater Malek. Bod of as ran in dark stinki korners of de barn desperetli luking after stupid sau. Raning bek Emilko flip over an sliperi flor, puling mi vit him. His gogels endet in de stinki bru. Insted tu trit as laik a hiros, vi bod godet anader lod of blesin and mas chench autsait.

"Dont ju samtaim ask jor self, hau meni blesing maste hev as holi Piter, befor hi godet gop an de geit?" tok Emilko, med an Malek.

"Luket det from positiv sait. Vi are mach mor kloser tu heven nau, als befor."

Vos she stolen? No, det vos as pater Malek chrch sau! Samting laik det kud bi not stolen. Vi ar non lak a gud parishment, dei liv endlis dei chrch saus in pis.

Vel, mis Pigi kam in Malek laif vit lak. Jes, lak. He vin hr an lital taun loteri, an St. Florian dei, auer protektor of faer. Auer volunter faerfaiter briged disaidet tu sho ab in de chrch in dei hevi dark blu juniform. Tu mek a rili gud inpreshen dei brodet a old stachu of a St. Florian in de chrch tu bi blest from as Malek.

---

blessed, Emilko and me tried to please our lovely Pater Malek. Both of us ran to the dark stinky corners of the barn desperately looking for the stupid sow. Running back, Emilko flipped over on the slippery floor, pulling me with him. His goggles ended up in the stinky brew. Instead of treating us like heroes, we both got another load of blessing and had to change outside.

"Don't you sometimes ask yourself how many blessings our holy Peter must have had before he got his job at the gate?" asked Emilko, mad at Malek.

"Look at it from the positive side. We are much closer to heaven than before."

Was she stolen? No, that was Pater Malek's church sow! Something like that could not be stolen. We are known as a good parish, which at least leaves the church sows in peace.

Well, Miss Piggy came into Malek's life with luck. Yes, luck. He won her in a little town lottery on St. Florian's Day, our protector against fire. Our volunteer fire brigade decided to show up in the church in their heavy dark blue uniforms. To make a really good impression they brought an old statue of St. Florian to church to be blessed by Malek.

Iven as faerfaitars diden engoet de mes tu vel, sveting laik a piglec, as St. Florian kuden hev beter taim. Hi engoet de kraud of vorshiper and hepili raid an as devels beks. For meni jers nau, noubadi tuk him daun from his ples over de big dor an entrenc from faerhol. Iven hi vos a rili peshent sent and diden main brds malesting, inaf is inaf. After blesing de lital stachu of St. Florian, vi blesed de big tu, det olveis ste in auer chrch.

Over hepi faerfaiter kolet as pater Malek det ivning tu de big denc in de faer-faiter hol. Vit fresh blesed sent over de entranc vi ol hev a bjutifol taim, veiding an loteri. Gipsis vos pleing laik kresi and iven as svit pater Malek kuden resist. Hi denc vit grenmamichka Hlivovec. Ven dei start tu trn fest, vi kidc soet for frst taim, vait fit of auer taun prich. Den ven gipsis vos iting dei big mil tu mek dem strong for rest of a nait, loteri viner vos kolt. Auer ticherin godet a chiken, as Hot Zuzi de big trki and als sopreis, auer pater Malek godet a pigi. Ven de Orel Bachi vos cheking de seks of det pur litel slipi kricher, he jal in de kraud.

◎◎◎◎◎◎◎◎◎◎◎◎◎◎◎◎◎◎◎◎◎◎◎◎◎◎◎◎◎◎◎◎◎◎◎◎◎

Though our firefighters didn't enjoy the mass too well, sweating like piglets, our St. Florian couldn't have had a better time. He enjoyed the crowd of worshippers and happily rode on our devil's backs. For many years now, nobody had taken him down from his place over the big door at the entrance to the firehall. Even though he is a really patient saint and didn't mind the birds' molesting, enough is enough. After blessing the little statue of St. Florian, we blessed the big one too, the one that always stays in our church.

Our happy firefighters called our Pater Malek that evening to the big dance in the fire hall. With a fresh-blessed saint over the entrance, we all had a beautiful time waiting for the lottery. Gypsies were playing like crazy and even our sweet Pater Malek couldn't resist. He danced with Grandmamichka Hlivovec. When they started to spin fast, we kids saw for the first time the white feet of our town priest. Then, when the gypsies were eating a big meal to make them strong for the rest of the night, the lottery winners were called. Our teacher got a chicken, our Hot Zuzi a big turkey, and to our surprise, our Pater Malek got a piggy. When Orel Bachi checked the sex of that poor little sleepy creature, he yelled to the crowd.

◎◎◎◎◎◎◎◎◎◎◎◎◎◎◎◎◎◎◎◎◎◎◎◎◎◎◎◎◎◎◎◎◎◎◎◎◎

"Shi is a grl.l.l.l! Ha ha ha. Mai dir pater Malek is det not tu dengeres for ju? Ha ha ha."

"Dontju ever vori ebaut mi, mai brader. I am blest, and pei tu kip aut de trobel," ancer lital tipsi taun prich, haging det lital mis. Sait den dei vos olveis frends. Mis Pigi vos frst laif ting det onli belong tu him. Evriting als he vos shering vit as, bad des litel kjut mis vos onli his. He disaidet tu tek ker of her, so long ven he is a laif.

Na, an des point is nidet a lital korekchen. As bjutifol mis Pigi akcheli teket ker abaut as belavet pater Malek. She help im tu sorvaiv des bladi maut from his meid vich tro dem aut an de sters of de chrch haus. Dei vos sliping an des hard ston for mos of de erli moning. Onli hr skviging an emti stamak push Marishka tu chench her main. Ven de simpatetik dranks going dei homs start tu gedern bisaid snoring Malek, shi hes inaf. Marishka brod hr in hr barn and giv hr fud. Hr anjuzuali oner desapir in det big haus for rest of a dei. Tu tenk as svit Misi hi vos olveis bringing sam of des kukis det hi gedet bai visiting taun sols tu hr.

🌀🌀🌀🌀🌀🌀🌀🌀🌀🌀🌀🌀🌀🌀🌀🌀🌀🌀🌀🌀🌀🌀🌀🌀🌀🌀🌀🌀🌀🌀🌀🌀🌀

"She is a girlllllll! Ha ha ha. My dear Pater Malek, is that not too dangerous for you? Ha ha ha."

"Don't you ever worry about me, my brother. I am blessed, and paid to keep out of trouble," answered the slightly tipsy town priest, hugging that little miss. Since then they were always friends. Miss Piggy was the first live thing that belonged only to him. Everything else he shared with us, but this little cutie was only his. He decided to take care of her so long as he is alive.

Now, at this point a little correction is needed. Our beautiful Miss Piggy actually took care of our beloved Pater Malek. She helped him to survive the bloody mouth of his maid, who threw them out on the stairs of the church house. They were sleeping on the hard stone for most of the early morning. Only her screeching on an empty stomach pushed Marishka to change her mind. When the sympathetic drunks going to their homes started to gather beside the snoring Malek, she'd had enough. Marishka took her to the barn and gave her food. Her unusual owner disappeared into that big house for the rest of the day. To thank our sweet Missy, he would always bring her some of the cookies that he got from visiting town souls.

Never befor vi soet as direst lord srvent hepier den des taim. Onesli, his lav tu groing mis vos so big det hi iven skip a plezers of taun bar. Bad, ven ju tenk ju hevin ol ju start tu lus sam. Problem start tu gedert ven Marishka sed tu as pater Malek, det Mis nidet a men. Et frst hi ignor des.

Na hau shud Marishka nju, det his bjutifol Mis nidet a bor? She is not van of dem, det foling in lav. She is a virgen, and det she stei. Bad a big groning kaming from Mis kvoters teling him, det Mis is rili in trobel. Det nait hi giv ol preer tu his lavli pigi, bad ven a jang dei vek de taun ab, Mis vos vorser den befor.

As pur pater Malek hardli itet samting for brekvust, lisening his meid toking. "Direst pater Malek, she is a normal sau and she nidet a bor, simpel laik des," luk a pur Marishka red in de chiks.

Demet, his holi chrch properti is not sam kain of Sodoma and Gomora. Vot if auer lord dont laik det mis Pigi behevju and destroi de chrch? Vai des mis kud bi not a normal virgen, safering hr laif evei. Nau him de lords srvent

---

Never before had we seen our dearest lord's servant happier than at this time. Honestly, his love for the growing miss was so big that he even skipped the pleasures of the town bar. But, when you think you've got it all you start to lose some. The problems started when Marishka told our Pater Malek that his Miss needed a man. At first he ignored this.

Now how should she know that his beautiful Miss needed a boar? She is not one of those that falls in love. She is a virgin, and that she'll stay. But a big groan coming from Miss's quarters told him that Miss is really in trouble. That night he gave all his prayers to his lovely pig, but when the young day woke the town up, Miss was worse than before.

Our poor Pater Malek hardly ate anything for breakfast, listening to his maid talking. "Dearest Pater Malek, she is a normal sow and she needs a boar, it's that simple," said poor Marishka red in the cheeks.

Dammit, his holy church property is not like some kind of Sodom and Gomorrah. What if our lord didn't like Miss Piggy's behaviour and destroyed the church? Why couldn't this miss be a normal virgin, suffering her life away. Now he, the lord's servant,

mas go eraund tu esk for devels plesher in taun det vans hi tich holi behevju. De pipel bi sun lefing, chakling bihain his bek. "Luk, det is a Malek, det kud not proventet his on mis Pigi of satans filing and hi van tu tich as hau tu liv." Sun de kic bi raning after him troing him a bed apels. Demet, ol dos jers of holi tiching daun de drein. And for vat? Bikos mai mis refjus tu bi a sinpel from god skeri virgen!

So breking his holi hed vit det sekshual isju he olmos mis de dor of as taun bar. Drinking sloli evei his lavli main, hi veidet for as Orel bachika tu giv him adveis an des isju. Orel vos dem gud sol, and evribadi in taun laik him. Hi vos a farmer, men der vos femos for his praktikaliti. Ven hi eraivt pater Malek kol for a badel of vain and der sedaun tu diskaset des metar.

"Vel mai dir belavet Malek, I no hau ju fil. Bad jor mis nidet a mister," sed Orel svoloing his lef.

"Mai Mis is vrgen and stei virgen!" jal bek as pater Malek, luking an dos gedert sols det veiding an lef.

"Bad pater Malek, she is in des gud eg, ju no? Vel ju soet jor self vot for trobel she hes," traing tu eksplein as lavli Orel bachika.

⊚⊚⊚⊚⊚⊚⊚⊚⊚⊚⊚⊚⊚⊚⊚⊚⊚⊚⊚⊚⊚⊚⊚⊚⊚⊚⊚⊚⊚⊚⊚⊚⊚⊚⊚⊚

must go around to ask for the devil's pleasure in the town that wants him to teach holy behaviour. "Look, there is Malek, who could not prevent his own Miss Piggy from Satan's feeling and he wants to teach us how to live." Soon the kids would be running after him throwing bad apples at him. Dammit, all those years of holy teaching down the drain. And for what? Because my miss refuses to be a simple God-fearing virgin!

His holy head was so bursting with this sexual issue that he almost missed the door of our town bar. Slowly drinking away his lovely mind, he waited for Orel Bachika to give him advice on this issue. Orel was a damn good soul and everybody in town liked him. He was a farmer, a man who was famous for his practicality. When he arrived, Pater Malek called for a bottle of wine and sat down there to discuss this matter.

"Well, my dear beloved Malek, I know how you feel. But your miss needs a mister," said Orel, swallowing his laughter.

"My Miss is a virgin and will stay a virgin!" yelled back our Pater Malek, looking at the gathered souls waiting to laugh.

"But Pater Malek, she is at that age, you know? Well, you saw yourself what her trouble is," our lovely Orel Bachika tried to explain.

⊚⊚⊚⊚⊚⊚⊚⊚⊚⊚⊚⊚⊚⊚⊚⊚⊚⊚⊚⊚⊚⊚⊚⊚⊚⊚⊚⊚⊚⊚⊚⊚⊚⊚⊚

Marijan Megla

"Pein. I am in pein tu and safere a long," ancer pater Malek.

"I dont andestan ju. Ju a peit for steing aut de trobel," se de old Orel.

"Mai direst Orel bachika, I ask ju hau ju kud provent det lav and not hau ju ekorig des, and I am viling tu pei for det," sed Malek hef stending bai de teibel.

"Vel, or ju vam overhepi misis or sed vrgen, det is jor problm. Bad, I tel ju she is shor redi tu hev a laver," sed hi foling in lef.

"And she gene not gedet!"

"O..o..o..o, dont bi so. If is eniting chencht bai des bisnis, bi kavert vit de tel. She ken stil kerit holi shin eraund hr big heri hed," lefing encer de Orel bachika.

"Na gud, dem sau shud hev de fan, bad vot vi du vit dem, dei folo?" asking chok vait Malek, toking olmos in Orels ir.

"Vel, dei bi jors truli engels," sei lait as Orel bachika raning evei from Malek flaing vain krug.

Pur pater Malek retrn tu his chrch. Hi vos totali drank an des ivning ven Mis vos teken tu Orels big bor, for breking

---

"Pain. I am in pain too and have suffered long," answered Pater Malek.

"I don't understand you. You are paid for staying out of trouble," said old Orel.

"My dearest Orel Bachika, I asked you how you could prevent that love, not how you encourage it, and I am willing to pay for it," said Malek, half standing by the table.

"Well, either you want an overjoyed Missus or a sad virgin, that is your problem. But I tell you, she is sure ready to have a lover," he said with a laugh.

"And she's not gonna get it!"

"Ooohhh, don't be like that. If anything is changed by this business it will be covered by the tail. She can still carry her holy halo around her big hairy head," laughingly answered Orel Bachika.

"Okay then, the damn sow should have some fun, but what will we do with those that follow?" asked the chalk-white Malek, talking almost in Orel's ear.

"Well, they will be your true angels," Orel Bachika said lightly, running away from Malek's flying wine jug.

Poor Pater Malek returned to his church. He was totally drunk on the evening when Miss was taken to Orel's big boar to break hr svit virginiti. Sun after as lavli Malek vos praud onkel and pipel in de taun bar stil rememberet brsdei parti for seven piglec.

Frendship never safer mach bikos misis Pigi step in rong direkshen. She stil engoet iting oversvit kukis, strudels, chiken mit, bisaid hrs on fud. On des dei of hr desapiring she vos praudli pushing hr 550 blesed paund. For as oltar bois det vos luking for hr in des frst hefen auer det vos shoking. Never befor vos eniting stolen from as chrch. Na preheps lital holi vota, or sens, bad det is a meiger kraim. Misis Pigi vos lavt from ol of as and kud bi gast chopt in sam kain of gulash. Vi ar living in hepi taun of katolik and gus and not in sam god ferseken gipsi vileg. Katolik and gus for det metar, never ever stilet eniting. Spesheli not sacha inportant enimal laik misis Pigi, de chrch sau. Pipel gedering in shok eraund as blesed chrch, diskasing hu kud du sacha tings tu as misis Pigi.

"De gipsi danet," jaling de hef med taun gosop. "Grenmamichka Hlivovec soet de bladi bastats vit de fol sek keriing samting aut de vileg."

⊚⊚⊚⊚⊚⊚⊚⊚⊚⊚⊚⊚⊚⊚⊚⊚⊚⊚⊚⊚⊚⊚⊚⊚⊚⊚⊚⊚⊚⊚⊚⊚⊚⊚⊚

her sweet virginity. Soon after, our lovely Malek was a proud uncle and people in the town bar still remember the birthday party for the seven piglets.

Their friendship didn't suffer much because Missus Piggy stepped in the wrong direction. She still enjoyed eating over-sweet cookies, strudels, chicken meat, besides her own food. On the day she disappeared she was proudly pushing her 550 blessed pounds. For us altar boys looking for her in the first half hour, it was shocking. Never before was anything stolen from our church. Oh, perhaps a little holy water or incense, but this was a major crime. Missus Piggy was loved by all of us and couldn't just be chopped in some kind of goulash. We live in a happy town of Catholics and Jews and not in some God-forsaken gypsy village. Catholics and Jews, for that matter, never ever steal anything. Especially not such an important animal as Missus Piggy, the church sow. People gathered in shock around our blessed church discussing who could do such things to our Missus Piggy.

"The gypsies did it," yelled the half-mad town gossips. "Grandmamichka Hlivovec saw those bloody bastards with a full sack carrying something out of the village."

⊚⊚⊚⊚⊚⊚⊚⊚⊚⊚⊚⊚⊚⊚⊚⊚⊚⊚⊚⊚⊚⊚⊚⊚⊚⊚⊚⊚⊚⊚⊚⊚⊚⊚⊚

Marijan Megla

Fresh horses vos putet in de kerich and as svit Malek, stil pel from shok, vit de sex strong bois. Tu kip dem vorm and in best mental chep, dei tuket demigon of red vain and badel of slivovic. Old tutlos grenis start tu prei for fest ending of des misteri. Dos gais ar anstapebel. "Bladi gipsis, dei bi never stiling egen as chrch sau." Dei overlodet kerich olmos trn over in de big kurv an end of a taun. "Go and bring Misis hom," jaling vi kidc raning bisaid de kerich.

Bad, in ol pur vilag of gipsis, dei vos onli van mister pig, vich bols vos kat. Hi vos so skini det ju kud si evri lital bon det help him muv in his stinki kvoter. Iven droing de kraud of in de hri vekt ab sols, det in hasti putet hevi shus vos gedert eraund des svain skeleton tu protekt him from dranks, diden duet eni gut. Misis Pigi vos not faundct.

Dei retrn let des nait drank lak mader erd, and vit dilema. Hu kud posible stolet de chrch sau and vot tu du nekst. Dei start tu diskaset bai hot vain in Marishka kichen dei nju taktik. Ven de old gosop vos sloli retrning hom, dei step an big dilema. Shor, dei kud go tu si

Fresh horses were harnessed to the carriage for our sweet Malek, still pale from shock, and six strong boys. To keep them warm and in the best shape, they took a demijohn of red wine and a bottle of slivovica. Old toothless grannies started to pray for a fast end to this mystery. Those guys were unstoppable. "Bloody gypsies, they'll never be stealing our church sow again." Their overloaded carriage almost turned over on the big curve at the edge of town. "Go and bring Missus home," we kids yelled, running beside the carriage.

But in the whole poor village of gypsies there was only one mister pig, whose balls had been cut. He was so skinny that you could see every little bone that helped him move in his stinky quarters. Even drawing a crowd of hurriedly-woken-up souls, who in their hastily-put-on shoes gathered around this swine skeleton to protect him from the drunks, didn't do any good. Missus Piggy was not found.

They returned late that night drunk as mother earth, and with a dilemma. Who could possibly steal the church sow, and what to do next? They started to discuss their new tactics by the hot wine in Marishka's kitchen. When the old gossips were slowly returning home, they were stopped by a big dilemma. Sure, they could go see evrivans pig barn and noubadi bi med, bad pig bi pigs and dei ol luk de seim vans rolt in de mad. It vos pig kiling sison and Malek nju his chens tu faund de mising misis Pigi a veri slim. Shi probebli voching oredi des blesed vorld in chep of a gud hot sosich or sun inaf laik a hjuch smoket hem. Miting endet ven Marishka troet evri singel drank aut of kichen. "Noubadi shud sing ven misis Pigi is not faundet."

Pipel faund as pater Malek meni taim in tirs, preing blo de virgen Meri. Preheps det is lord panishment tu misis Pigi det chos not tu bi vrgen. Meni taim hi svor revench tu de kiler of his misis. Auer gronabs traet evriting tu chir im ab. Dei givin from dei on kilings, fresh sosiches, blad sosiches, hed chis. Dei order de gipsis tu plei his most feveret songs belo his vindos. Nating, apsolutli nating, simstu chir im ab. Iven his srvises in de chrch vos short and vit aut mjusik.

"Pipel, des kud bring onli lord panishment aponas," jaking de old gosop. "Meibi de lord kiling as krops, and hu nos auer vainplantash." Living vit aut vain and slivovic

---

everyone's pig barn and nobody would be mad, but pigs are pigs and they all look the same once they're rolled in the mud. It was pig killing season and Malek knew his chance of finding his missing Missus Piggy were very slim. She was probably already seeing the world in the shape of a good hot sausage, or soon enough as a huge smoked ham. The meeting ended when Marishka threw every single drunk out of the kitchen. "Nobody should sing when Missus Piggy is not found."

People found our Pater Malek in tears many times, praying beneath the Virgin Mary. Perhaps this is the lord's punishment to Missus Piggy who chose not to be a virgin. Many times he swore revenge against the killer of his Missus. Our grownups tried everything to cheer him up. They gave from their own killings, fresh sausages, blood sausages, head cheese. They ordered the gypsies to play his favourite songs below his windows. Nothing, absolutely nothing, seemed to cheer him up. Even his church services were short and without music.

"People, this could only bring the lord's punishment upon us," yakked the old gossips. "Maybe the lord will kill our crops, and who knows about our vineyards." Living without wine and slivovica would

bi laik safering sam kain of "sol femen" and des taun kud lus sam multi fain mens in des stragel.

Hm..m..m. Taun shor chench kvik in sacha misheps. Der vos dasent amachurs self proklemt detektivs raning laik vet horsis kros de taun. Auer svit baterflai Istvan de taun polismen diden slip for a vik or so, investigeting tausend foni reports. Ven ever sambadi kilet de pig, streng shedo bi voching evri bucher muvment. Stro stek bi muving, and korn stek bi toking and teking noc.

Hu nos hau long bi det sich of taun going an, if de Orel bachika diden spatet samting anjuzuli. "Hau kam det as drank Josef, lord never giv him de engels vings, hev sacha hjuch hem tu smok det vinter?"

Den van kuld dei its hepen. From auer chrch tauer ol seven bels vos never staping benging. Pipel kroset dem self and tenk an vorst, det preheps a vor is breking ab. Demet hu shud meket nau de vor? As grendedishkin kaiser is det, as Rashien zar is det, de bladi Hitler brn him self tu det, end vi hev onli ten jers of pis.

ⓔⓔⓔⓔⓔⓔⓔⓔⓔⓔⓔⓔⓔⓔⓔⓔⓔⓔⓔⓔⓔⓔⓔⓔⓔⓔⓔⓔⓔⓔⓔⓔⓔⓔⓔ

be like suffering some kind of soul famine, and this town could lose some mighty fine men in the struggle.

Hmmmm. The town sure changed quickly in such a situation. There were a dozen amateur self-proclaimed detectives running like wet horses across town. Our sweet butterfly Istvan the town policeman didn't sleep for a week or so, investigating a thousand phoney reports. Whenever somebody killed a pig, a strange shadow would be watching the butcher's every movement. Straw stacks moved, corn stalks talked and took notes.

Who knows how long that siege of town would have gone on if Orel Bachika hadn't spotted something unusual. "How come our drunk Joseph, lord never give him angel's wings, has such a huge ham to smoke this winter?"

Then one cold day it happened. From our church tower all seven bells wouldn't stop banging. People crossed themselves and thought the worst, that perhaps a war is breaking out. Dammit, who should make war now? Our grandeduchkin Kaiser is dead, our Russian Czar is dead, bloody Hitler burned himself to death, and we've only had ten years of peace.

ⓔⓔⓔⓔⓔⓔⓔⓔⓔⓔⓔⓔⓔⓔⓔⓔⓔⓔⓔⓔⓔⓔⓔⓔⓔⓔⓔⓔⓔⓔ

Tru chrch dors, a feroshes faiting and svering continju from insait. Preheps tu satans atek as pur Malek and hi mei daing for onar of his chrch. Kidc hed vos blest and kriskrost from skeri grenmamichkas. Gosop regrut im self tu sturm lords haus and sho de bladi satans hu is de bos hir. De hevi dors a open and de gais dei kud teket pik foling in lef. Roling over chrch sters laik a vundet solger. Sun evribadi lef. Tu strong gais helping as baterflai Istvan sabdu de med Malek. His onli vil is tu rich vit his fet hends fet Rosi, tu strengel hr. Hr self faund de refjug in big pot of holi vota det stei an entrenc of a chrch. Siting der laik sam ist India elefant, bai voshing.

Maleks lital meid Marishka desperatli trai tu push him in his nos a open badel of smeling solt. Insted tu kam im daun de bladi badel mek him mor kresi. An de holi flor of a chrch spredet ol over ar sosishes, blad sosiches, smoket rips and a hjuch hem.

In a holi tauer as drank Josef ganp laik med Tarsan from van bel rop tu ader direkted vit Orel bachikas old kaiser sors. For frst taim old gai sho as hau mach gud dirigent hi kud bi, ven hi med is.

◎◎◎◎◎◎◎◎◎◎◎◎◎◎◎◎◎◎◎◎◎◎◎◎◎◎◎◎◎◎◎◎◎◎◎◎◎

Through the church doors was heard ferocious fighting and swearing from inside. Perhaps two Satans attacked our poor Malek and he's maybe dying for the honour of his church. Kids heads were blessed and crossed by scared grandmamichkas. The gossips regrouped to storm the lord's house and show bloody Satan who is the boss here. The heavy doors opened and the guys who could take a peek fell down laughing. They rolled over the church stairs like wounded soldiers. Two strong guys were helping our butterfly Istvan subdue the angry Malek. With all his will he wanted to reach fat Rosie with his fat hands to strangle her. She herself found refuge in the big pot of holy water at the entrance to the church. She sat there like some East Indian elephant, bathing. Malek's little maid Marishka desperately tried to push an open bottle of smelling salts under his nose. Instead of calming him the bloody bottle made him more crazy. All over the holy floor of the church were spread sausages, blood sausages, smoked ribs and a huge ham.

In the holy tower our drunk Joseph jumped like a mad Tarzan from one bell rope to the other, directed by Orel Bachika's old kaiser swords. For the first time the old guy showed us what a good conductor he could be when he was mad.

◎◎◎◎◎◎◎◎◎◎◎◎◎◎◎◎◎◎◎◎◎◎◎◎◎◎◎◎◎◎◎◎◎◎◎◎◎

Marijan Megla

Vans a pater Malek vos put in his soft bed and dor lokt, living him droming an old ok dor, fet Rosi vos transportet hom tu chench hr big anderver and rumi skrt. De drank Josef vos eskortet tu baterflai Istvan klin ofis. Orel bachika vos kult daun in taun bar and it vos nidet seven krugs befor hi start tu tok normali.

Ven as polismen vish his svet and regein sam of his pauer, investigeshen start. "Vel drank Josef, vai? Vai ju stolet, nating als bat de holi chrch sau?" ask hi skribeling an pis of peper.

"I dont nou, mai dir blesed Istvan. Ju shud no des befor ju bit mi an mai blesed skini barom vit jor hevi belt. I dont no hau es hepen," tok kvaetli de bladi drank, masazing his taet boni hends. "I remember det hi giv mi sam pig det dem moning, for help mi aut kros de vinter. Ju no, I hev 8 kids and fet Rosi, mai blesed vaif tu fid. Den vi vent tu Malek seler tu trost an det and laik juzuli I gon drank. Ven mai Rosi kam tu transpotet de given pig hom, I simpli fergat vich pig is mir given. Rosi sho mi det bigvan, and I tenk det

@@

Once Pater Malek was put in his soft bed and the door locked, leaving him drumming on the old oak door, fat Rosie was transported home to change her large underwear and roomy skirt. Drunk Joseph was escorted to butterfly Istvan's clean office. Orel Bachika was cooled down in the town bar, and it took seven jugs before he started to talk normally.

When our policeman washed off his sweat and regained some of his power, the investigation started. "Well drunk Joseph, why? Why did you steal, and nothing but the holy church sow?" he asked, scribbling on a piece of paper.

"I don't know, my dear blessed Istvan. You should know this before you beat me on my blessed skinny bottom with your heavy belt. I don't know how it happened," the bloody drunk said quietly, massaging his bony hands. "I remember that he gave me some pig that morning, to help me through the winter. You know I have eight kids and fat Rosie, my blessed wife, to feed. Then we went to Malek's cellar to toast to it and like usual I got drunk. When my Rosie came to take the gift pig home, I simply forgot which pig we were given. Rosie showed me the big one and I thought that

@@

bi orait for as. Vi ar de big femili and nid laca mit. Vi kl hr emidiatli and ven dei diskaver det she is mising, shi vos oredi in pigs heven."

"So vot hepen den?" ask de taun polismen.

"Vel, jestudei kam tu as de Orel bachika and ask, and ask sam mor so long til I dont edmitet tu kil det bladi chrch sau. So, tu dei mi and mai blesed Rosi, lord bles evri paund ovet, bring hef of misis Pigi bek."

"And vot hepen?" ask de gud luking polisman.

"Vel, if I bi not ganping so brevli from rop tu rop, dei mek mi preheps tu oks," sed de taun drank voching de hol in his penc krach. "I dont no vot dei du tu mai Rosi, bad shi vos shor skriming a lat."

As polisman baterflai Istvan kipet as taun drank Josef for dei or tu. Vans pater Malek vos kult daun inaf he relis him. For panishment noubadi bi giving him eni bus for det vinter. Bisaid, vot is laif? Vot kam an des erd mas go van dei bek. Sun pater Malek vos kuking de dranks sosiches and dei vere veri gud. It vos normal — de mit vos from as blesed misis Pigi.

⊚⊚⊚⊚⊚⊚⊚⊚⊚⊚⊚⊚⊚⊚⊚⊚⊚⊚⊚⊚⊚⊚⊚⊚⊚⊚⊚⊚⊚⊚⊚⊚⊚

would be all right for us. We are a big family and need lots of meat. We killed her immediately, and when we discovered she was missing she was already in pig's heaven."

"So what happened then?" asked the town policeman.

"Well, yesterday Orel Bachika came and asked, and kept asking so long as I didn't admit killing the bloody church sow. So today me and my blessed Rosie, lord bless every pound of her, brought half of Missus Piggy back."

"And what happened?" asked the good-looking policeman.

"Well, if I hadn't jumped from rope to rope so bravely they might have made me into an ox," said the town drunk, looking at the hole in the crotch of his pants. "I don't know what they did to my Rosie, but she was sure screaming a lot."

Our policeman butterfly Istvan kept our town drunk Joseph for a day or two. He released him once Pater Malek had cooled down enough. For punishment, nobody would give him any booze over the winter. Besides, what is life? What comes onto this earth must go back one day. Soon Pater Malek was cooking the drunk's sausages and they were very good. It was to be expected — the meat was from our blessed Missus Piggy.

⊚⊚⊚⊚⊚⊚⊚⊚⊚⊚⊚⊚⊚⊚⊚⊚⊚⊚⊚⊚⊚⊚⊚⊚⊚⊚⊚⊚⊚⊚⊚⊚⊚

Auer chrch vos bildet an end of eitint senchuri from auer pesent masel, bishofs mani, and blesing of auer lord in citadel. Hi disaidet not tu kol dos pesenc tu sandei vork, vich helpet an hr konstrakshen. She vos sinpel, laik pipel der bildet hr, and strong laik dei ver. Hr properti vos soraundet vit hai vait vol. Auer chrch vos laik lital frenli fortres, hevenli ailend in de si of kranbelt sols.

Auer chrch vos a big hol, vich siling and vols vos peintet. Evrivan of det fresk luked so sed, in enormes safering, bring as pur sols in big dilema. Hau an erd heven soposto bi sacha hepi ples if evrivan is safering der. An rait sait of a mein rum vos plest tu lital oltars. Van of dem vos dediketet tu as mader vrgen Mcri. Il vos mosli fimel domein. Dei bi laitening dei kendel belo hr stachu so she help dem resolv dei problems. Broken meriches or tu erli maderhut, vit aut noing hu is de hepi fader, vos komen kos.

~~~

Our church was built at the end of the eighteenth century from our peasant muscle, bishop's money, and the blessing of our lord on high. He decided not to call those peasants to work on Sunday, which helped in her construction. She was simple, like the people who built her, and strong like they were. Her property was surrounded by a high white wall. Our church was like a friendly little fortress, a heavenly island in the sea of crumbled souls.

Our church was a big hall with paintings on the ceiling and walls. Everyone in its frescos looked so sad, in enormous suffering, that it brought us poor souls to a big dilemma. How on earth is heaven supposed to be such a happy place if everyone is suffering there? On the right side of the main room were placed two little altars. One of them was dedicated to our mother Virgin Mary. It was mostly a female domain. They'd light their candles below her statue so she'd help them solve their problems. Broken marriages or premature motherhood without knowing who is the father were common causes.

Ader lital oltar vos for as St. Florian, sever from faer. Hi vos most lonliest stachu in de chrch for mosli of de jers det I spendet der. Onli ven meiger faer destroi blok or tu of kau barns verd his egsistenc eknolegt. For mant or tu hi bi engoing bjutifol flauer det as sols bring him. Over mein entrenc tu de chrch vos bildet a larch balkoni, an vich stud a hjuch organ. It nidet olmos ol evelebal spec, taching vit his hajeste paips de peintet chrch siling. In front of det monster vos plest a register fest tu de meiger oltar an de ader sait of a hol. Siting an de larg bench ju hed an inpresiv vju of ol chrch. For as kids, det vos most preshes part of a chrch, vich ju kud rich only jusing de tauer sters. I mas edmitet det nating in det hevenli fortres vere mor inportant for as taun kidc, det never hes plesher tu plei an dei on pianos or orgen.

Shor, vi vos heving fan tu go kemjunjen olmost evri sandei, baiting as pater Malek for his holi fingers. Hi bi saimtaim troing de gesus bodi in as devels maut from kvait distanc, skert from as sharp tit. Bad bisaid puling an de bels befor mes,

---

The other little altar was for our St. Florian, saviour from fire. He was the loneliest statue in the church for most of the years that I spent there. Only when a major fire destroyed a block or two of cow barns was his existence acknowledged. For a month or two he'd be enjoying the beautiful flowers that our souls brought him.

Over the main entrance to the church was built a large balcony on which stood a huge organ. It needed almost all the available space, touching with its highest pipes the painted church ceiling. In front of that monster was a register fastened to the main altar on the other side of the hall.

Sitting on the large bench you had an impressive view of the whole church. For us kids, that was the most precious part of the church, which you could reach only by using the tower stairs. I must admit that nothing in that heavenly fortress was more important to us town kids, who never had the pleasure to play on their own pianos or organs.

Sure, we had fun taking communion almost every Sunday, biting our Pater Malek's holy fingers. He would sometimes throw the body of Jesus at our devil's mouths from quite a distance, scared of our sharp teeth. But beside pulling the bells for mass,

Marijan Megla

orgen vos as feveret obgekt in as chrch. I stil tudei remembering hau mach fan and pein kud bring as de sandei mes. Ven de oltar bois vere bisi vit chenching dci klos, tu mek dem for des auer de chosen engel, vi from de kor bi vit dikan Pino going redi for singing. Dikan Pino vos jang siti boi. Bisaid his mjusik and big lav tu St. Florian, gardien of faer, hi vanet tu bi as saker koch. Hi kam in as taun tu lern holi gop, and if lord vil, van dei reples as pater Malek, de lord srvent in as taun. Hi vos preing a lat belo stachu of St. Florian, hoping det hi kud kil de faer in his mens chest. His kain of faer startet ven hi soet a bjutifol jang ticherin Mira. She tu muv in as taun and vos veri lonli.

Vel, his vish tu plei de saker ver sun grentet ven auer taun nidet a nju saker koch. His faer in chest eksplodet in a katasliufal brn aut, from vich iven as vuden sent tuket de refjug. Seving his braun skrt and safering badi hi liv him alon tu Miras faer. Vot betrif his mjusik, preheps she diden ran evei, bad vos shor destroit from as taun kidc. Hi gast kuden menagt for lav of as gud lord his chrch kor. Iven vi

the organ was our favourite object in our church. I still remember today how much fun and pain the Sunday mass gave us. When the altar boys were busy changing their clothes to make them the chosen angels for this hour, we in the choir would be with Deacon Pino getting ready to sing.

Deacon Pino was a young city boy. Besides his music and deep love for St. Florian, guardian of fire, he wanted to be our soccer coach. He came to our town to learn the holy job, and if the lord willed one day he would replace our Pater Malek, the lord's servant in our town. He was praying a lot below the statue of St. Florian, hoping that he could kill the fire in his man's chest. His kind of fire started when he saw the beautiful young teacher, Mira. She too had moved to our town and was very lonely.

Well, his wish to play soccer was very soon granted when our town needed a new soccer coach. His fire in the chest exploded in a catastrophic burnout from which even our wooden saint took refuge. Saving his brown skirt and suffering body, he left him alone to Mira's fire. What became of his music, at least it didn't run away, but it sure was destroyed by us town kids. He just couldn't manage, for the love of our good lord, his church choir. Though we kidc nju vot trobel he hes vit as pater Malek, tu eksplen him as misbehevju, temteshen tu plei an de orgen bisaid him vos mach mor biger.

Des moning Emilko and mi kam laid juzuali letst. As dikan Pino vos aredi traing tu sort aut as kor det ran eraund him in smol spec det vos left inbetvin orgen and balkoni fens. Puling his her samtain, turning vit his big ais hi desperatli trai tu kip his nrvs and kontrol over det devel kraut.

"Soprano! Plis gedert in midel of de organ. Plis bi pisfol. Soprano van! Plis gedert an mai left sait. Pis, I sed, ju lital devels. Tenors shud kam an mai rait sait. I sed rait sait, ju godlos ship of auer gesus. Ar der Toni and Drago an de pedels? Go plis, and cheket bihain de orgen." Den, ven noubadi vuden chek hi svift go tu vords de onli dor of balkoni, to si in dark korner if det tu gais panping de air.

"Gais, ar ju redi?"

"Jes dikan, ve hev oredi sam presher!"

"So vi kud start?"

"Je, je. Vi kud start."

kids knew what trouble he was having with Pater Malek explaining our misbehaviour to him, the temptation to play the organ beside him was too great.

That morning Emilko and me came last as usual. Our Deacon Pino was already trying to sort out the choir that ran around him in the small space that was left between the organ and the balcony rail. Pulling his hair sometimes, turning away his big eyes, he desperately tried to keep his nerve and his control over that devil's crowd.

"Sopranos! Please gather at the centre of the organ. Please be peaceful. Soprano one! Please gather on my left side. Peace, I said, you little devils. Tenors should come on my right side. I said right side you godless sheep of our Jesus. Are Tony and Drago on the pedals? Go please and check if they're behind the organ." Then, when nobody would check, he swiftly went towards the only door on the balcony to see in the dark corner if those two guys were pumping air.

"Guys, are you ready?"

"Yes deacon, we already have some pressure!"

"So we can start?"

"Ya, ya. We can start."

"Shhh!" Puting his long finger an his bleset maut, he lukt so holi, laik St. Florian, protektor of faer.

Komoshen vos hai and pur dikan Pino vos stil divaiding soprano from soprano van and tenors, ven sambadi skrimet.

"Pater Malek is kaming, vit his oltar bois!"

"O mai god!" toking skert dikan Pino, pushing an de sait as lital satans, det laik hrd of ship raning eraund him. Faunding de shorteste vei tu orgen hjuch register, he sank his ten bjutifol fingers intu de kibord.

Glories mjusik sprang from de orgen, an vich lital fet pink angels vit broken vings henget. The mjusik vos so nais, so overvelmt, det veri sun evrivan van tu bi part of des mjusikal aleluja. At frst evri brev chaild det kud rich eni part of registar pleet onli vit van finqer, or tu. Bad de mjusik vos so bjutifol, so fol of magik, det sun evrivan jused ol fingers det kud rich det mjusikal heven.

Vi faitet for det konvinien plesis. Evri trik no metar hau lo vos just tu gedert ples bisaid as holi dikan Pino. Samtaim in des enormes anprofeshenal efert, in vich ol dikan Pinos

⟨⟨

"Shhhh!" Putting his long finger on his blessed mouth he looked so holy, like St. Florian, protector of fire.

The commotion was high and poor Deacon Pino was still dividing soprano from soprano one and tenors when somebody screamed.

"Pater Malek is coming with his altar boys!"

"Oh my God!" said the scared Deacon Pino, pushing aside us little satans who like a herd of sheep were running around him. Finding the shortest way to the organ's huge register, he sank his ten beautiful fingers into the keyboard.

Glorious music sprang from the organ, on which little fat pink angels with broken wings hung. The music was so nice, so overwhelming, that very soon everyone wanted to be part of this musical hallelujah. At first every brave child that could reach any part of the register played with only one finger, or two. But the music was so beautiful, so full of magic, that soon everyone used all the fingers that could reach that musical heaven.

We fought for the convenient places. Every trick, no matter how low, was used to get a place beside our holy Deacon Pino. Sometime in this enormous unprofessional effort, in which all of Deacon Pino's holi finger vos envolvt, his tu legs, and armi of streng fingers and leks of as kids, mjusik rapidli chench. Meni legs belonging tu devels bodis for vich vos no rum an de bench bisaid de dikan laing daun an de holi chrch flor. Tengelt vit ol dos gais dei stendet, pushet or torcheret for beter ples, dei idiotikli kiket an van or tu bas pedal. Crashing samtaim vit as dikan Pinos soft enkels dei fol in dip lef.

Evri sacha kresh, vit sam of streng aninvaidet leks, hi register vit vait open eis and his red chiks fol bloen vit his on holi er. Jaling samting tu his felo musishen. Protesting? Svering? I dont no. I vos bisi pleing de hjuch orgen.

Srdenli! Vem! Vem! Auch! Auch! Bambu...u...u...us! Det vos hot njus. En emidiatli reakshen ken sev ju a bruses. Pino vos femos for his bambus, end hi diden seving noubadi finger. De armi of streng fingers desapiring in a hri. Ganping an beks of dos belo an chrch flor dei koset meiger kraing vev, and evakueshen of dei devels bodis. Mjuzik inpruvt rapidli, and sun afterverc evrivan vos singing.

<hr/>

holy fingers were involved, his two legs, and an army of strange fingers and legs of us kids, the music rapidly changed. Many legs belonging to devil's bodies for which there was no room on the bench beside the deacon were lying on the church floor. Tangled with all those guys they stood on, pushed or tortured for a better place, they idiotically kicked one or two bass pedals. Crashing sometimes with our Deacon Pino's soft ankles, they fell into deep laughter.

Every such crash with some of the strange uninvited legs, he registered with wide open eyes and red cheeks full blown with his own holy air. Yelling something to his fellow musicians. Protesting? Swearing? I don't know. I was busy playing the huge organ.

Suddenly! Wham! Wham! Ouch! Ouch! Swat! That was hot news. An immediate reaction could save you a bruise. Pino was famous for his swats, and he didn't save anybody's finger. The army of strange fingers disappeared in a hurry. Jumping on the backs of those down on the church floor they caused a major crying wave, and evacuation of their devil's bodies. The music improved rapidly, and soon afterwards everyone was singing.

Marijan Megla

I gru ab after de vor, and elektrisiti vos samtaim kat tu as taun. Elektrisiti vos bedli nidet for as indastri det vos sloli kaming bek. Meibi bikos vi vos never srten vot taim vi bi no mor heving elektrisiti, as pater Malek orderet tu biger gais tu pedelet an orgen er soplai. It vos nating rong vit des. Pedeling diden kil no chaild det hev non farm chors. Onli stedi pushing of pedal kud soplai inaf er, and det kud bi ekomlisht rili isi.

For long taim nau, Toni and Drago vos kot in des posishen. Dei vos tu jang to goin de saker klab and chenchet dei vois, so dei kud not sing in de chrch kor. But, vit chenching dei voises, dei chenchet dei apinien over sam gerls det hepen to bi bolk of auer kor. So in sted pedeling dei ol konsern vos tu muv kloser tu det godlos harem. Bad duing det, dei mas abendct dci pcdcling ples bihain de orgen.

It vos onli meter of taim befor Pinos orgen ran aut of er, end letct krai of a tin paip sloli dai. Daun belo as dei vos stil singing and sloli van bai van kvaet daun. Skert pipel trning dei heds laik a gus akspekting sam atek from de skai. Pater Malek is kot laut mamling, and de oltar bois

---

I grew up after the war, and electricity was sometimes cut to our town. Electricity was badly needed for our industry that was slowly recovering. Maybe because we were never certain when we'd have no more electricity, our Pater Malek ordered two bigger guys to pedal the organ's air supply. There was nothing wrong with it. Pedalling didn't kill a child who'd known farm chores. Only a steady pushing of the pedal could supply enough air, and that could be accomplished really easily.

For a long time now, Tony and Drago were caught in that position. They were too young to join the soccer club, and their voices had changed so they couldn't sing in the church choir. But, with the change of their voices, they changed their opinion of some girls who happened to be the bulk of our choir. So instead of pedalling their only concern was to move closer to that godless harem. But doing that, they had to abandon their pedalling place behind the organ.

It was only a matter of time before Pino's organ ran out of air, and the last cry of a tin pipe slowly died. Down below us they were still singing and slowly one by one they quieted down. Scared people turned their heads like a goose expecting an attack from the sky. Pater Malek was caught mumbling aloud, and the altar boys

komenting lets njus in saker geim. Sambadi hev a sevir hikabs. In des prfekt sailenc as dikan svering laik letst kucher, pushing as dei vos in his vei ran behain de orgen. Nachurli noubadi vos der. Ven hi vos puling des tu biger gais aut of des godlos tinager harem, his ples bai registar vos emidiatli okupait. Kor members okupait evri evelebal ples, ankering dei fingers in evri evelebal ki. De hikab prson god his konpanien, vich snis endlis for taim, kosing an overvelming "God bles ja" from sopreis parishener. Pater Malek trning raund put his hevi hends an his fet vest. Ju kud hr de roseris trning nervesli in de tutlos grenis hends. Bihaind de orgen meiger vor is breking ab.

Splesh! Auch!

"Ju dem bist, sekshuli antikrais huligan, if I ketch ju vans mor in mai kor I kat jor bols."

Splesh, splesh.

"Auch, liv mi alon, demet. I promis no mor tu tach jor dem vrgens."

"Ju promis det letct vikend, ju boso."

"I pedeling oredi demet, vot mor ju van?"

●◎●◎●◎●◎●◎●◎●◎●◎●◎●◎●◎●◎●◎●◎●◎●◎●◎●

were commenting on the latest news on the soccer game. Somebody had severe hiccups. In this perfect silence our deacon was swearing like the last teamster, pushing us out of his way as he ran behind the organ. Naturally, nobody was there. When he was pulling those two bigger guys out of that godless teenaged harem, his place at the register was immediately occupied. Choir members occupied every available place, anchoring their fingers in every available key. The hiccuping person got a companion, who sneezed at least four times, causing an overwhelming "God bless you" from the surprised parishioners. Pater Malek turned around and put his heavy hands on his fat waist. You could hear the rosaries turning nervously in the toothless grannies' hands. Behind the organ, major war was breaking out.

Splash! Ouch!

"You damn beasts, sexual antichrist hooligans, if I catch you in my choir once more I'll cut your balls."

Splash, splash.

"Ouch, leave me alone, dammit. I promise not to touch your damn virgins any more."

"You promised that last weekend, you bozo."

"I'm pedalling already, dammit, what more do you want?"

◎◎◎◎◎◎◎◎◎◎◎◎◎◎◎◎◎◎◎◎◎◎◎◎◎◎◎◎◎◎◎◎◎◎◎◎

"Det ju never stap, never, ju boso."

Nau, evrivan nju det vos gasta meter of taim, ven presher bildel ab. Ol tasten ar okupaid. Faineli, de roring orgen shetart de kvaetnis of a chrch. In des revolushen of voisis, Haiden, Wagner or Bach bi gast apiring als sekend best. Dikan Pino flaing aut behaid de orgen laik frst dencer of Bolshoi teatr. Hi jal samting, bad his vois ist svolo from des glories musik det bringing ol chrch vindos tu dengeres vibreishen. Daun in de chrch evribadi, I minet evribadi, luk ab tu si vot is hepening. As svit pater Malek kavert his holi iers. Olter bois lefing and veving tu as an de balkoni.

In des moments a big evakueshen from de orgen register start. Badis of de devels sols pailed an de oposit sait of Pinos ofensiv. Penik. Kids kraing and lefing an de scim taim. Evrivan hu kud and is not hoplos fertengelt vit ader devels badis muv. Shemfoli trai tu sev his lucifer sol in his korpus de likti. Sun tri or for leas of badis, ganping laik freshli kot smol fish in vuden basket, totali blokt de eskep. De sorendet kidc teking de hit of meiger ofensiv. Wem... wem... wem! Auch... auch... auch!

"That you never stop, never, you bozo."

Now, everyone knew that it was just a matter of time until the pressure built up. All the keys were occupied. Finally, the roaring organ shattered the quietness of the church. In this revolution of voices, Hayden, Wagner or Bach would appear second best. Deacon Pino flew out from behind the organ like the first dancer in the Bolshoi Ballet. He yelled something, but his voice was swallowed by the glorious music that was taking all the windows to a dangerous level of vibration. Down in the church everybody, and I mean everybody, was looking up to see what was happening. Our sweet Pater Malek covered his ears. The altar boys were laughing and waving to us up on the balcony.

In these moments a big evacuation from the organ register started. Bodies of the devil's souls piled up on the opposite side of Pino's offensive. Panic. Kids crying and laughing at the same time. Everyone who could, and was not hopelessly tangled with other devil's bodies, moved. Each shamefully tried to save his Lucifer soul in his corpus delecti. Soon three or four layers of bodies, jumping like freshly caught minnows in a wooden basket, totally blocked the escape route. The surrounded kids took the heat of a major offensive. Wham... wham... wham! Ouch... ouch... ouch!

"Ju lital satans, I sho ju," jal hi tu skert bois det hev no chens tu eskep.

"Vi sori dikan, onest tu got. Auch! Dem ju, not iven frst krishchen diden safern so mach. Auch."

"Krishchen? Ju gais put juself in de seim kategori vit as and mi? Na. Na. Ju devels sid!"

Musik inpruving vans egen. Mocart, Smetana or Chaikovski ar nau de meiger hits. Bad komoshen in as kor is far from over. Meni of kidc kaunting dei skars and stregen dei heds hau tu kaver dem. Sam of dem krai, bad mosli sinking in histerikal lef. Meni of biger grls chuing dei volen keps gast not tu lef. Nating helps. After konteminetet ol kor, laf brok in ol his fors in des laif. Sam of de litel bois vet dei penc and lital fani peches of vota apir an klin chrch flor. Vi hardli menagt tu sing "Amen" an end of a mes.

Raning lak hrd of baisons daun de stip sters, vi lefing and vividli komenting as ekonplishment. Vans aut, biger grls formet dei lital grups lefing histerikali over sam koments of des tu biger gais det stil diden kam daun.

"You little Satans, I'll show you," he yelled at the scared boys who had no chance to escape.

"We're sorry deacon, honest to God. Ouch! Damn you, not even the first Christians suffered so much. Ouch."

"Christians? You guys put yourself in the same category as them and me? No. No. You're on the devil's side!"

The music improved once again. Mozart, Smetana or Tchaikovsky are now the major hits. But the commotion in our choir was far from over. Many of the kids were counting their scars and straining their heads to work out how to cover them. Some of them cried, but most sank into hysterical laughter. Many of the bigger girls chewed their woollen caps to keep from laughing. Nothing helped. After contaminating the whole choir, laughter broke out in all the force it has in this life. Some of the little boys wet their pants and funny little patches of water appeared on the church floor. We hardly managed to sing "Amen" at the end of the mass.

Running like a herd of bisons down the steep stairs, we laughed and vividly commented on our accomplishment. Once out, the bigger girls formed their little groups, laughing hysterically over some comment of those two bigger guys who still hadn't come down.

Litelvans eshemt of dei vet penc luk for sefti in mamas or grenmamichka hends. De onli hostail luks geding de bois in dei praud tent jer of a laif. Vi never danet nating vrong. Shor vi vos traing tu help dikan Pino, bad ta cet.

"Vai an erd bois so gud laik vi ar kud not ganpt from ten tu tventi," sed mai best fren tu mi. "I am sik and taet tu bi blemt for trobels det akcheli grls startet."

"O vel, de trut bi non van dei," sed I filosofikal, voching mai grended finger keching mai irs.

"Vot ju vos promising mi letct sandei? Hm?" sed hi tvisting mai irs.

"I am sori, I vos brav singing and never danet eniting vrong. Ask Emilko!" tok I laut, tvisting mai devels hed.

"Hi is rait! Vi never danet eniting vrong," sed Emilko, chusing de vorts so det mai grenpa liv mi alon.

From chrch open dors kam krai of det tu biger bois, det hev plesher tu trai pater Maleks hend.

"Auch! Auch!"

"Ju tu gut for nating eshols, nekst taim I skrepet jor

ⓔⓔⓔⓔⓔⓔⓔⓔⓔⓔⓔⓔⓔⓔⓔⓔⓔⓔⓔⓔⓔⓔⓔⓔⓔⓔⓔⓔⓔⓔⓔⓔⓔ

Little ones ashamed of their wet pants looked for safety in their mama's or grandmamichka's hands. The only hostile looks were for the boys in their proud tenth year of life. We never did anything wrong. Sure we were trying to help Deacon Pino, but that's it.

"Why on earth can't boys as good as we are just jump from ten to twenty," said my best friend to me. "I am sick and tired of being blamed for troubles that actually the girls started."

"Oh well, the truth will be known one day," I said philosophically, seeing my granddad's finger catching my ears.

"What were you promising me last Sunday? Hm?" he said, twisting my ears.

"I'm sorry, I was bravely singing and never did anything wrong. Ask Emilko!" I said loudly, twisting my devil's head.

"He's right! We never did anything wrong," said Emilko, choosing his words so that my grampa left me alone.

From the church's open doors came the cries of the two bigger boys who'd had the pleasure of trying Pater Malek's hand.

"Ouch! Ouch!"

"You two good for nothing assholes, next time I'll scrape your

ⓔⓔⓔⓔⓔⓔⓔⓔⓔⓔⓔⓔⓔⓔⓔⓔⓔⓔⓔⓔⓔⓔⓔⓔⓔⓔⓔⓔⓔⓔⓔⓔ

krach. It is inposibel dos deis put van gud grl in kloster from as vileg. Is shem bat trut. Dei kudn iven rich dei merich nait vit aut bi malestet. Tventi 'fater unser' and tumoro an babtaising. Is det klir? Dikan, vi hev a tok."

"Jes pater Malek."

"Det is de letct taim det I help ju vit de kidc. No kor, no saker geim. Is det klir Pino?" sed med pater Malek.

"Jes pater Malek. I andestan.... Ooooo, I bi klining orgen and preheps prei a litel, so dont veid an mi vit lanch."

"Go du des, I bi seing det tu slo Marishka," sed de pater Malek, sheking vit de hed, sloli voking tu de sakristai.

Vi litel bois veidet in shed of a hjuch chesnac befor chrch. Tu go hom vos tu dengeres, so long ven de oldervans dont kul daun. Kaunting as bruses, vi plen de nekst sandei mes fan. Auer or so leter, ven vi faineli hev de kurich to liv sefty of vaild chesnac tris, vi spatet as ticherin Mira kaming from the chrch tauer dor, kising gud bai as dikan Pino. Vi duk tugeder, peshentli veiding det strit vos emti.

⊚⊚⊚⊚⊚⊚⊚⊚⊚⊚⊚⊚⊚⊚⊚⊚⊚⊚⊚⊚⊚⊚⊚⊚⊚⊚⊚⊚⊚⊚⊚⊚⊚⊚

crotch. It is impossible these days to put one good girl in cloister from our village. It's a shame but true. They couldn't even reach their marriage night without being molested. Twenty 'our father's' and tomorrow confession. Is that clear? Deacon, we'll have a talk."

"Yes Pater Malek."

"That is the last time that I help you with the kids. No choir, no soccer game. Is that clear Pino?" said the angry Pater Malek.

"Yes Pater Malek. I understand.... Oooohh, I'll be cleaning the organ and perhaps praying a little, so don't wait for me with lunch."

"Go do that, and I'll tell slow Marishka," said Pater Malek, shaking his head as he slowly walked toward the sacristy.

We little boys waited in the shade of a huge chestnut in front of the church. To go home was dangerous, so long as the older ones hadn't cooled down. Counting our bruises, we planned our fun for next Sunday's mass. An hour or so later, when we finally had the courage to leave the safety of the wild chestnut trees, we spotted our teacher Mira coming from the church tower door, kissing our Deacon Pino goodbye. We ducked together, patiently waiting for the street to empty.

⊚⊚⊚⊚⊚⊚⊚⊚⊚⊚⊚⊚⊚⊚⊚⊚⊚⊚⊚⊚⊚⊚⊚⊚⊚⊚⊚⊚⊚⊚⊚⊚⊚⊚

Marijan Megla

Bisaid chrch and bar, saker klab vos onli institushen in vich vi stud junaited behain as St. Jelena. I dont van tu deminisht as holi chrch kontribjushen tu des taun, bad saker klab has plesentli kombein bar, sport, and religen. In taim ven vi vos fesing strong enimis an de saker pleigraunt, vi vos most fanatik ketolik ever. If vi vin, de parti det vi tro for as sakers in as taun bar kuden bi fergoten for long taim.

Ju si, I groing ab in de taim ven as chrch vos eprishietet, bad she alon kuden provaidet det nidet "zest" tu kip as onli in her vols. As taun bar vos tu leking of det "samting" det kip as onli in der. Preheps det vos mosli as folt. Vi kuden sorveiv not iven van bladi denc vit aut faiting vit ichader, and frenli demolish as hepi feses.

Tu bi member of det inportant taun institushen, as pesents most onli frikt aut an evri geim det as saker klab plei. And frikt aut dei did. Vi vos femos tu

---

Besides the church and bar, the soccer club was the only institution behind which we stood united in St. Helena. I don't want to diminish the church's contribution to our town, but the soccer club pleasantly combined bar, sport and religion. At the time we were facing strong enemies on the soccer playing ground, we were the most fanatic Catholics ever. If we won, the party that we threw for our soccer players in the town bar wasn't forgotten for a long time.

You see, I grew up in a time when our church was appreciated, but when she alone couldn't provide that needed "zest" to keep us only in her walls. Our town bar lacked that same "something" to keep us only there. Perhaps that was mostly our fault. We couldn't survive even one bloody dance without fighting with each other, and friends demolished each other's happy faces.

To be a member of that important town institution, we peasants must only freak out at every game our soccer club played. And freak out they did. We were famous for

provaid as siti hospital vit fresh peshent det kontribjutet tu as defid. Samtaim, in agoni of defid, vi masaz de soft ribs of ol saker tim from ader taun inkluding de gag. Never in mai laif I soet kviker slaiding in betvin pis and vor laik an de sandei saker geim. Meni taim I tenk it vos de gulash and hevi vain det vi drink det mek as det vei.

Det partikulari sison, vi hev not van jet not iven van singel geim. Det sandei vi vos lusing egen and as gosop disaidet tu du samting. No, vi vos not med an auer bois. Dei traet hart inaf tu sorvaiv det shemfol daunslai. Dos gais skin trning red iven after ten minit of fest voking. After evri geim dei luket mor als safern bist bisaid properti lain after long vorking auers. Det dei vos St. Jelena praim bois, rest for raning, kud not iven vi emegin. Taun sols faineli edmitet tu dem self, vit aut a gud trener, no saker. Vit aut saker klab, laif in taun bi anberebel.

Samhau vi ol felt not getinget inaf aut for det vot vi akcheli investet. For evri trening, as old sols preper a rostet piglec or endlis faif galon a gud strong gulash for as tim. De trening

providing our city hospital with fresh patients who'd contributed to our defeat. Sometimes, in the agony of defeat, we'd massage the soft ribs of the whole soccer team from the other town, including the referee. Never in my life have I seen a quicker slide from peace to war than in the Sunday soccer game. Many times I think it was the goulash and strong wine we drank that made us that way.

This particular season, we had not yet won a single game. That Sunday we were losing again and our gossips decided to do something. No, we were not mad with our boys. They tried hard enough to survive the shameful downslide. Those guys' skin turned red even after ten minutes of fast walking. After every game they looked like suffering beasts at the property line after long hours of work. That they were St. Helena's prime boys, raised for running, not even we could imagine. The town souls finally admitted to themselves that without a good trainer there would be no soccer. Without a soccer club life in town would be unbearable.

Somehow we all felt we weren't getting enough for what we actually invested. For every training session, our old souls prepared a roast piglet and at least five gallons of good strong goulash for our team. The practice sun trn tu luk mor als sam hepi piknik, ver de saker bol samtaim not iven vans tach de grin gras. As trener soft Polika meket vit des polisi preheps strong bois, bad saker dei vere not. Na, onesli ... verd ju raning vit part of a sakeli piglec in jor tami, and tri for krugs of vain? No, ju bi resting, cheking jor bladpresher and hart bit evri fju minit. Boj, and dei did rest. Samtaim in midel of a trening ju kud emegin tu hr "Faterland soldaten" snoring in der kaiser bets. Trning dei godlos beks tu as grendedushkin Kaiser pikcher an de vol, vich fud dei gast hepen tu daigest in dei barom los stamaks.

St. Jelena nidet a koch. Meni det vos konsideret lent ab. Sam of dos mens vos seing det if vi van tu hev sakers, vi nid tu hev 7 jer of meiger femen, so vi ol go skinier. Den, kaming hom from de letst saker geim in long kolons of baisikels, as belavet greni Hlivovec hev an aidija. Shi sed tu desapointet saker fens, det brevli raidet dei baisikels tu vords hom: "Pipel, as jang dikan vanet tu bi a saker koch."

ⓔⓔⓔⓔⓔⓔⓔⓔⓔⓔⓔⓔⓔⓔⓔⓔⓔⓔⓔⓔⓔⓔⓔⓔⓔⓔⓔⓔⓔⓔⓔⓔ

soon began to look more like some happy picnic where the soccer ball sometimes didn't even touch the grass once. Our trainer soft Polika perhaps made strong boys with this policy, but they were not soccer players. Now, honestly ... would you run with part of a suckling pig in your tummy, and three or four jugs of wine? No, you'd be resting, checking your blood pressure and heartbeat every few minutes. Boy, and did they rest. Sometimes in the middle of training you could imagine you were hearing "Faterland soldaten" snoring in their barracks bed. Turning their godless backs to our granduchkin Kaiser's picture on the wall, whose food they just happened to be digesting in their bottomless stomachs.

St. Helena needed a coach. Many that were considered begged off. Some of those men were saying that if we wanted soccer players we'd need seven years of major famine so we'd all get skinnier. Then, coming home from the last soccer game in long columns of bicycles, our beloved Granny Hlivovec had an idea. She said to the disappointed soccer fans, who were bravely riding their bicycles toward home: "People, our young deacon wants to be a soccer coach."

ⓔⓔⓔⓔⓔⓔⓔⓔⓔⓔⓔⓔⓔⓔⓔⓔⓔⓔⓔⓔⓔⓔⓔⓔⓔⓔⓔⓔⓔⓔⓔⓔⓔ

"O kaman, gud greni. Hau kud a dikan bi a koch," ancer as old Orel bachika luking apatikli in bek of ader baisiklist. "Demet, dikans ar meid for chrch. Ju no, long skrts, krucefiks an de sait."

"Ju rong, mai dir belavet Orel bachika. Belo des skrt der is de seim mens blesing laik ju engoet. Na, preheps litel beter."

"And hau ju soposto no det?" ask de old gai.

"Hi is stil vrgen ... and for shor fol lodet," ancer de old greni, sopreising hr self vit dos vorts.

"Ha ha ha. Let mek streit vi nid de saker koch, and not sam lodet mens blesing, kavert vit his vrginiti," ancer de old gai.

"His hobi is saker geim and hi plei in his skul gast det," sed de old greni medli, keching biger spid.

"O vel greni, I bi asking as saker komiti if dei vanet de holi dikan Pino for der koch. Bad remember, der is a pater Malek ... and I teling ju, he bi not laiket det."

Bai des taim vi ol nju det onli a holi hend kud pul as aut at des sport miseri. It vos olmos inposibel tu go in sam anadar taun vit aut geting big lef from pipel. Gosop start,

---

"Oh come on, good grannie. How could a deacon be a coach," answered old Orel Bachika looking apathetically at the back of the other bicyclists. "Dammit, deacons are made for church. You know, long skirts, a crucifix on the side."

"You're wrong, my dear beloved Orel Bachika. Under that skirt there is the same men's blessing that you enjoy. Perhaps a little better."

"And how are you supposed to know that?" asked the old guy.

"He is still a virgin ... and for sure fully loaded," answered the old granny, surprising herself with these words.

"Ha ha ha. Let's make it straight that we need a soccer coach, and not some loaded men's blessing, covered with its virginity," answered the old guy.

"His hobby is soccer and he played just that game at his school," the old granny said angrily, speeding up.

"Oh well granny, I'll ask our soccer committee if they want holy Deacon Pino for their coach. But remember, there is Pater Malek ... and I'm telling you he won't like it."

By this time we all knew that only a holy hand could pull us out of that sports misery. It was almost impossible to go into some other town without getting a big laugh from the people. Gossip started

det in as taun evri blaind hors kud plei saker beter den vi. So, as sols of St. Jelena disaidet during det vik det holi koch is preheps not det det vi ol vanct, bat det vot vi kan gedet. As belavet pater Malek egri onli hef hartig. He andestud det de taun moral is daun, and he vos gled det dei ask chrch for help. Bad Pino and saker geim? No, det hepen never befor. Dikan is boren for chrch and not tu stand an de sait of a pleigraund svering laik a kucher. Bat, tu trn bed omen from as taun, he egri.

An auer sopreis, as dikan vos not bed et ol. Vi stil diden vin de geim, bad auer bois start tu plei ofensivli. Trening vos held sikretli in de svamps and evri rostet piglec vos retrned tu his sopreist doner. Insted tu hev a piknik dei ranet samtaim eraund de taun, eskortet vit dikan Pino an his baisikel. Nois det dei meking is olmos inposible tu lisen vit aut risking tirs. Dei droning samtaim lak as Astro-Hangerian hangri solgers, kepchert in Rashien vorking kemps. Sam of de atlets maders vanet tu protest tu pater Malek ebaud des sevich trening polisi of his dikan. Bad, ven dei soet as sakers in beter chep dei fergodet ol ebaut.

ⓔⓔⓔⓔⓔⓔⓔⓔⓔⓔⓔⓔⓔⓔⓔⓔⓔⓔⓔⓔⓔⓔⓔⓔⓔⓔⓔⓔⓔⓔⓔⓔ

that in our town every blind horse could play soccer better than we. So, we souls of St. Helena decided during that week that a holy coach wasn't what we all wanted, but it was what we could get. Our beloved Pater Malek agreed only half-heartedly. He understood that town morale was down, and he was glad that they asked the church for help. But Pino and the game of soccer? No, that had never happened before. The deacon is born for church and not to stand at the side of the field swearing like a teamster. But to turn the bad omen away from our town, he agreed.

To our surprise, our deacon wasn't bad at all. We still didn't win the games, but our boys started to play offensively. Training was held secretly in the swamps and every roasted piglet was returned to its surprised donor. Instead of having a picnic they sometimes ran around the town, escorted by Deacon Pino on his bicycle. The noise they made was almost impossible to bear without risking tears. They would drone sometimes like hungry Austro-Hungarian soldiers, captive in Russian working camps. Some of the athletes' mothers wanted to protest to Pater Malek about the savage training policy of his deacon. But when they saw our soccer players in better shape they forgot all about it.

ⓔⓔⓔⓔⓔⓔⓔⓔⓔⓔⓔⓔⓔⓔⓔⓔⓔⓔⓔⓔⓔⓔⓔⓔⓔⓔⓔⓔⓔⓔ

Gast ven as gud taun sol faineli akceptet de holi koch, dei gedet a nju koch asisten. It vos noubadi als als de jang komjunist ticherin, Mira. If ju tenk vi vos staunt vit dikan koching, den ju kud emegin hau vi ol felt vit det jang grl so klos tu as dikan. Vel bisaid de pater Malek, evrivan als akceptet det blesing. Never befor vos rekordet sacha gud koopereshen in betvin chrch and komjunist parti. It kud bring as onli gud and hu nos, meibi nju beter sakers. In auer neks saker geim vi vanet and belivet or not, vi vanet ever senc. St. Jelena vos no mor de gulash kapital, vi vos faineli akceptet laik gud saker pleiers. Lefing stap and auer men kud praudli go an de markets in ader tauns.

St. Jelena hev for frst taim a sakers det kud bring as in ader liga. Vi ol stil kud frik aut if vi vanet tu, bad biting de enimis blek and blu vos no mor nidet.

For mosli of as taun sols, det vos de vork of as streng koch duo. Shor vi diden andesten frst his holi torcher an as sakers bikos as soft Polika vos heving so diferent taktik in trening. Dos deis ven as bjutifol ticherin and Pino pesing

Just when our good town souls finally accepted the holy coach, they got a new coach's assistant. It was nobody else but the young Communist teacher, Mira. If you think we were stunned to have a deacon coaching, then you can imagine how we all felt with that young girl so close to our deacon. Well, other than Pater Malek, everyone accepted that blessing. Never before was recorded such good co-operation between the church and the Communist party. It could only bring us good and, who knows, maybe new better soccer players. In our next soccer game we won and believe it or not we won ever since. St. Helena was no more the goulash capital, we were finally accepted as good soccer players. The laughing stopped and our men could proudly go through the markets in other towns.

St. Helena had for the first time a soccer team that could advance to the next league. We all still could freak out if we wanted to, but beating the enemies black and blue wasn't necessary any more.

For most of our town's souls, this was the work of our strange coaching duo. Sure, at first we didn't understand his holy torture of our soccer players because soft Polika had such different training tactics. Those days, when our beautiful teacher and Pino passed

Marijan Megla

bai, folot vit as saker, evrivan hepili salut. It vos gast nais tu si him an his big blek milkman baisikal and his skrt pult ab eraund his vest, folot bai Mira in hr sport short penc. Vi hev stil lital trobel hau tu grit dem and tu hu shud vi sei frst halo. "Gud ivning mai dir belavet dikan Pino. Gud ivning mis ticherin. Jast giv him a raund ekstra so det dei kud vin in de geim."

And Pino bi praudli encering: "Bles ju lord, mai gut sol, blesju!"

And Mira bi encering: "Viva Marshal Tito and komjunist parti!" After dos vorts Pino vos juzuli meking lital krucefiks in di er.

Pater Malek egri onli anisi an des koching of saker klab, and he vos speshili suspishes an des ticherin. Noing det and remembering his pur proformenc vit chrch kor, Pino vos raning tin lain to kep Malek hepi.

No meter hau mach Pino vos preing, hau onesli, hau hart he vos traing ... he gast kuden get de grip of as singing engels. Bisaid ol des trobels hi hes det brning faer in his chest det iven as St. Florian protektor of faer kuden kilet.

@@

by, followed by our soccer players, everyone happily saluted. It was just nice to see him on his big black milkman's bicycle with his skirt pulled up around his waist, followed by Mira in her short sport pants. We had a little trouble deciding how to greet them and to whom we should say hello first. "Good evening my dear beloved Deacon Pino. Good evening Miss Teacher. Just give them one more lap so they can win the game."

And Pino would proudly answer: "Lord bless you, my good souls, bless you!"

And Mira would answer: "Viva Marshal Tito and the Communist Party!" After those words Pino would usually make a little cross in the air.

Pater Malek agreed only uneasily to this coaching of the soccer club, and he was especially suspicious of this teacher. Knowing that and remembering his poor performance with the church choir, Pino was running a thin line to keep Malek happy.

No matter how much Pino prayed, or how honestly or how hard he tried ... he just couldn't get a grip on us singing angels in the choir. Beside all those troubles, he had that burning fire in his chest that even St. Florian, protector of fire, couldn't kill.

@@

Seving him self, hi liv Pino alon in hends of ticherin Mira. Emilko and mi hir him toking, vans ven vi vos haiding in bush of det dark shortkat, ver dei in vorm let ivning hev dei kising auer: "Mira, ... in jor hends I si de vorld."
"Det is shor samting. Hau kud a gai kising a vumen in dark korner of a taun siet hol vorld?" sed de shokt Emilko.
"Sh ... sh. Bi kvaet. Dei mei hir as. Bisaid hau ju no, det never trai tu kis a grl, vich hiden pauer ju kud diskaver in jor devels badi?" sed I, stering in dei fertengelt siluet.
"So vai hi dont sei as vot taim is in de Honkong? Der is nau moning and hi kud faind sam pablik voch," tok hi, chesing de big moskitos, not andestan de romantik lav.
"A ju rili tenk det der is nating vot ken ju du als, as raning behain sam pablik voch in Honkong, ven ju in grls hends?" ask I.
"Vel, endlis vi nju den ken hi si de vorld ... or not," ancer Emilko, skraching de moskito bait.
"Dem, Emilko, dei hev romentik taim and not sam auer of geografi," sed I, olmos svoloing van moskito.

Saving himself, he left Pino alone in the hands of Mira the teacher. Emilko and me heard him talking once, when we were hiding in the bush of that dark shortcut where they, in the warm evening, had their kissing hour: "Mira, in your hands I see the world."
"That is sure something. How could a guy kissing a woman in a dark corner of town see the whole world?" said the shocked Emilko.
"Sh ... shh. Be quiet. They may hear us. Besides, how would you know, who's never kissed a girl, what hidden power you could discover in your devil's body?" I said, staring at their entangled silhouette.

"So why doesn't he tell us what time it is in Hong Kong? It's morning there now and he could find some public clock," he said, chasing big mosquitoes, not understanding romantic love.
"Are you really thinking that there is nothing else you can do, other than running behind some public clock in Hong Kong, when you're in a girl's arms?" I asked.
"Well, at least we'd know if he can see the whole world ... or not," answered Emilko, scratching a mosquito bite.
"Dammit Emilko, they're having a romantic time and not some hour of geography," I said, almost swallowing a mosquito.

"Hu kers, it is boring. And de moskito kiling mi."

Des ivning, siting kvaetli in des dem bush, vi hr Pino kraing. "I gast ken no mor duet. I dont no vot shud I du vit dos gais in kor. Malek sed tu mi van mistek mor and hi bi no mor giving mi promishen tu tren de sakers."

Mira stud der vit tirs in hr ais toking tu him. "I vish I kud help. Dem kidc dei are samtaim rili pen in de nek. Mai onli pauer is hevi homvork. From det dei are skert, and if nating helps det bring him bek tu normal. Hau ebaut if ju ask de Malek for sam help det ste vit ju an de kor, during de mes?"

"I traet oredi. Hi dont bag. He tel mi det sam nans hev hert det samting bed going an vit his dikan. Ju no if det kam aut, iven de ekselenci bi noing. Preheps, Malek hev skert from det."

Des ivning vi godet penc fol from as grenmamichkas, bikos vi kam tu let hom. Iven dei egsistet an teling de trut vi bot lai. Vi diden vanet to tel noubadi vot vi soet an dark shortkat.

An end of des saker sison, vi vos holding a frst ples. If vi vining a geim vit letct in de nekst lig, des ivning, vi

---

"Who cares, it is boring. And the mosquitoes are killing me."

That evening, sitting quietly in this damn bush, we heard Pino crying. "I just can't do it any more. I don't know what I should do with those guys in the choir. Malek told me one more mistake and he would no longer give me permission to train the soccer players."

Mira stood there with tears in her eyes talking to him. "I wish I could help. The damn kids are sometimes a real pain in the neck. My only power is heavy homework. Of that they are scared, and if nothing helps, that brings them back to normal. How about you ask Malek for some helpers to stay with you and the choir during mass?"

"I tried already. He won't budge. He told me that some nuns have heard that something bad is going on with his deacon. You know if that comes out even His Excellency will know. Perhaps Malek is scared of that."

That evening we got our pants whipped by our grandmothers because we came home too late. Even though they insisted we tell the truth we both lied. We didn't want to tell anybody what we'd seen on that dark shortcut.

At the end of soccer season, we were holding first place. If we won a game with the last place team in the next league, this evening, we'd bi pleing in rigen liga. For frst taim in auer long histori of as lavli taun vi erchiv samting vot is vort tu remember.

Nau ven de dikan Pino vos mosli nidet tu bi vit as sakers, hi got in de fait vit pater Malek. Disciplin in chrch kor vos so bed in de moning mes, det pater Malek maste stap meni taim in his sandei srvis. Iven juzuali kam mader oversierin kuden haidet hr ernoiment. Kidc lefing, ganping eraund orgen — du eniting, gast not singing. In moment or tu det vos mor jer market als lords mes.

Vel, it vos hard inaf evri ader sandei tu risk vochin de geim, bad des taim hi cud posibel sit at hom. Pino kuden faund de risen for as behevju in de chrch kor and vanet onli bi left alon in his miseri. After a big lanch det his nerves stamek regektet hi disaidet tu du best of spoilet ivning. Tu eskep pater Malek granpinis hi klaim de chrch tauer ver hi kud si endlis de geim.

Erli des ivning evrivan det hev tu gud leks vos daun in de pablik pashcher, or chrch tu prei for as bois. Meni of as sols gedert an as pleigraund miset dikan and ticherin.

⊙⊙⊙⊙⊙⊙⊙⊙⊙⊙⊙⊙⊙⊙⊙⊙⊙⊙⊙⊙⊙⊙⊙⊙⊙⊙⊙⊙⊙⊙⊙⊙⊙⊙⊙⊙⊙⊙

be playing in the regional league. For the first time in the long history of our lovely town we'd achieved something worth remembering.

Now, when Deacon Pino was most needed to be with our soccer players, he got into a fight with Pater Malek. Discipline in the church choir was so bad in the morning mass that Pater Malek had to stop many times in his Sunday service. Even the usually calm Mother Superior couldn't hide her annoyance. Kids were laughing, jumping around the organ — doing anything except singing. In a moment or two it was more like the annual market than the lord's mass.

Well, it was hard enough every other Sunday to risk watching the game, but this time who could possibly sit at home. Pino couldn't find the reason for our behaviour in the church choir and wanted only to be left alone with his misery. After a big lunch that his nervous stomach rejected, he decided to make the best of his spoiled evening. To escape Pater Malek's grumpiness he climbed the church tower where he could at least see the game.

Early this evening everyone who had two good legs was either down in the public pasture or at church to pray for our boys. Many of our souls gathered at the field missed the deacon and the teacher.

⊙⊙⊙⊙⊙⊙⊙⊙⊙⊙⊙⊙⊙⊙⊙⊙⊙⊙⊙⊙⊙⊙⊙⊙⊙⊙⊙⊙⊙⊙⊙⊙⊙⊙⊙⊙⊙⊙

Marijan Megla

"Demet, ver dei are nau? Preheps he shud bles as tim kruket leks befor geim and shi kud giv sam masaz."

Ven auer tim lostet de geim and de chens lu go in ader biger liga, noubadi kud faund as dikan and his seksi helper. Dei simpli desapir from de fes of de erd.

"Tja det is olveis so vit chrch and goverment. Ven ever vi nidet mosli dei help, dei kud not bi faundet," tok as groen abs desapointet.

Hardli eniting kud push de moral of auer taun daun so mach laik des lost geim. Ven de bed njus rich de taun, grenmas roseris start tu spin fester. Pater Malek never vos saker fen, bad filig des hevi veit tragedi, hi disaidet tu srv a mes for ol det in tirs nided lords help. Dikan Pino det never mis eni of sacha hepenings, kud bi not faundet. Streng njus start tu cirkulet kros de taun end chrch. "Dikan Pino kil him self probebli ... bikos vi lost de geim." Histeri sloli bad shorli spredet eraund. Sam of old gosop svor det dei soet Pino living de taun in tirs. "I teling ju, hi keri onli his big krucefiks and his roseri."

⦿⦿⦿⦿⦿⦿⦿⦿⦿⦿⦿⦿⦿⦿⦿⦿⦿⦿⦿⦿⦿⦿⦿⦿⦿⦿⦿⦿⦿⦿⦿⦿

"Dammit, where are they now? Perhaps he should bless our team's crooked legs before the game and she could give some massage."

When our team lost the game and the chance to advance to the next league, nobody could find our deacon and his sexy helper. They'd simply disappeared from the face of the earth.

"Tcha! That's always how it is with church and government. Whenever we need their help most they cannot be found," said our grownups disappointedly.

Hardly anything could push the morale of our town down as much as this lost game. When the bad news reached the town, grandmas' rosaries started to spin faster. Pater Malek never was a soccer fan, but feeling this heavyweight tragedy, he decided to serve a mass for all those who in tears needed the lord's help. Deacon Pino, who never missed any such happenings, could not be found. Strange news started to circulate across the town and church. "Deacon Pino killed himself probably ... because we lost the game." Hysteria slowly but surely spread. Some of the old gossips swore that they saw Pino leave town in tears. "I'm telling you, he carried only his big crucifix and his rosary."

"Jang men soposto folo him and bring him hom, det or laif."

"O..o..ooo ... der in svanp of river Drava is a jang ketolik kiling him self and noubadi is der tu help him."

Faineli de fresh horsis vos putet befor big vegen and tventi gais vapnet vit vain and slivovica drov tu de river Drava tu piket ab Pinos badi.

In de meiger penik det strak de taun a lital chrch bel in de tauer start tu bel. Hol griving sosaeti ran in tu de barom of de tauer, bad der vos noubadi det pul de bel and rop vos not muving.

"Det is Pinos sol kaming hom. O. O. Ooo, fergiv as svit lord," jaling de old grenis.

De flok ov vimen ni daun and preing laut veidet for pater Malek blesing. Hi diden hev a van minic pis sait det bladi geim. "Is evribadi kresi in des taun," tenk hi for him self. "Hau is posebel det van stupid geim kud chench so meni personaliti in so short taim. Kud shoing of as mader virgen hev de seim efekt an dos bladi heds?"

ⓢⓢⓢⓢⓢⓢⓢⓢⓢⓢⓢⓢⓢⓢⓢⓢⓢⓢⓢⓢⓢⓢⓢⓢⓢⓢⓢⓢⓢⓢⓢ

"The young men are supposed to follow him and bring him home, dead or alive."

"O..o..oooh ... there in the swamp of the River Drava a young Catholic is killing himself and nobody is there to help him."

Finally fresh horses were harnessed to a big wagon and twenty guys armed with wine and slivovica drove to the River Drava to pick up Pino's body.

In the midst of the major panic that struck the town a little church bell in the tower started to peal. The whole grieving society ran to the bottom of the tower, but there was nobody pulling the bell and the rope was not moving.

"That is Pino's soul coming home. Oh. Oh. Ohhhhh, forgive us sweet lord," yelled the old grannies.

The flock of women kneeled down and, praying loudly, waited for Pater Malek's blessing. He hadn't had one minute's peace since that bloody game. "Is everybody crazy in this town," he thought to himself. "How is it possible that one stupid game could change so many personalities in so short a time. Could an appearance of our mother virgin have the same effect on those bloody heads."

Taini bel kontinju tu ring, samtaim rapidli, samtaim remein kvaet for a ten minitc. Auer chrch remein fol in laits laik ven gast nau as svit gesus is boren. As tvanti gais retrnet hom emti hendet and drank laik a mader erd. Pater Malek nervs are an dei end. Hi sedaun apatikli in korner of a chrch end bles evrivan dei stil muvt. Pancha olter bois slip an de benches. Evri singel henkerchips is vet of krokodais tirs det floing aut meni ais. Egsostet sol siting in de chrch and prei.

Den de dors of de sters tu de tauer openet vit big kresh. De morning stap emidiatli. Pater Malek stend ab from his ples and bles him self. Pur olter bois veking ab raning eraund vit slipi ais, tu rich pater Malek. In dor stendet as belavet Orel bachi holding de dikan Pino belo de arm. Ol morener inkluding pater Malek, vich insenc faer vos kold, raning tu help. Onli Orel bachikas strong vois staped des stanpid det kud push dem bod an de graund. Ven de Pinos holi badi vos transportet in de siti hospital and Orel bachika godet his krug of vain hi tel de kraud vot hepen.

ⓔⓔⓔⓔⓔⓔⓔⓔⓔⓔⓔⓔⓔⓔⓔⓔⓔⓔⓔⓔⓔⓔⓔⓔⓔⓔⓔⓔⓔⓔⓔⓔⓔ

The tiny bell continued to ring, sometimes rapidly, sometimes remaining quiet for ten minutes. Our church was lit up as brightly as if our sweet Jesus had just now been born. Our twenty guys returned home empty handed and drunk as mother earth. Pater Malek's nerves were at their limit. He sat down apathetically in the corner of the church and blessed everyone that still moved. A bunch of altar boys slept on the benches. Every single handkerchief was wet with the crocodile tears flowing from many eyes. The exhausted souls sat in the church and prayed.

Then the doors to the stairs up the tower opened with a big crash. The mourning stopped immediately. Pater Malek stood up from his place and blessed himself. The poor altar boys woke up and ran with sleepy eyes to reach Pater Malek. In the door stood our beloved Orel Bachi holding Deacon Pino by the arm. All the mourners including Pater Malek, whose incense fire was cold, ran to help. Only Orel Bachika's strong voice stopped this stampede that could push them both to the ground. When Pino's holy body had been transported to the city hospital and Orel Bachika had his jug of wine he told the crowd what had happened.

ⓥⓥⓥⓥⓥⓥⓥⓥⓥⓥⓥⓥⓥⓥⓥⓥⓥⓥⓥⓥⓥⓥⓥⓥⓥⓥⓥⓥⓥⓥⓥ

"Vel ... mai sisters and braders ... I never beliv det sol, speshili sacha skinivan, kud so long benging an de bel. So, ven evrivan vos brevli roteting his roseris I gon ab and faun de dikan det vit his broken lek ledaun an de flor belo de bels. Hi vos voching de geim from der and ven vi start tu lus hi benget medli in vol," sed old gai.

"So vot hepen den," ask sambadi from de kraut.

"I brod him daun," ancer taet Orel bachika.

Vot de old gai diden soet det ivning, deskaveret vi kidc. Ven de old gosop vos kiling dem self helping as Pino, vi soet as lavli ticherin kaming from de tauer. Shi lef an as and fest desapir in de darknis of a strit.

"Hm ... I teling ju mai neibar, samting is vrong! Tu nau dei shoet gas as kidc dei lav gribs. Nau iven as gesus no for det," tok mai frend Emilko.

"Vot ju no vot dei danet in de tauer?" ask I laut.

"Hmm ... for shor not preing," sed taet Emilko.

"Ju min ... "

"I dont min nating, bad .... did ju si det hepi fes of as

***

"Well ... my sisters and brothers ... I never believed that a soul, especially such a skinny one, could bang on a bell so long. So, when everyone was bravely rotating his rosaries I went up and found the deacon with his broken leg laying down on the floor below the bells. He was watching the game from there and when we started to lose he banged madly on the wall," said the old guy.

"So what happened then?" asked somebody from the crowd.

"I brought him down," answered the tired Orel Bachika.

What the old guy didn't see that evening we kids discovered. When the old gossips were killing themselves helping our Pino, we saw our lovely teacher coming from the tower. She laughed at us and quickly disappeared into the darkness of the street.

"Hmmm ... I'm telling you neighbour, something is wrong! Until now they've showed just us kids their love grips. Now even our Jesus knows about that," said my friend Emilko.

"What do you know about what they were doing in the tower?" I asked loudly.

"Hmmm ... for sure not praying," said tired Emilko.

"You mean ... "

"I don't mean anything, but ... did you see the happy face on our

Marijan Megla

ticherin? Det fes shi hes det dei ven vi kam tu let tu voch, and soet onli fiksing hr skrt," sed Emilko fiksing his lital raund gogels.

"Svit gesus ... det min meibi vi hev merich in de taun," sed I praudli.

In kaming deis of dikan rekavering meni vos chench. Pater Malek vos pusht tu respekt de taun nids for saker koch and auer perenc svor solatli tu tek a trn an de voch of chrch kor. Auer sexi koch kuden bi hepier vit det.

Auer taun giv said den meni big saker pleers. Vi pleing nau in van of de best liga in de kaunti, and hev a nju stedium. A nju koncert hol is stil not skegul, partli bikos noubadi meket big in de mjusik.

---

teacher? That was the face she had that day when we came too late to watch, and only saw her fixing her skirt," said Emilko, adjusting his little round glasses.

"Sweet Jesus .. that means maybe we'll have a marriage in the town," I said proudly.

In the coming days of the deacon's recovery many things changed. Pater Malek was pushed to respect the town's need for a soccer coach and our parents swore solidly to take turns watching the church choir. Our sexy coach couldn't be happier with that.

Our town since then has produced many big soccer players. We're playing now in one of the best leagues in the county and have a new stadium. A new concert hall is still not scheduled, partly because nobody ever made it big in music.

Zuzika

vos veri femos for hr sekshuali cheritis tu ol men det vilingli sekrifais dei taim an hr badi. Det brod hr reder streng neim, "Hot Zuzi". Bisaid hr hasbend, det simstu hev mach mor setisfekshen in fol vainkrug als in hr pink badi — ver hi ligali belong — she hes meni aders. Baterflai Istvan, de taun polisman, vos van of dem. Fet bucher Martin and Ferike de menijak hev dei fan tu. Tu spesifai evri singel mens neim det profitet in des gud neiberhud seks bi inposebel. Auer gosop insist det endlis hefe mels population in auer taun pendelt iligali over neket "Hot Zuzi" endlis vans in dei laif.

Den in fol, olmos tu jers ego, hr bladi hasbent disaidet tu dai from overdosis of slivovica. Hi liv as sed, bikos hi vos bisaid his drinking a gud gai. And laik his deparcher in heven vere not inaf trobel for as, he liv as vit van big problem. Vot tu du vit "Hot Zuzika"? Hr sekshuli apetait kud bi onli setisfai if ol auer men in best eg pinch tugeder vit dei devels erg.

Zuzika was very famous for her sexual charity toward any man who would willingly sacrifice his time on her body. That brought her the rather strange name, "Hot Zuzi". Besides her husband, who seemed to have much more satisfaction in a full wine jug than in her pink body — where he legally belonged — she had many others. Butterfly Istvan, the town policeman, was one of them. The fat butcher Martin and Ferike the maniac had their fun too. To tell the name of every single man who profited in this good neighbourhood sex would be impossible. Our gossips insist that at least half the male population of our town dawdled illegally over the naked "Hot Zuzi" at least once in their life.

Then in fall, almost two years ago, her bloody husband decided to die from overdoses of slivovica. He left us sad because, his drinking aside, he was a good guy. And as though his departure to heaven wasn't enough trouble for us, he left us with one big problem. What to do with Hot Zuzika? Her sexual appetite could only be satisfied if all our men in their prime pitched in with their devil's urge.

Sacha non atecht hot vumen cud cos lots of trobel in de lokal ekonomi. Men of ol eges ver isi prei in her hends. Dei spended mach mor taim an de properti of de jang vido, den in der on filds. Jang bois der are redi for merich bi veiding belo hr svit vindos tu geder veri inportant primerich ekspirienc. Der vere jang grls old inaf tu bi merit and friet from dei sed vrginitis, dei nau veidet tu bi old spinstres. Dei vere gipsis det kud plei an eni merich and probebli starv tu det. As taun of St. Jelena stud befor bigeste problem ever. An tape of ol des, vors pater Malek anhepi vit ruint meriches, les matremonis, and les bebi baroms tu bles.

Atek vos akspektet sun or leter, from as heserdes gosop. De kveshchen vos sinpel. Vot mas bi dan vit de Hot Zuzika, and hau dei shud duet. "It hestu bi dan fest, befor Lucifer breid menagt tu destroi de hol komjuniti. Tu sev de St. Jelena grum mas bi faund. Bad hu is viling tu hev a vaif det hardli ever hev a taim for kuking, or a kvaet ivning et hom?" Ven as gosop kveshchenet de flok of rusters, vich deli krused eraund hr ples tu meri hr, evrivan bek aut.

⊚⊚⊚⊚⊚⊚⊚⊚⊚⊚⊚⊚⊚⊚⊚⊚⊚⊚⊚⊚⊚⊚⊚⊚⊚⊚⊚⊚⊚⊚⊚⊚⊚⊚⊚⊚⊚⊚⊚

Such an unattached hot woman could cause lots of trouble in the local economy. Men of all ages were easy prey in her hands. They spent much more time on the property of the young widow that in their own fields. Young boys ready for marriage would be waiting below her sweet windows to gather very important premarital experience. There were young girls old enough to be married and freed from their sad virginities, now looking forward to being old spinsters. There were gypsies who could play at every marriage and still starve to death. Our town of St. Helena stood before its biggest problem ever. On top of all this, Pater Malek was unhappy with broken marriages, fewer weddings and fewer babies' bottoms to bless.

An attack was expected sooner or later from our hazardous gossips. The question was simple. What must be done with Hot Zuzika and how to do it. "It has to be done fast, before Lucifer's bride manages to destroy the whole community. To save St. Helena a groom must be found. But who is willing to have a wife that hardly ever has time for cooking or a quiet evening at home?" When our gossips asked the flock of roosters which cruised around her place if one would marry her, everyone backed out.

⊚⊚⊚⊚⊚⊚⊚⊚⊚⊚⊚⊚⊚⊚⊚⊚⊚⊚⊚⊚⊚⊚⊚⊚⊚⊚⊚⊚⊚⊚⊚⊚⊚⊚⊚⊚⊚⊚

Des long kold vinter, an dei feder rupfen ivnings, vumen faineli faun det van prson for des gop. Koper smid Polika, de saker koch, det vi ol kol Soft Polika. Hi vos in his let fortis and his kontribjushen tu taun seks laif vos veri pur, or not egsisting. Des deficit in lav, tu as svit taun fimels, never konsrn as Polika mach. His onli interest vos tu bild a hevi strong sakers bois, det hardli ever vin de geim. Das de soft Polika spend inkredibal taim masazing as sakers badis vos never as konsrn. As taun sols tenket det hi is gast eshemt tu esk a grls for fevers. Dei tot det giving soft Polika in Zuzikas hends evriting bi dan. Noing det hr sekshul femens vere never longer den a dei or tu, dei trast her blesed devels erg tu inform de felo an des ishju.

Pipel hopt det Polika hes inaf big stemena tu sorvaiv des sekshuli huriken. He vos dam inaf tu bi not badert vit posebel apirenc of neket frendli neibars in his bedrum. Iven den if die hapen to heve bjutifol taim in konfertebel bet vit his nu vaiv. Vot for a neibers der, als helping ichader? Vi

During the long cold winter, on their feather plucking evenings, the women finally found the one person for the job. Polika the coppersmith, the soccer coach we all called Soft Polika. He was in his late forties and his contribution to the town's sex life was very poor, or non-existent. This deficit in love to our sweet town females never concerned Polika much. His only interest was to build big strong soccer boys that hardly ever won a game. That soft Polika spent an incredible amount of time massaging our soccer players' bodies was never our concern. Our people thought he was just ashamed to ask girls for their favours. They thought that simply putting soft Polika into Zuzika's hands would do it all. Knowing that her sexual famines were never longer than a day or two, they trusted her blessed devil's urge to inform the fellow on this issue.

People hoped Polika would have enough stamina to survive this sexual hurricane. At least he was dumb enough not to be bothered by the possible appearance of naked friendly neighbours in his bedroom. Even if they happened to have a beautiful time in the comfortable bed with his new wife. What are neighbours for but to help each other? We

hop det hi vos strong inaf tu kip hr daun, so long ven evrivan als ist not der. And, he vos rich inaf tu kip hr hepi. O vel, as Zuzika shud not ekspektet mirikal. She vos in her trtis, and hr figjur safer a latc in des sefen jer of open dor polisi det she self hepili inpos.

De dil kud brod Polika for instanc a vaif and risen tu his long vorking auers. Hi kud faineli sit inbetvin mens, ven de pater Malek hes his sandei mes. Hi spend, god nos, inaf taim an de bois benches in chrch.

Vel, it vos isi tu plen so, bad hart tu ekonplisht des. As soft Polika vos pusht tu tok vit Zuzika, bring hr de flauer, svits from taun stor, bad nating als ever hepend. She tuket evriting, smail a lital, and giv tu bojs det mek hr hepi. Luking an des sirios problem, as old gosop trn for help tu as blesed pater Malek. Sambadi hes tu stap Lucifer braid and hu is beter ekvipt als as taun prist?

Van let ivning a grup chosen from auer taun gosop fain de vei tu de Malek haus sters. It vos a kvaet ivning and dei kud hir pater Malek goking vit his lavli meid slo

hoped he would be strong enough to keep her down when everyone else was not there. And that he would be rich enough to keep her happy.

Oh well, our Zuzika shouldn't expect a miracle. She was in her thirties and her figure had suffered a lot in the seven-year open door policy she'd happily imposed upon herself.

The deal could bring Polika a wife for once and a reason for his long working hours. He could finally sit between men when Pater Malek says Sunday mass. He's spent, God knows, enough time on the boys benches in church.

Well, it was easy to plan but hard to accomplish. Our soft Polika was pushed to talk with Zuzika, to bring her flowers or sweets from the town store, but nothing else ever happened. She took everything, smiled a little, and gave it to the boys who made her happy. Looking at this serious problem, our old gossips turned to our blessed Pater Malek for help. Somebody has to stop this Lucifer's bride and who is better equipped than the town priest?

One late evening a group chosen from among the town gossips found their way to the stairs of Malek's house. It was a quiet evening and they could hear Pater Malek joking with his lovely maid, slow

Marijan Megla

Marishka and dikan Pino. Marishka bi samtaim foling in big laut lef repiding olveis det vorts: "O pater Malek, dont bi sili. Det ken posibel bi tru. Preheps ju gast meidct ab tu mek mi lef."
After laut noking slo Marishka openet de dor. She envaidet dem in. In midel of super klin kichen stud big teibel. From de big bol an de hevi teibel, smel of chiken paprikash kud invaid iven as det Kaiser for saper. Pino, as dikan, vos hepi tu si de visitors. He kud stapet tu eksplen sam baiblikal stori in vich he vos not shor and not akspektet visit help him tu bek aut, not lusing his fes.
"Gud ivning ledis, vot kan I du for ju?" ask Malek polaitli, hoping det evriting kud bi solvt fest. In hefen auer he mas bi bai Orel bachika haus, ver dei plei de karts vit grendedushkin Sablanich. Hi miset oredi tu taim des mant bikos Lords bisnis kam olveis ekros.
"As ju no mai svit dir pater Malek, Zuzi is stil spreding hr satans bret over des taun," tok de old grenmamichka Hlivovec, meshering from de sait his holi tais, "and vi ..."

@@@

Marishka, and Deacon Pino. Marishka would occasionally break into loud laughter, always repeating these words: "Oh, Pater Malek, don't be silly. That can't possibly be true. Perhaps you just made it up to make me laugh."

After a loud knocking, slow Marishka opened the door. She invited them in. In the middle of the super clean kitchen stood a big table. From the big bowl on the heavy table came the smell of chicken paprikash that could invite even our dead Kaiser for supper. Pino, our deacon, was happy to see the visitors. He could stop explaining the biblical story he wasn't sure about and the unexpected visit helped him back out without losing face.

"Good evening ladies, what can I do for you?" Malek asked politely, hoping that everything could be solved fast. In half an hour he was to be at Orel Bachika's house to play cards with Grandeduchkin Sablanich. He'd already missed twice this month because the lord's business always came up.

"As you know my sweet dear Pater Malek, Zuzi is still spreading her satan's breath over this town," said old grandmamichka Hlivovec, sizing up his holy thighs from the side, "and we ..."

"Dir belavet ledis. Jes I du fil det det is bed, bad I hev onli krucefiks, roseri and holi vota. And det vos ap tu nau selten vorking an taun heds, laik vi ol no," encer de Malek, voching an de klak.

"Bisaid, dont push evriting in hr shus ledis," miks him self dikan Pino in konverseshen. "If de men hes inaf romentik hom for grab, dei bi not raning eraund de Hot Zuzika haus," sed hi tu grup of vumen dei trai hard tu ignor his edveis.

"And gast hau ar ju sacha ekspert in det?" askt pater Malek.

"Its kam from lord noleg," sed Pino svoloing de big shishkerl.

"Vi dont ker vot ju bi duing, gast go tu hr and sei hr tu stap," toking ol dos old vimen, laik a viches eraund de faer.

"Ven ju go der mai svit pater Malek, go in tait long gons, gast in..." Slo Marishka trn red in hr fes.

"Gast in ... vat?" ask de Malek chok pel.

"Vel, so meni of as best mens gon der, in gut feit, and endet droping dei anderver. Preheps, if ever hepen tu ju mai dir Malek, long gons ar hevier tu drop," sed Marishka.

<hr />

"Dear beloved ladies. Yes, I do feel that that is bad, but I have only the crucifix, rosary and holy water. And up to now they have seldom worked on the heads in this town, like it or not," answered Malek, watching the clock.

"Besides, don't put it all in her shoes," said Deacon Pino, mixing himself into the conversation. "If the men had enough romance at home they wouldn't be running around to Hot Zuzika's house," he said to the group of women who tried hard to ignore his advice.

"And just how are you such an expert in this?" asked Pater Malek.

"It comes from the knowledge of the lord," said Pino, swallowing hard.

"We don't care what you do, just go to her and tell her to stop," said all the old women, talking like witches around a fire.

"When you go there my dear sweet Pater Malek, go in tight long johns, just in..." Slow Marishka's face turned red.

"Just in ... what?" asked Malek, chalk pale.

"Well, so many of our best men have gone there, in good faith, and ended up dropping their underwear. Perhaps, if it ever happened to you my dear Malek, long johns are heavier to drop," said Marishka.

"Dei meibi hevier tu drop, bad dei hev biger hol over bod blesings," sed sanbadi in gosop komiti. Ven de Pino vos chuing an his gaket sliv, gast not tu lef as prist Malek vos eksplodet. Neibers hiret an des ivning Malek vois laik hi vos siting in dei homs. "I am lord servent and blest from barom tu tape of mai hed. Sacha prson laik mi hev nating tu fir from Zuzi hot blesing! Ist det klir?" Hi push de old gosop an de strit and tel dem det he prsoneli bi luking after gud devel det tikling dos old viches for rest of dei laifs. As slo Marishka ran intu hr kvoter kraing laik a lital bebi. Pino desapir in de dark chrch.

Des nait vos pater Malek lusing de geim of shnaps. Orel and Sablanich bachika tuket evri dinar det hi hes in his poket. "Na hau kud sambadi koncentreting an karts det hev, gast hefen auers ego, meiger atek an his kredebiliti laik taun prich." Med laik a satan, hi stap an Zuzi sters an de vei hom.

"Zuzika! Is pater Malek! Tro sam of des godlos rusters aut. If I faund enibadi vit his blesing aut of his anderver, I

@@

"They may be heavier to drop, but they have bigger holes over both blessings," said someone in the gossip committee.

As Pino was chewing on his jacket sleeve, just to keep from laughing, our priest Malek exploded. That evening the neighbours heard Malek's voice as if he was sitting in their homes. "I am the lord's servant and blessed from my bottom to the top of my head. A person such as I has nothing to fear from Zuzi's hot blessing! Is that clear?" He pushed the old gossips out to the street and told them he would personally be looking after the good devil who would be tickling those old witches for the rest of their lives. Our slow Marishka ran into her quarters crying like a little baby. Pino disappeared into the dark church.

That night, Pater Malek was losing the game of schnaps. Orel and Sablanich bachika took every dinar he had in his pocket. "Now how could somebody concentrate on cards who had, just half an hour ago, a major attack on his credibility as town priest." Mad as Satan, he stopped on Zuzi's stairs on the way home.

"Zuzika! It's Pater Malek! Throw some of those Godless roosters out. If I find anybody with his blessing out of his underwear I'll

@@

bi jusing mai krucefiks tu brek his svit belonging," jal Malek det ol neibarhud vos hiring his holi vois. After long komoshen, overtron frnach, svet Zuzi ran an hr sters vit a lemp. Hr klos vos putet in de hri, and skrt diden kaveret hr long bjutifol legs vich as Malek simstu laiket.

"Ooooo, pater Malek, bles ju mai dir belavetvan. A ju kaming in fet, or gud fet? Na vot ever bi jor risen tu kam for visit, ju piket fain taim. I am ol jors, redi tu bi blest," tok she svit.

"Vel mai dir belavet," start Malek, svoloing de big shishkerl. "A ju viling tu teket hir de blesing, or vi hev a tok insaid?"

"Vel, it is not det I kud not teket hir, bad insait vi hev mor pis. Ju no, not evri dei kam de sakrament in de haus. So, I van tu du mai best tu help ju," sed Hot Zuzi, puling dengeresli hr skrt ab bai skreching hr self.

Vot dei toket vos onli non from bucher Martin. He spendet des long nait stafet in hr smol kichen kabert. After hi kud strech his badi in taun bar, hi tol de kraud over sam kain

use my crucifix to break his sweet belonging," Malek yelled, loud enough for the whole neighbourhood to hear his holy voice.

After a long commotion and overthrown furniture, sweet Zuzi ran onto her stairs with a lamp. Her clothes had been put on in a hurry, and her skirt didn't cover her long beautiful legs, which our Malek seemed to like.

"Ooooo, Pater Malek, bless you my dear beloved one. Are you coming in faith or in good faith? Now whatever your reason for coming here, you picked a fine time. I am all yours, ready to be blessed," she said sweetly.

"Well, my dear beloved," Malek started, swallowing hard. "Are you willing to take a blessing here, or shall we have a talk inside?"

"Well, it is not that I couldn't take it here, but inside we'll have more peace. You know, it's not every day the sacrament comes into the house. So, I want to do my best to help you," said Hot Zuzi, pulling her skirt up dangerously by scratching herself.

What they talked about was only found out from Martin the butcher. He spent that long night stuffed in her small kitchen cupboard. After he could stretch his body in the town bar, he told the crowd of some kind

of a dil det Zuzi and Malek meid. "Ju no mai bjutifol sister,"
tel de Malek tu hr, "ju shud meri de Polika, de taun kapersmid.
I no hi is kain of fani, bad is beter den nating." Ven des erli
moning Zuzi vos blest, she promis as Malek bi a gud grl. Sun
after Malek order Polika tu mek slivovica boiler for Zuzi.

So, van vorm dei letct fol, as "soft Polika" teket ol his
kapersmid hemers tu hr haus. Hi vandering vai an erd shi
nid det bladi boiler if she dont hev a plam tris. Bad, for seg
of a bisnis and tu plis de Malek hi never ask eni kveshchens.
Sun after neibers hiret hepi hemering an de koper. It vos
gud sain for sols of auer taun. She invaidet him vit open
arms tu stei der. Iven slip in seim rum vit hr. She fid him
laik a trki short befor killing.

Ol dos hobi mech mekers det plenet det start tu releks.
St. Jelena vos vans egen a veri hepi taun. As harvest vos
finisht in rekord taim and pis retrn tu de taun. Bad, van dei
in de lanch taim, samting hepen det noubadi, iven de
bigeste pesimist, diden ekspektet eni mor. Hot Zuzika lost hr
temper, and befor help kud eraivt, auer Polika svit tenking

🙵🙵🙵🙵🙵🙵🙵🙵🙵🙵🙵🙵🙵🙵🙵🙵🙵🙵🙵🙵🙵🙵🙵🙵🙵🙵🙵🙵🙵🙵🙵🙵🙵

of deal that Zuzi and Malek made.
"You know my beautiful sister,"
Malek told her, "you should marry
Polika, the town coppersmith. I
know he's kind of funny, but he's
better than nothing." When Zuzi
was blessed early that morning, she
promised Malek to be a good girl.
Soon after Malek ordered Polika to
make a slivovica boiler for Zuzi.

So, one warm day last fall, our
soft Polika took all his
coppersmith hammers to her
house. He was wondering why on
earth she needed the bloody boiler
if she didn't have any plum trees.
But, for the sake of business and
to please Malek he didn't ask any
questions. Soon after, neighbours

heard happy hammering on
copper. It was a good sign for the
souls of our town. She invited him
with open arms to stay there. Even
to sleep in the same room with
her. She fed him like a turkey just
before killing.

All the hobby matchmakers
who'd planned this started to
relax. St. Helena was once again a
very happy town. Our harvest was
finished in record time and peace
returned to the town.

But one day at lunch time,
something happened that nobody,
even the worst pessimist, hadn't
expected. Hot Zuzika lost her
temper, and before help could
arrive our Polika's sweet thinking

boks vos luking laik skin of overboilet poteto, and Zuzika hes traet oredi ol his hemers. Laik a lital skeri piglec hi vos jaling, olovei tu de siti hospital. Befor doktor finished him, he vos heving 60 stiches and gud shev of his big soft hed. Bad auer svit Zuzika det vos stil not gut inaf. Shi tuk him tu kort, and after de kort faineli finisht vit Polika, hi lost evriting. Zuzi lojer argju and vin, portreting as soft Polika als sekshuali meniak. God greshest. Ju liv vit sambadi for so long, never so im vit eni vumen, nekst ting ju no hi is a seks meniak.

Shortli after as hot vido selt evriting and desapirt. Polika liv vit as anadar tu jers, never spok a vort tu eni fimel. Den van dei ven hi vos vorking vit de horsis van of dem tro im an fresh raf tinber. Hi kam tu konchens, bad hi mas bi breking samting in his badi. An his daing bet as Orel bachika vos toking vit him, Soft Polika edmitet tu him vot vos hepening des krushal lanch taim.

Hi vos siting an vorm teras, hepili hemering an his slivovica boiler. Hot Zuzika vok aut aut de haus keriing big

box was looking like the skin of an overboiled potato, and Zuzika had already tried all of his hammers. He yelled like a scared little piglet all the way to the city hospital. Before the doctor finished with him he had 60 stitches and a good shave of his big soft head. But that wasn't good enough for our sweet Zuzika. She took him to court, and after the court finally finished with Polika, he'd lost everything. Zuzi's lawyer argued and won, portraying our soft Polika as a sex maniac. Good gracious. You lived with somebody for so long, never saw him with any women, and next thing you know he is a sex maniac.

Shortly after, our hot widow sold everything and disappeared. Polika lived with us another two years, never speaking a word to any female. Then one day after he was working with the horses, one of them threw him onto a pile of fresh rough timber. He came to consciousness, but must have broken something in his body. On his deathbed, as Orel Bachika was talking with him, Soft Polika admitted to him what happened that crucial lunch time.

He was sitting on the warm terrace, happily hammering on his slivovica boiler. Hot Zuzika walked out of the house carrying a big pleit of fresh meid chis polachinka. Shi vos klodet onli in hr soft pink skin. Kaming klos tu him, shi sailend sed hevili briding, "Nau ju kud du evriting det ju van tu du." Insted tu bait in Evas epel and chos de misforchin of merit mens, he disaidet tu kip his enchen virginiti. Boj, samtaim flaing penc kud ekonplishing mor als ol taun sols tugeder. Endlis des vos tru in Polikas kes. Vel, sturms an veri hot deis ar femos for dei fors, and Zuzi vos hot. Ven hi tuket de big polachinka and trnet eraund heven fol daun. Hi diden iven bait det bladi polachinka ven she strakt him vit de hamer — and de rest vi no oredi.

Zuzi never sho ab eni mor in taun. Iven tu as gosop vos hr desapirenc an open fail. After det insident noubadi in as taun vos beliving in mech meker eni mor. Tu meni laivs vos hrt and lost an des ishju.

⊚⊚⊚⊚⊚⊚⊚⊚⊚⊚⊚⊚⊚⊚⊚⊚⊚⊚⊚⊚⊚⊚⊚⊚⊚⊚⊚⊚⊚⊚⊚⊚⊚⊚⊚⊚⊚

plate of fresh-made cheese polachinkas. She was clothed only in her soft pink skin. Coming close to him, she whispered heavily, "Now you can do everything you want to do." Instead of biting Eve's apple and choose the misfortune of married men, he decided to keep his ancient virginity. Boy, sometimes flying pants can accomplish more than all the town souls together. At least this was true in Polika's case. Well, storms on very hot days are famous for their force, and Zuzi was hot. When he took a big polachinka and turned around, heaven fell down. He hadn't even bit the bloody polachinka when she struck him with the hammer — and the rest we know already.

Zuzi never showed up again in town. Even to our gossips her disappearance was an open file. After this incident nobody in our town believed in matchmakers any more. Too many lives were lost and hurt over this issue.

⊚⊚⊚⊚⊚⊚⊚⊚⊚⊚⊚⊚⊚⊚⊚⊚⊚⊚⊚⊚⊚⊚⊚⊚⊚⊚⊚⊚⊚⊚⊚⊚⊚⊚⊚⊚⊚

Onli de veri old sol remembering Pishtas mader. She vos stum grl, boren tu perenc dei pest gud eg of heving a children. Dei livet purli, bat veri hepi, in an broken daun old shed on auskrts of auer lital taun. Dei frst neibers vere krset vilos peshentli veiding an nekst flading. Ven ever a somer sturms brod mor als normal rehen, des properti vos fladet. It vos mach vorser in fogi spring and fol, ven de Drava pushet hr sisons hai vota. For des famili, fait vit flad vos vei of laif.

Ven hr perenc dai pur grl trai tu kip evriting hau et vos an hr tu ekar farm. It vos not isi. Meni taim pipel bi helping tu bring hr over de vinter, givin hr sam ekstra poteto or smoket beken. Samtaim dei iven kipet hr old kau for deis in dei barn, fiding her. In bed jers shi bi lusing hr hei and stro, so shi kuden fid hr. Pishtas mader vos after ol a gud grl, and hr onli mistek vos not noing hau tu spik. Tu evrivan der ever help hr, shi bi retrning in peing him vit hr

---

Only the very old souls remember Pishta's mother. She was a mute girl, born to parents past the healthy age for having children. They lived poorly, but very happily, in a broken-down old shed on the outskirts of our little town. Their first neighbours were the cursed willows patiently awaiting the next flooding. Whenever summer storms brought more than the normal rain, their property was flooded. It was much worse in the foggy spring and fall, when the Drava pushed her seasonal high water. For this family, fighting with floods was a way of life.

When her parents died the poor girl tried to keep everything as it was on her two-acre farm. It wasn't easy. Many times people would help her through the winter, giving her some extra potatoes or smoked bacon. Sometimes they'd even keep her old cow and feed it for days in their barns. In bad years she would lose her hay and straw so she couldn't feed the cow. Pishta's mother, after all, was a good girl whose only mistake was not knowing how to speak. Everyone who helped her she paid back with her own hends. Samtaim vos des bebisiting, vorking an de fil in harvest taim, or gedering de ti for vumens signis. Sols of auer taun never vos tu rich, bad dei shor du de best tu help as grl in trobel.

Van somer, auer blest kaiser solgers vere in taun. Dei drinket, marcht, and laik olveis luket for trobel. Meni taim, akording an auer gosop, dei gast sveret, or singt, giving pur sols taim tu haid jang fimels. In sacha taim a jang gud luking grl bi putet in old grenis klos, and smirt vit ash tu mek hr anapiling tu de solgers.

Pur stum grl vos retrning tu hr old shed from hevi fild vork an van of de farmer. Iven she vos stum, shi vos an gud luking grl. Dei spatet hr ven shi vos krosing de strit not far from taun bar, and folo hr. Frst dei vos gast horsing, "Guten abent main Freulain," or "Wie gets inen". Bat des chench ven shi rich svams. Not noing det shi vos folot, she vos sopreist in atek. Pipel sed dei hir hr skriming, bat dei kuden help if dei dont vanet bi self in trobel.

An neks moning, ven dei trup faineli liv de taun, dei

hands. Sometimes it was babysitting, working in the fields at harvest time, or gathering tea for women's sicknesses. The people of our town were never too rich, but they sure did their best to help our girl in trouble.

One summer, our blessed kaiser's soldiers were in town. They drank, marched, and like always looked for trouble. Many times, according to our gossips, they just swore or sang, giving our poor souls time to hide the young females. In such a time a young good looking girl would be put in old granny's clothes and smeared with ash to make her unappealing to soldiers.

The poor mute girl was returning to her old shed from heavy field work for one of the farmers. Though she was mute, she was a good looking girl. They spotted her when she was crossing the street not far from the town bar and followed her. First they just horsed around, "Guten abent mein fraulein," or "Wie gets inen." But this changed when she reached the swamps. Not knowing that she was being followed, she was surprised in the attack. People said they heard her screaming, but they couldn't help if they didn't want to get in trouble themselves.

The next morning, when the troops finally left town, they

Marijan Megla

faund hr. She vas biten and left hef neket belo krset vilo. She vos in shak, and big pein. De old vumen vosht hr and putet an hr fit.

Samer pest and fol rehen faund hr in hop of a chaild. Jes she vos pregnet vit sam of dos bladi solger, det nau marching samver als, spreding dei miseri.

Let des fol Drava vos flading laik never befor. Pushing hr big stamak, shi desperatli trai tu sev hr lital shek. In taim of flading evri femili is left alon tu sevet dei on. Votar vos evriver, in beisments, jards, kaubarn, strits. Shi vos left alon, bikos as sols asjum det she probebli draun. Hr lital haus kolepset and dei tenket she dai inet. Ven de vota supsidet and dei get tu hr, shi vos an enibadi sopreis stil a laiv. Totali vet, she vos siting an krset vilo voching remeins of hr shek in dip madi vota. Vans egen, shi vos pept ab end sorvaivt. Vinter kam erli and ais breket det lital left of hr hom. Kreshing de vols and chimni det stil stud laik sam taet solger an grev of his mader dei dai in his apsenc.

Den, van nait, old grenis vos gedering in hr lital rum in

found her. She was beaten and left half naked below a cursed willow. She was in shock and serious pain. The old women washed her and put her on her feet.

Summer passed and the fall rain found her expecting a child. Yes, she was pregnant by one of those bloody soldiers, now marching somewhere else, spreading their misery.

Late that fall the Drava flooded like never before. Pushing her big stomach, she desperately tried to save her little shack. During floods, every family is left to save their own. Water was everywhere, in basements, yards, cow barns, streets. She was left alone because our people assumed that she had probably drowned. Her little house had collapsed and they though she'd died in it. When the water subsided and they got to her, to everybody's surprise she was still alive. Soaking wet, she was sitting in a cursed willow looking at the remains of her shack in the deep muddy water. Once again she was pepped up and survived. Winter came early and the ice broke up what little was left of her home, crashing the walls and chimney that still stood like some tired soldier at the grave of his mother who'd died in his absence.

Then, one night, the old grannies gathered in her little room in taun. Children of a haus vos putet bai neibars. In long noisi leber, a chaild vos boren. Dei given him de neim Pishta, after de farmer hu giv hr de rum in de taun. Old vumen diden sei mach ven dei drinket dei lital slivovic in bar, after de nju mader vos put tugeder vit hr chaild. Bad, sam ov dem kuden resistet tu tel dei apinijen ebaut de Pishtika. Dei tenk de chail is krset. Ven Pishtika vos faif, evrivan in taun njuet hi vos hendikept. Hi vos sacha hensam felo det evrivan giv him tu it or tu slip, noing det his mader going from van depreshen tu aders, living Pishta meni taims alon for meni deis. Pipel helpet hau dei kud. Pishta vos olveis a chaild der dont belong tu noubadi, bat evrivan vori ebaut him.

Hau Pishtika's pur mader endet hr trobelt laif, noubadi rili nos. Shi gast desapir van dei, living as hr Pishtika. In hol taun, I diden no eni prson det akcheli het him, iven hi vos den in his sikstis. Evri vinter hi godet his buc, preheps not njuvan, bat stil a buc vurdi of de sno. Hi godet his long gons, ekstra shrt, glavs laik enibadi als. Akcheli I never soet enibadi giving him samting. It vos mor or les

town. Children of the house were put with the neighbours. After a long, noisy labour, a child was born. They gave him the name Pishta, after the farmer who gave her the room in the town. The old women didn't say much as they drank their little slivovica in the bar after the new mother was put together with her child. But some of them couldn't resist telling their opinion about Pishtika. They thought the child was cursed.

When Pishtika was five, everyone in town knew he was handicapped. He was such a handsome fellow that everyone gave him food or a place to sleep, knowing that his mother was going from one depression to another, often leaving Pishta alone for many days. People helped how they could. Pishta was always a child who didn't belong to anybody, but everyone worried about him.

How Pishtika's poor mother ended her troubled life, nobody really knows. She just disappeared one day, leaving us her Pishtika. In the whole town, I never knew any person who actually hated him, even though he was by then in his sixties. Every winter he got his boots, perhaps not new ones, but still boots worthy of the snow. He got his long johns, an extra shirt, and gloves like anybody else. Actually, I never saw anybody give him something. It was more or less

laik hi hes fergoten det in his kabert, in des haus. Pishta vos onli gai det hev kabert in evri haus.

Noubadi nos vai, bat his gop vos keriing as hef nekel Jesus an proseshen and finerals. Sam of de older pipel asket isklusivli, an dei daing bet, for Pishtika krucefiks. "Hi hed ... sacha sed luk, and hi stil truli beliv in auer lord. So plis dont spend mach an kofin ... get him."

Pishtika livet his on laif, keriing ol taun sikrits in on hart. It vos preheps not olveis van of hepier laivs, bad noubadi so him ever kraing. He vos an evri merich, jubileum, femili rejunien, taun fjesta, det ever vos helt in taun of St. Jelena. Onli hi denct vit evri vumen in taun, no meter hau smol or big or old dei ver. Pishta vos most femes saker chirer. In taim ven vi vos lusing hi bi jaling, troing his kep, iven preing befor ol pipel. Hi vos as self inpost orkestra dirigent, no meter if dei gipsi pleet or as taun bras. Dei iven edmitet, ven hi ganp eraund and vevs vit his hends evriting is mach mor beter.

Pishta vos as kort jester, faerfaiter, komedian, best

---

that he'd forgotten something in his cupboard, in this house. Pishta was the only guy who had a cupboard in every house.

Nobody knows why, but his job was carrying our half-naked Jesus in processions and funerals. Some of the older people asked exclusively, on their deathbed, for Pishtika's crucifix. "He had ... such sad luck, and he still truly believes in our lord. So please don't spend much on a coffin ... get him."

Pishtika lived his own life, carrying the whole town's secrets in his heart. It was perhaps not always one of the happiest lives, but nobody ever saw him crying. He was at every marriage, jubilee, family reunion and town festival that was ever held in the town of St. Helena. Only he would dance with every woman in town, no matter how small or big or old they were. Pishta was the most famous soccer cheerer. When we were losing he'd be yelling, throwing his cap, even praying in front of all the people. He was our self-appointed orchestra director, no matter if it was the gypsies who were playing or the town brass. They even admitted that when he jumped around and waved with his hands everything was much better.

Pishta was our court jester, our firefighter, comedian, best katolik, and taun idiot. Vi lav him and defendet him. Auer sols tuk him evri jer tu de bleset Mader vrgen from Bistrica, and vetet his hed in holi vota. Hi miset onli fju taims de pilgremich, simpli bikos hi vos not der ven de fetfol living an fut de taun. Old sol teling det going vit him tu Bistrica vos fan, and evrivan vos kraing tirs from lefing.

Vans, long taim ego, vi olmost lostet him in madi Drava. Kaming tu de river de big grup of pilgrems hedet tu Maria Bistrica mas split, bikos vos no rum for evrivan an de feri. So ven de pater Malek and mosli of old vidos vos transportet to ader sait of de river, sambadi of jang bois kam an veri gud aidija. "Vai ve kud not mek sam fan, and sho as grls hau de St. Piter vos voking an de vota?" Sun aidija vos akceptet, and proper log and pis of old rop faundet. For hepinis of ol, Pishta egri tu bi voking sent.

Ven de feri retrnt for rest of a pilgrems evriting vos redi. Pishtika hes his rop oredi and log vos emidietly putet so det hi rag over de feri fens. Pur feri kepten vandert vai an erd jang pipel from St. Jelena keriing a log insted of krucefiks

Catholic, and town idiot. We loved him and defended him. Our people took him every year to the Blessed Mother Virgin of Bistrica and wet his head with holy water. He only missed the pilgrimage a few times, simply because he was not there when the faithful left town on foot. Old people say that going to Bistrica with him was fun, and everyone would cry tears of laughter.

Once, a long time ago, we almost lost him in the muddy Drava. Coming to the river, a big group of pilgrims headed to Maria Bistrica had to split up because there wasn't room for everyone on the ferry. So while Pater Malek and most of the old widows were being transported to the other side of the river, some of the young boys came up with a very good idea. "Why shouldn't we have some fun and show the girls how St. Peter walked on water?" Soon the idea was accepted and the proper log and a piece of old rope found. For the happiness of all, Pishta agreed to be the walking saint.

When the ferry returned for the rest of the pilgrims everything was ready. Pishtika had his rope ready and a log was immediately put so that it reached over the side of the ferry. The poor ferry captain wondered why on earth the young people of St. Helena were carrying a log instead of a crucifix

an de pilgremich ... bad it is a fri vorld. Prehaps is des nau a nju trent. Luking over an de ader sait, hi miset sam of de hesti akshen an bord. Ven de hed of proseshen vos erekting the brodet krucefiks and as chrch flags, prepering to junaitet march tu Bistrica, bois and grls vos kleping oredi tu Pishtika.

Dei bindet eraund Pishtikas vest a rop end rop an de big log det ragt aut. Et frst vos evriting orait, and as belavet kresi pilgrem vos rili voking an de vota. His oversaist boni bar fit, meking big crkels an de shaini serfes of a svift river. Hi lavet. Iven kepten kud not resist to smail. Bad kaming tu ader bich, rop slip and as bleset Pishtika desapir in de madi vota. Ven de shokt pilgrems det voch det proformenc skrimet, only de kvik reskju of de kepten sev him from det. De shokt taun bois vos panisht vit keriing de Pishtika, det faineli rekaver, sveing for ol dei an dei beks on de vei tu pilgremich. Na vot be des for de taun det lost his vileg idiot, pleing St. Piter over de kold Drava? For rest of a pilgremich he liv laik a king.

on their pilgrimage ... but it's a free world. Perhaps this is a new trend. Looking over the other side, he missed some of the hasty action on board. When the head of the procession was erecting the crucifix they'd brought and the church flags, preparing to march united to Bistrica, the boys and girls were already applauding Pishtika.

They'd tied the rope around Pishtika's waist and looped it over the big log that reached out. At first everything was all right, and our beloved crazy pilgrim was really walking on the water. His oversized bony bare feet made big circles on the shiny surface of the swift river. He loved it. Even the captain couldn't resist smiling. But coming to the other beach the rope slipped and our beloved Pishtika disappeared in the muddy water. When the shocked pilgrims watching the performance screamed, only a quick rescue by the captain saved him from death. The shocked town boys were punished by having to carry Pishtika, who'd finally recovered, swaying all day on their backs on the way to the pilgrimage. Now, what would become of a town that lost its village idiot playing St. Peter over the cold Drava? For the rest of the pilgrimage he lived like a king.

It vos let van samer ven bed njus spred kros auer taun. Pishtika, de taun ful, daing in old grenmamichka Hlivovec kichen. Evrivan hu kud, end vos not in midel of a hevi sison vork, ran tu si him. Tu mi and Emilko vos given komend tu faund as svit pater Malek. Grenma Hlivovec haus vos in as blok, so vi hev tu du evriting tu plis as neiber.

Raning tu de chrch haus vi vander vot kud sei as taun prist tu des Pishtika daing bisnis. Hi vos not hom. "De onli ples det hi kud bi in des taim of a dei is bai Orel bachika haus. If de Orel nenika is not hom, go luking in de vainceler. Dei probebli plei de karts vit grenpa Sablanich," jal after as de slo Marishka, de prist meid.

Vi faineli faund as bleset pater Malek in Orel bachikas kul vain seler. Hi vos hepi laik vi never so him befor. After long, long taim hi vos faineli vining sam of his mani bek of det tu old fuls.

"Dem Malek, dont fergat det ju de prist and not sam profeshenel pleer," sed Orel bachi puting de nikel an de big hil of penis an de teibel.

◎◎◎◎◎◎◎◎◎◎◎◎◎◎◎◎◎◎◎◎◎◎◎◎◎◎◎◎◎◎◎◎◎◎◎◎◎◎

It was late one summer when bad news spread across our town. Pishtika, the town fool, was dying in old Grandma Hlivovec's kitchen. Everyone who could, and who was not in the middle of the season's hard work, ran to see him. Emilko and I were commanded to find our sweet Pater Malek. Grandma Hlivovec's house was in our block, so we had to do everything to please our neighbour.

Running to the church house we wondered what we could say to our town priest about this Pishtika's dying business. He was not home. "The only place he could be this time of day is Orel Bachika's house. If Orel isn't home, go looking in his wine cellar. They're probably playing cards with Grampa Sablanich," slow Marishka, the priest's maid, yelled after us.

We finally found our blessed Pater Malek in Orel Bachika's cool wine cellar. He was happier than we'd ever seen him before. After a long, long time he was finally winning some of his money back from those two old fools.

"Dammit Malek, don't forget that you're the priest and not some professional player," said Orel Bachi, putting a nickel on the big hill of pennies on the table.

◎◎

Marijan Megla

"Ja, diden de lord tich ju det never teket de peni from pur pipel?" ask sed Sablanich, fergeting det he juzuli vin an sacha geims.

"O shadap, vil ju? I never van a geim in jers," sed de pater Malek trning his atenchen tu as, dei anpeshentli veidet ven de geim is over. "And vich plesher bring des tu jang gentelman tu as?"

"Plesher of daing!" tok laut mai busom badi Emilko.

"Vat? A ju kresi Emilko? Daing is never de plesher," sed de pater Malek. "Hu is daing?"

"Ja, tel. Hu is daing?" ask de Orel bachika.

"As blesed Pishtika de taun idiot!" sed I.

"I njuet. I njuet. I vos vining, lord, kud ju not ferspon det prsons daing? No? Ju Sablanich dont tach de kart, I kam bek. No! Beter ju kam vit mi, and ju Orel bachika klos de vainseler and giv mi de ki. So. Nau, in vich haus is de Pishtika de taun ful daing?"

"Bai grenmamichka Hlivovec. Hi is so preokupaid vit det bisnis det hi lostet iven his penc in des stragel," sed I tu Malek and Sablanich det vok behaind as.

⦾⦾⦾⦾⦾⦾⦾⦾⦾⦾⦾⦾⦾⦾⦾⦾⦾⦾⦾⦾⦾⦾⦾⦾⦾⦾⦾⦾⦾⦾⦾⦾⦾⦾

"Yeah, didn't the lord teach you never to take a penny from poor people?" asked sad Sablanich, forgetting that he usually wins these games.

"Oh shut up, will you? I never won a game in years," said Pater Malek, turning his attention to us, who waited impatiently for the game to be over. "And which pleasure brings these two young gentlemen to us."

"Pleasure of death!" my bosom buddy Emilko said loudly.

"What? Are you crazy Emilko? Dying is never a pleasure," said Pater Malek. "Who is dying?"

"Yeah, tell. Who is dying?" asked Orel Bachika.

"Our blessed Pishtika the town idiot!" I said.

"I knew it. I knew it. I was winning, lord, could you not postpone that person's dying? No? You, Sablanich, don't touch the cards, I'm coming back. No! Better you come with me, and you Orel Bachika close the wine cellar and give me the key. So. Now, in which house is Pishtika the town fool dying?"

"Grandma Hlivovec's. He was so preoccupied with that business that he even lost his pants in the struggle," I said to Malek and Sablanich, who walked behind us.

⦾⦾⦾⦾⦾⦾⦾⦾⦾⦾⦾⦾⦾⦾⦾⦾⦾⦾⦾⦾⦾⦾⦾⦾⦾⦾⦾⦾⦾⦾⦾⦾⦾

It vos sed siing Pishtika so gasping for er and so meni fimels laut krain ven vi brod de Malek and Sablanich. Grenmamichka Hlivovec, an hr nis besaid de bet, vos van of laudeste morner. Old gosop vos gedering in de hri and vit Malek vandering, vot vos Pishtika duing in de kichen drest onli in his long gons? Det vos vel respektet vidow haus. Vit aut eni vidnis from vrong duing, de meter vos putet an hold.

Auer or so leter, as belavet Pishtika dai, vit help of auer pater Malek. Ven de old grenis voshet his laiflos badi, grendedushkin Sablanich vos putet in charg of fineral.

Dei nju tu vel det evri hjumen bin kost mani, and ded spescheli. Ven dei gedert an Pishtika letct parti in as vido grenmamichka Hlivovec haus, evrivan ekspektet tu bi askt for mani. Hi vos a pur sol, nevr merit and nating tu diwaid, and no vaif tu hold bek an vain. Tu meket des nait wurdi of kraing dei brod dei on buz.

It vos big los, laca sednis and laca buz vos nidet tu izi de pein for lost Pishtika. Weri sun alkohol level in heds of sed sols ros. Los of taun ful trned in tu big hepi parti. It

It was sad seeing Pishtika gasping so hard for air and so many females crying loudly when we brought in Malek and Sablanich. Grandma Hlivovec, on her knees beside the bed, was one of the loudest mourners. The old gossips gathered in a hurry, and with Malek wondered, what was Pishtika doing in the kitchen dressed only in his long johns? This was a well-respected widow's house. Without any witness of wrong-doing, the matter was put on hold.

An hour or so later, our beloved Pishtika died with the help of our Pater Malek. When the old grannies had washed his lifeless body, Grandeduchkin Sablanich was put in charge of the funeral.

They knew too well that every human being costs money, dead especially. When they gathered at Pishtika's last party at the widow Grandma Hlivovec's house, everyone expected to be asked for money. He was a poor soul, never married and nothing to divide, and no wife to hold him back on the wine. To make the night worthy of crying, they brought their own booze.

It was a big loss, and lots of sadness and lots of booze were needed to ease the pain over lost Pishtika. Very soon the alcohol level in the heads of the sad souls rose. The loss of the town fool turned into a big happy party. It

is not det des vos destrbing auer Pishtika, hi vos hepili sliping in his kofin. Hi diden main iven auer pater Malek singing, after ol hi laik tu si as hepi an his letct erdli parti. Bat samhau, hi vos akspekting samting bed. Ol dos bjutifol rosis and des lavli kofin, des bi gast tu gut tu bi tru. Hi vos onli taun ful and so mach atenchen tu him vos never grentet from as. Samting is vrong. Preheps dei tuket a rong kofin, or so.

"Sei mi, mai frend Milchi, is det kofin not lital tu ekspenciv for as Pishta?" ask Emilko, hepili itng de big buftlin an de flor bisaid de kofin.

"Vel, I dont no. Iven as old grendedushkin diden hev sacha bjutifol staf eraund him ven hi disaidet tu go in de skai. I shor hop dei no hau mach kan det kost as," sed I, manching an big pis of apel strudel.

"I samhau tenk as Pishtika is in de trobel. I gast no det," sed Emilko.

After the taun chrch klok strak midnait, de kveshchen det ol veiding for vos faineli askt. "Hau mach cost det kofin and dekor?" Old grendedushkin Sablanich simstu nid tu ader gais tu help

***

didn't disturb our Pishtika, who was happily sleeping in his coffin. He didn't even mind our Pater Malek's singing, after all he'd like to see us happy at his last earthly party. But somehow, he was expecting something bad. All those beautiful roses and this lovely coffin were just too good to be true. He was only the town fool and we'd never granted him so much attention. Something was wrong. Perhaps they'd taken the wrong coffin, or something.

"Tell me, my friend Milchi, is that coffin not a little too expensive four our Pishta?" asked Emilko, happily eating a big bismark on the floor beside the coffin.

"Well, I don't know. Even our old grandedushkin didn't have such beautiful stuff around him when he decided to go up into the sky. I sure hope they know how much this can cost us," I said, munching a big piece of apple strudel.

"I somehow think our Pishtika is in trouble. I just know it," said Emilko.

After the town church clock struck midnight, the question we were all waiting for was finally asked. "How much did that coffin and decorations cost?" Old Grandeduchkin Sablanich seemed to need two other guys to help him stend ab tu proklem des hai kost. It is interesting vot ken du a laud spoken nambar, tu drank pipel det nating befor stapet of toking. Sailends spredet imediatli, iven in betvin as children. Ais of ol kraut traet tu loketet in des ochen of smok and alkohol smel des bladi idiot Sablanich.

"Jesus Meri and Josef," faineli rekaver de pater Malek. "A ju med grendedushkin? A ju bringing a taun idiot in grev or kantri minister vit his fet beli? Lord fegiv mi, I toking ebaut ded sol," tok as belavet pater Malek, straking kofin vit his fet hend so hart det pur Pishtika olmos vok ab. Malek kip protesting laudli and aders goinet. I kuden beliv mai ais and mai irs. Des are de pipel det gast jestudei vos so frenli tu as Pishtika?

"Pipel!" tok auer prist, sveting laik a fet gus in oven. "Der vil bi no harm dan if vi bring tumoro des dekor bek. De ader det sol bi for shor hepi vit it."

Grendedushkin Sablanich an van sait vit hefe taun and pater Malek auf ader sait vit old gosop, japing and ganping laik tu jang rusters, paunding an des pur kofin.

⦾⦾⦾⦾⦾⦾⦾⦾⦾⦾⦾⦾⦾⦾⦾⦾⦾⦾⦾⦾⦾⦾⦾⦾⦾⦾⦾⦾⦾⦾⦾⦾

him stand up to proclaim the high cost. It is interesting what a loudly spoken number can do to drunk people whose talking can't be stopped by anything else. Silence spread immediately, even among us children. The eyes of the whole crowd tried to locate the bloody idiot Sablanich through the ocean of smoke and smell of alcohol.

"Jesus, Mary and Joseph," Pater Malek finally said. "Are you mad grandeduchkin? Are you burying a town idiot or a country minister with his fat belly? Lord forgive me, I'm talking about a dead soul," said our beloved Pater Malek, striking the coffin with his fat hand so hard that poor Pishtika almost woke up. Malek kept protesting loudly and others joined. I couldn't believe my eyes and ears. These are the people that just yesterday were so friendly to our Pishtika?

"People!" said our priest, sweating like a fat goose in the oven. "There will be no harm done if we take these decorations back tomorrow. The other dead souls will certainly be happy with it."

Grandeduchkin Sablanich, on one side with half the town, and Pater Malek on the other side with the old gossips, were yapping and jumping like two young roosters, pounding on the poor coffin.

⦿⦿⦿⦿⦿⦿⦿⦿⦿⦿⦿⦿⦿⦿⦿⦿⦿⦿⦿⦿⦿⦿⦿⦿⦿⦿⦿⦿⦿⦿⦿⦿

Meni taims des nait laining of a kofin vos tron aut and veri sun it luk laik siti peper in de laiberi after vik of jus. Nju chip svit, det auer Pishtika hev for frst taim in his erdli laif, vos stripet from his laiflos badi. At van moment hi olmost kam bek from his big hevenli treinstation. Frenli laik hi olveis vos, hi van tu pointet an his toren penc. Der ver hi go sun, ju kan hardli raning eraund vit toren penc. Iven his anderver, de letct vol of praivasi, vanet Malek tu retrn tu de siti stor or teket for praivat jus. Onli de smart muv of grendedushkin Sablanich sev de Pishtika shem from veri interestet taun fimels. Sablanich argju det des partikular anderver vere meid for speshal big mans blesing, and if is tru vot his jang meid sed, Malek is not van of dem. Auer pater Malek svolo de big shishkrl. His fes and nek koloret red. Den siing det noubadi peing atenchen an des nonsens, hi askt Sablanich:

"Em I taun bul or taun prist?"

"Taun prist," retrnet de Sablanich sarkastik.

"So, den gagmi for mai hart and not for sais of mai anderver."

 ⊚⊚⊚⊚⊚⊚⊚⊚⊚⊚⊚⊚⊚⊚⊚⊚⊚⊚⊚⊚⊚⊚⊚⊚⊚⊚⊚⊚⊚⊚⊚⊚⊚

Many times that night the lining of the coffin was thrown out and very soon it looked like a city paper in the library after a week of use. A new cheap suit that our poor Pishtika had for the first time in his earthly life was stripped from his lifeless body. At one moment he almost came back from his big heavenly train station. Friendly as he always was, he wanted to point out his torn pants. Where he was going soon, you can hardly be running around in torn pants.

Even his underwear, that last wall of privacy, Malek wanted to return to the city or store or take for his private use. Only a smart move by Grandeduchkin Sablanich saved Pishtika's shame from the very interested town females. Sablanich argued that this particular underwear was made for an especially big men's blessing, and if it's true what his young maid said, Malek's wasn't one of them. Our Pater Malek swallowed hard. His face and neck coloured red. Then seeing that nobody was paying attention to this nonsense, he asked Sablanich:

"Am I the town bull or town priest?"

"Town priest," Sablanich retorted sarcastically.

"So, then judge me for my heart and not for the size of my underwear."

 ⊚⊚⊚⊚⊚⊚⊚⊚⊚⊚⊚⊚⊚⊚⊚⊚⊚⊚⊚⊚⊚⊚⊚⊚⊚⊚⊚⊚⊚⊚⊚⊚⊚

"Den ju liv him de bladi anderver?" ask de Sablanich, stanping vit his hend an de kofin. His ais vere gast a inch evei of pater Malek mustash, so hi trai tu pul him self ab. "Jes, ju old blad saker," sed med Malek. "Ar ju nau setisfai?"

"Jes, I am setisfai," sed de old men.

Wit tri auers tu go befor living tu simentari de hol taun faineli disaidet tu giv evriting tu pur Pishtika. Hi vos putet in de kofin for letct taim, soraundet vit his drti kofin laining. Rait afterverc, grendedushkin Sablanich pushed tu long nels inet, gast tu meket shor det no dils ar erlaut eni mor. Sloli pipel releksing. Sanbadi kam auf gut aidija tu open ol vindos. Fresh er fri meni of as from anvantet ankonchens, vich kost rov end rov of smoket cigaret. De letzt glasis vos emtiet. De strong trkish moka, vich onli van lital sip kud kos hartatak, vos srvt. Toking egen pisfoli sam of dos hef det gais rekaver.

Tu sho him de taun lavt him after ol, dei kraet egen. I am not shor, and dont van tu spred bed gosop, bad sam of

⊚⊚⊚⊚⊚⊚⊚⊚⊚⊚⊚⊚⊚⊚⊚⊚⊚⊚⊚⊚⊚⊚⊚⊚⊚⊚⊚⊚⊚⊚⊚⊚⊚⊚⊚⊚⊚⊚⊚

"Then you'll leave him the bloody underwear?" asked Sablanich, stomping with his hand on the coffin. His eyes were just an inch away from Pater Malek's moustache, so he tried to pull himself up.

"Yes, you old bloodsucker," said the angry Malek. "Are you satisfied now?"

"Yes, I am satisfied," said the old man.

With three hours to go before leaving for the cemetery the whole town finally decided to give everything to poor Pishtika. He was put into the coffin for the last time, surrounded by his dirty coffin lining. Right afterwards, Grandeduchkin Sablanich pounded two long nails into the lid, just to make sure no more deals would be allowed. People slowly relaxed. Somebody came up with the good idea of opening all the windows. Fresh air freed many of us from the unwanted unconsciousness brought on by pack after pack of smoked cigarettes. The last glasses were emptied. Strong Turkish mocha, which could cause a heart attack with only one little sip, was served. Talking peacefully again, some of those half-dead guys recovered.

To show him the town loved him after all, they cried again. I am not sure, and I don't want to spread bad gossip, but some of

⊚⊚⊚⊚⊚⊚⊚⊚⊚⊚⊚⊚⊚⊚⊚⊚⊚⊚⊚⊚⊚⊚⊚⊚⊚⊚⊚⊚⊚⊚⊚⊚⊚⊚⊚⊚⊚⊚⊚

dem kraet des moning from vori det as Pishta dont tok bed in lords kindem. Na vat bi des for taun, det kud not bring his taun idiot in pis tu simenteri.

Let des moning de blek shaini vegen, vit pink, fet angels, kam tu grenmamichka Hlivovec haus. For strong men piket ab de Pishtikas kofin and keriing aut intu de vegen. Greni Hlivovec and ader old gosop gedert bihain de vegen vit de horsis. Pishtikas kofin vos kavert vit flauers det bai evri slaiseste muv of a vegen vibreting and shiftetet. Sloli bat shorli, fineral proseshen vos formt. Old tutlos grenis, anebel tu muv dei skini badis an long distanc, vevet Pishtika gudbai. Den, de tirs overkam des old sols, klodet in blak klos, noing det dei ven dei bi going is no mor far evei. An end of proseshen a kau vegen vas piking des bodis dei in agoni of alkohol poisening kuden vok eni mor. Sopreisingli, bat iven auer pater Malek vos traveling an des sol sever. Pishtikas hevenli expres vos veri slo, tu ekomidet de taet pipel vich spend de nait in bus and sin. After long march in vorm dei dei vos hepi tu si open grev.

⊚⊚⊚⊚⊚⊚⊚⊚⊚⊚⊚⊚⊚⊚⊚⊚⊚⊚⊚⊚⊚⊚⊚⊚⊚⊚⊚⊚⊚⊚⊚⊚⊚

them cried that morning in hope that Pishta wouldn't talk bad in the lord's kingdom. Now, what kind of town would it be that couldn't take its town fool in peace to the cemetery.

Late in the morning a black shiny wagon with pink fat angels came to Grandma Hlivovec's house. Four strong men picked up Pishtika's coffin and carried it out to the wagon. Granny Hlivovec and the other old gossips gathered behind the horse-drawn wagon. Pishtika's coffin was covered with flowers that vibrated and shifted with even the slightest movement of the wagon. Slowly but surely, the funeral procession was formed.

Old toothless grannies, unable to move their skinny bodies a long distance, waved Pishtika good-bye. Then, tears overcame these old souls clothed in black, knowing that their time to go is not far away. At the end of the procession a cow-drawn wagon was picking up the bodies that in the agony of alcohol poisoning couldn't walk any more. Surprisingly, even our Pater Malek was travelling in this soul saver. Pishtika's heavenly express was very slow, to accommodate the tired people who'd spent the night in booze and sin. After a long march in the warm day they were happy to see the open grave.

⊚⊚⊚⊚⊚⊚⊚⊚⊚⊚⊚⊚⊚⊚⊚⊚⊚⊚⊚⊚⊚⊚⊚⊚⊚⊚⊚⊚⊚⊚⊚⊚⊚

Vajolin

De gipsi, kolet in de hri from de taun bar, pleet Pishtikas feveret chardash. Dei so him stil laik dirigent and hi vos onli sol in St. Jelena vit dei vos rili klos. Old gipsi Laci, det sorvaiv as femos vajolina plejer Janoshi Bachi, orderet tu ol member of orkestra tu bi de best det dei kud bi. And plei dei did. De morener vek ab, and auer pater Malek olmos denc vit greni Hlivovec an de sait of de grev. Onli laut protesting of a pipel stapet des.

Ven de chip cros was pushet intu de erd pipel start retrning dei homs. Pishta vos olveis remembert, and vit him his foni ending. In taun vos gulash srvt and evrivan vos der, onli de Orel bachika, grendedushkin Sablanich and, an sopreist of meni, as belavet Malek. Ven de gosop vos krainting dei tongs for risen, Emilko and mi nju det der vos a geim tu finish. Frst ven evrivan als vos egsostet dosing in de shedos of dei greps det kaver evri jard, spreding over chip vuden kostrakshen eraund de haus, vi soet pater Malek kaming hom svering laik a satan.

"Dir lord is des so mach tu vish from ju, dont kol

Gypsies, called in a hurry from the town bar, played Pishtika's favourite chardash. They still thought of him as their conductor and he was the only soul in St. Helena with whom they were really close. The old gypsy Laci, that survived our famous violin player Janoshi Bachi, ordered all the members of the orchestra to be the best they could be. And play they did. The mourners woke up, and our Pater Malek almost danced with Granny Hlivovec on the site of the grave. Only loud protests from the people stopped them.

When the cheap cross was pushed into the earth, people started returning to their homes.

Pishta was always remembered, and with him his funny ending. In town, goulash was served and everyone was there except Orel Bachika, Grandeduchkin Sablanich, and to the surprise of many, our beloved Malek. When the gossips were grinding their tongues for a reason, Emilko and I knew that there was a game to finish. When everyone else was exhausted and dozing in the shadows of the grapevines that covered every yard, spreading over cheap wooden structures around the houses, we saw Pater Malek going home swearing like Satan.

"Dear lord, is it to much to wish from you that you don't call

Marijan Megla

noubadi in jor heven ven I plei de kart! Bikos I am sik and taet tu lus, I am sik and taet tu bi robt from det tu huligan. Plis lord encer mi! Or ju tu hev a snuz?"

De rest of a somer pest in vork. Taun gosop iven aktiv an des metar simstu bi anebel tu faund eni vrong duing in Pishtikas det. It vos in let fol ven de kveshchen retrn tu as sols vans egen. In taim of brning slivovica, vich kud bi rili peinfol, voching dos dei drink hr vorm from de kaper destilir boiler, lusing dej hepinis or stamaks. Long naits bai vorm destilir devais and never ending soplai of bus, meket iven as sols tu detektivs, redi to krek de Pishtikas misteries letct auer of erdli laif.

Dei traet des teori an den des or sam ader, bat olveis vos samting mising. Dei iven ask de grenmamichka vai de hel Pishtika vos gast in his anderver an his det, bat shi olveis faund sam risen not tu explen.

Des kaming kold vinter bring ol pipel tu de grenmamichkas haus tu plik hr feders. It is a vork presrvt mosli for vumen bad de gais shod ab tu. It vos anjuzuli

e e e e e e e e e e e e e e e e e e e e e e e e e e e e e e e e e e e e

anybody into your heaven when I'm playing cards! Because I am sick and tired of losing. I am sick and tired of being robbed by those two hooligans. Please lord, answer me! Or are you too having a snooze?"

The rest of the summer passed in work. The town gossips still active on the matter seemed unable to find any wrong-doing in Pishtika's death. It was in late fall when the question returned to our people once again, in the time of burning slivovica, which could be really painful, watching those that drank it warm from the copper distiller boiler, losing their happiness or their stomachs. Long nights by the warm distiller device and the never-ending supply of booze made even our people into detectives, ready to crack the mystery of Pishtika's last hour of earthly life.

They tried this theory and then this or some other, but something was always missing. They even asked the granny why the hell Pishtika was just in his underwear at his death, but she always found some reason not to explain.

The coming of cold winter sent all the people to the granny's house to pluck her feathers. It is work reserved mostly for women but the guys showed up too. It was an unusual

trnab of a pipel for des emaunt of feders. Des nait mas bi trut spoken, or evriting fergoten. Dei tok eraund de teibel, ebaud pigs or kaus, ebaut normal deli laif. Bad ven evar sambadi spendet litel mor als juzuli an dei meting behevju, old greni chench de tema. Gedart kraut vos lusing de betel. De old greni dont bag an eniting. Laik a hevi veit bokser, vich refjus tu giv ab in 13 raund, shi stil ganping in des congrigeshen ring. In des lo panch fait, shi simstu hes onli van gop for det ivning — fiding and komforting as bleset pater Malek. An van point hi vas rili eshemt an des fani atenchen.

"Mai dir belavet grenmamichka Hlivovec," sed hi klining his hends in vait kichen reg. "It is nais det ju vori ebaut mi, bat, I hev no nid tu it so mach."

"O mai bjutifol pater Malek, onien kan du mirikals bai a men in jor eg," sed de grenmamichka, softli smailing. "Men is laik a bul ... vot ju put intuet, ju gedet from et," tok shi, teping him an his bir beli. "Lord blesed jor badi, evri paund ovet."

turnout of people for that amount of feathers. This night, the truth must be spoken or everything will be forgotten. They talked around the table, about pigs or cows, about normal daily life. But whenever somebody spent a little more time than usual talking about mating behaviour, the old granny changed the topic. The gathered crowd was losing the battle. The old granny didn't budge on anything. Like a heavyweight boxer who refused to give up in 13 rounds, she was still jumping around in this congregational ring. In this low-punch fight she seemed to have only one job for the evening — feeding and comforting our blessed Pater Malek. At one point he was really ashamed about all this fawning attention.

"My dear beloved Grandmamichka Hlivovec," he said, cleaning his hands on a white kitchen rag. "It is nice that you worry about me, but, I have no need for so much of it."

"Oh, my beautiful Pater Malek, an onion can do miracles for a man of your age," said the grandmamichka, softly smiling. "A man is like a bowl — what you put into it, you get out of it," she said, tapping him on his beer belly. "The lord blessed your body, every pound of it."

Marijan Megla

"Bad grenmamichka!" protesting de old grendedushkin Sablanich. "Hau kam ju ar not konsrn over mai flesh?" "Vel, in jor eg, evrivan shud no kud not bi akspektet mirekals. Iven beg of oniens kud not chencht nating," encer de smailing grenmamichka.

"Bad I am olmos de seim eg laik auer Pishtika, god giv him best ples in heven," sed de old grended, smeling viktori. Sailenc strak de rum. Evrivan vanet tu no gast van ting. Vot hepend des krushel nait in de samer in des rum? Auer lavli greni faineli sorendet. Vit tirs in hr ais, shi nit bisaid de pater Malek redi tu edmit hr mistek.

An des inportant dei ven auer pur Pishtika dai, shi kud hev faineli lital lav from him, tu kolekt samting bek for hr gud gulash, hr mauntens of kukis, hr voris for him. Nachurali, after ten jers of sekshual femen, she vos lital tu vaild prehaps ... anpeshent. Bad befor ever samting hepen hi chench his kolor and grab his hart. Befor shi hev ol hr klos anet, and kud bring help, hi vos oredi daing. Nau shi hes des shemfol task tu tel des kongregeshen det shi is stil a

---

"But Grandmamichka!" protested old Grandeduchkin Sablanich. "How come you are not concerned over my flesh?"

"Well, at your age, everyone should know you can't expect miracles. Even a bag of onions couldn't change anything," answered the smiling grandmamichka.

"But I am almost the same age as our Pishtika, God give him the best place in heaven," said the old granddad, smelling victory.

Silence struck the room. Everyone wanted to know just one thing. What happened that crucial night in the summer in this room? Our lovely granny finally surrendered. With tears in her eyes, she knelt beside Pater Malek ready to admit her mistake.

On the important day when our poor Pishtika died, she was finally going to get a little love from him, to collect something back for her good goulash, her mountains of cookies, her worries for him. Naturally, after ten years of sexual famine she was a little wild perhaps ... impatient. But before anything happened his colour changed and he grabbed his heart. Before she could get her clothes on and could bring help, he was already dying. Now she had the shameful task of telling this congregation that she is still a jang vumen, vit srten nid. Big lef brstet in de rum. Plikt feders flaing eraund laik sam konfeti an jang merich. Iven auer pater Malek kuden sev his fes of enormes lef. Pipel living, and dei lef ju kud hir an de strit. Onli as pater Malek stei over tu kul as vido daun.

Bed tongs teling det auer prist liv des haus frst erli in de moning, living rili hepi vido an hr haus sters.

Gosop teling det der vos natin tu be eshemt foret. As grema vas gast hevili blest. Bad de old Sablanich tel de vorld det hi never hiret a noisier blesing in ol his laif, end hi vos old.

⊚⊚⊚⊚⊚⊚⊚⊚⊚⊚⊚⊚⊚⊚⊚⊚⊚⊚⊚⊚⊚⊚⊚⊚⊚⊚⊚⊚⊚⊚⊚⊚⊚⊚⊚⊚⊚

young woman, with certain needs.

Loud laughter broke out in the room. Plucked feathers flew around like confetti at a young marriage. Even Pater Malek couldn't save his face from an enormous laugh. People were leaving, and you could hear their laughter in the street. Only our Pater Malek stayed over to cool down our widow.

Bad tongues tell that our priest left the house in the first morning light, leaving a really happy widow on her house stairs.

The gossips tell that there was nothing to be ashamed about. Our grandma was just heavily blessed. But old Sablanich told the world that he'd never heard a noisier blessing in all his life, and he was old.

Dei vos gled det moning ven I sho ab tu voluntering in lokal ol foks hom. Old Vasja, Tatar, from got fergoten an des vorld, vos an ranpeig. Enibadi hu nju det temperament felo tuket kaver. Iven de strong Agnes, de nursing eid, diden der open his dor. Tu meni taim oredi de hiros bi gritet vit flaing obgekt.

"It is inposible tu dei tu meket pis vit him," tok tu mi vorit Agnes, traing tu kech mai spid of voking.

"So, ... vot hepen? Vot is vrong?" ask I ven vi bot kam tu his dor.

"I dont hev eni aidia. Hi gast start tu tro eniting an as, and vi ran for kaver," sed pel Agnes nervesli.

Vasja vos grei Tatar from siti Kasan an de Volga. His rili neim noubadi kud pronaunct, so vi ol setelt for Vasja. After long negociation, he faineli akceptet det. Long taim ego hi maste bi a veri strong men. Dos deis his badi shrinkt tu boni strakshen, klodet in

---

They were glad that morning when I showed up to volunteer in the local old folks home. Vasja, the old Tartar forgotten by God in this world, was on a rampage. Anybody who knew that temperamental fellow took cover. Even strong Agnes, the nursing aide, didn't dare open his door. Too many times already have heroes been greeted with flying objects.

"It is impossible today to make peace with him," said worried Agnes to me, trying to keep up with my speed of walking.

"So, what happened? What's wrong?" I asked when we both came to his door.

"I don't have any idea. He just started to throw anything at us, and we ran for cover," said pale Agnes nervously.

Vasja was a grey Tartar from the city of Kasan on the Volga. His real name nobody could pronounce, so we all settled for Vasja. After a long negotiation, he finally accepted that. A long time ago he must have been a very strong man. These days his body had shrunk to a bony structure clothed in

Vajolin

KRAING BALALAIKA

vrinkels. His stabernhait vos femos. Meni of inmeids beliv det onli det kip him a laif.

"Hei Vasja. Its mi, jor frend. Dont ju no mi eni mor?" sed I, opening de dor. Sliper gast mis mai hed.

"Ei, ju old Tatar, said ven ju fait a men vit aut vepen?"

"Oooo ... I am sori. I diden si ju," tok de hef klodet men aut his vilcher.

"So. Vot is det ol ebaudet?" ask I, pushing de Agnes evei, vich gladli desapir in long holovei.

"I tel ju, mai jang brader," tok nervesli old gai. "Dei tuket mai anderver vans egen. And laik juzuli, dei diden retrnet. Vot shud I du? Siting in des godlos vilcher neket? Lisening an shemfol lefing of old grenis ven hanger push mi in kafeteria?" tok hi medli, jusing his big heri hends.

I sit bisaid him tu eksplen him hau is isi tu lus samting so inportant laik his blesed anderver. Dei lostet probebli not atenchenli, and if dei faundet dei retrnet tu him. Bisaid, dei olveis ofer him a nju anderver, so hi rili dident nit tu bi vori, in taim ven hi go it his lanch hi

⊚⊚⊚⊚⊚⊚⊚⊚⊚⊚⊚⊚⊚⊚⊚⊚⊚⊚⊚⊚⊚⊚⊚⊚⊚⊚⊚⊚⊚⊚⊚⊚⊚⊚⊚⊚

wrinkles. His stubbornness was famous. Many of the inmates believed that only that kept him alive.

"Hey Vasja. It's me, your friend. Don't you know me any more?" I said, opening the door. A slipper just missed my head.

"Hey, you old Tartar, since when do you fight a man without a weapon?"

"Ooooh ... I am sorry. I didn't see you," said the half-clothed man from his wheelchair.

"So. What is this all about?" I asked, pushing away Agnes, who gladly disappeared into the long hallway.

"I'll tell you, my young brother," said the nervous old guy. "They took my underwear once again. And like usual, they didn't return it. What should I do? Sit in the godless wheelchair naked? Listen to the shameful laughing of old grannies when hunger pushes me into the cafeteria?" he said madly, using his big hairy hands.

I sat beside him to explain to him how it is easy to lose something so important as his blessed underwear. They lost it probably unintentionally, and if they found it they would return it to him. Besides, they always offer him new underwear, so he really didn't need to be worried — by the time he goes to eat his lunch he'll

⊚⊚⊚⊚⊚⊚⊚⊚⊚⊚⊚⊚⊚⊚⊚⊚⊚⊚⊚⊚⊚⊚⊚⊚⊚⊚⊚⊚⊚⊚⊚⊚⊚⊚⊚⊚

bi foli klost. I vos not shor if hi beliv mi det, bat endlis for nau, hi bi pisfol. It vos his juzuli autbrst of his enger, det hardli enibadi of personal kud andestan. Laik olvcis, after laudli kontenpleting over his problems, hi faineli kam daun. Als his ofer tu pis, hi gev mi an orang. Mosli de taim hi tuket det from kafeteria, haidinget in his kabert, onli for sacha okeshen.

Meni taim vi spend auers toking ebaut his and main homlend. Shor dei vos meni diferences, bat vot kip as tugeder vos as emigrant ekspirianc. Bisaid det I lav his balalaika, and lisen ebaut kantri det I never nju. Tu setisfai mi hi bi toking, miksing de trut vit his on vju, eksplening de politikal hepenings from des taim his on vei. It vos gut tu no hau ol des trobel taim soet van pur kerich draiver. An mai sopreis hi vos rait an meni plesis.

Samtaim, ven his artraitis erlau him, hi bi pleing his belavet balalaika. Iven his svoren enimis "nurses" engoet his mjusik. I remember ven mi and strong Agnes vos dencing an his mjsik. De hed nurs vos tenking det vi hev sam trobel vit

ⓔⓔⓔⓔⓔⓔⓔⓔⓔⓔⓔⓔⓔⓔⓔⓔⓔⓔⓔⓔⓔⓔⓔⓔⓔⓔⓔⓔⓔⓔⓔⓔⓔⓔⓔ

be fully clothed. I was not sure if he believed me, but at least for now he'd be peaceful. It was his usual outburst of anger that hardly any of the personnel could understand. Like always, after loudly contemplating his problems, he finally calmed down. As his peace offering, he gave me an orange. Most of the time he took them from the cafeteria, hiding them in his cupboard only for such an occasion.

Many times we spent hours talking about his and my homelands. Sure, there were many differences, but what kept us together was our immigrant experience. Besides, I loved his balalaika and hearing about a country that I never knew. To satisfy me he would be talking, mixing the truth with his own view, explaining the political happenings of that time his own way. It was good to know how all those troubled times were seen by one poor carriage driver. And to my surprise he was right in many places.

Sometimes, when his arthritis allowed him, he'd play his beloved balalaika. Even his sworn enemy nurses enjoyed his music. I remember when strong Agnes and I were dancing to his music. The head nurse was thinking that we had some trouble with

ⓔⓔⓔⓔⓔⓔⓔⓔⓔⓔⓔⓔⓔⓔⓔⓔⓔⓔⓔⓔⓔⓔⓔⓔⓔⓔⓔⓔⓔⓔⓔⓔⓔⓔⓔⓔⓔ

Vasja and shi kam tu help as. Siing as tu elefants dencing, shi goinet. I never soet Vasja mor hepi als den.

His balalaika vas laik a gitar vit tri strengs and draiengel vois boks. Shi vos hendelt from det grob gaent laik a vundet ai. Hi tel mi vans det I vos his best fren, bad tu rich de balalaika vos inposibel for mi. Shi vos antachebal for evri klining ledi, nurs, doktor. Preheps iven as belavet lord mas ask for his promishen tu plei onet. It vos old and inkredibli melodik, bildet vit grob bat laving hends. Shi vos hardli demicht if vi konsideret dengeresli tenper of hr master and long travel from Rashia.

Lisening tu his mjusik, I kud emegin his homlend. Vest forest, der for kilometers and kilometers strech ist of Volga, kavering lo hils befor Ural. Siet Vasja laik a jang boi, pleing his instrument. Kraud of pur sols dei gedert in e hri eraun him. Engoing vorm of his faer and his mjusik, dei dencet an pakt sno in der pur klos. Vasja heving a beter taim als his fader in stinki bar. Tja, ... him and his balalaika kud geder ol di pipel in shed of a big tris on bar properti, ver de vos veiding.

●⑤⑥⑤⑥⑤⑥⑤⑥⑤⑥⑤⑥⑤⑥⑤⑥⑤⑥⑤⑥⑤⑥⑤⑥⑤⑥⑤⑥⑤⑥⑤⑥⑤

Vasja and she came to help us. Seeing us two elephants dancing, she joined in. I never saw Vasja more happy than then.

His balalaika was like a guitar with three strings and a triangular voice-box. She was handled by that rough giant like a wounded eye. He told me once that I was his best friend, but to reach the balalaika was impossible for me. She was untouchable for every cleaning lady, nurse, doctor. Perhaps even our beloved lord must ask for his permission to play on it. It was old and incredibly melodic, built with rough but loving hands. She was hardly damaged, if we consider the dangerous temper of her master and the long travel from Russia.

Listening to his music, I could imagine his homeland. Vast forest that for kilometres and kilometres stretched east of the Volga covered the low hills before the Urals. See Vasja as a young boy, playing his instrument. A crowd of poor souls gather in a hurry around him. Enjoying the warmth of his fire and his music, they dance on packed snow in their poor clothes. Vasja was having a better time than his father in the stinky bar. Tcha! Him and his balalaika could gather all the people in the shelter of the big trees on the bar property, where they were waiting.

●⑥⑤⑥⑤⑥⑤⑥⑤⑥⑤⑥⑤⑥⑤⑥⑤⑥⑤⑥⑤⑥⑤⑥⑤⑥⑤⑥⑤⑥⑤⑥⑤⑥

Vasja end his fader vos transporting tinber for Kasan fektoris. Tu ern inaf tu fid dem self, horsis and rest of a femili, dei vorket evri singel dei. Hi beskraib mi soft rods karvt vit hevi vuden vils. Tu sols dak tugeder benit de hevi blanket, in endlos reni nait. Taet horsis tim det desapir in on fog in kold monings, living, laik stum vidnise, stimi hors apels an de rod. His fader, det rolt in de ship skins an vet raf tinber, sliping mosli de taim. Hi reaktet onli ven hi nidet de ader badel of votka, or tim stap. Hi bi draiving onli in kold vinter ven paks of hangri volvs folo de vegen tu klosli.

It is olmos seks tausend kilometer in betvin his and main homlend. So meni simulariti det I olmos emegin tu lisen mai on grended. Shor vi dont hev a volfs and tu log vinters, bad der a kerich dreiver det akt de seim, det transport de seim, sorvaiving an smokt beken and bus.

Vans I vanet tu tep his balalaika mjusik, for lisening et hom. It bi nais tu kipet samting from des old gaij, der so speshal is hir an preri flet. Strong Agnes and mi

⁂

Vasja and his father were transporting timber for Kasan factories. To earn enough to feed themselves, their horses, and the rest of the family, they worked every single day. He described to me soft roads carved with heavy wooden wheels. Two souls tucked together beneath the heavy blanket in the endless rainy night. A tired team of horses that disappear in their own fog on cold mornings, leaving, like dumb witnesses, steamy horse apples on the road. His father, rolled in sheepskins on the wet rough timber, sleeps most of the time. He reacts only when he needs another bottle of vodka, or if the team stops. He would drive only in cold winter when packs of hungry wolves followed the wagon too closely.

It is almost 6,000 kilometres between his and my homeland. So many similarities that I almost imagine I'm listening to my own granddad. Sure, we don't have wolves and too-long winters, but there are carriage drivers that act the same, that transport the same, surviving on smoked bacon and booze.

Once, I wanted to tape his balalaika music, to listen to at home. It would be nice to keep something from this old guy, who is so special here on the prairie flatlands. Strong Agnes and I nidet olmost tri vik tu put him in gud mud tu plei. Faineli, vi vos redi and hi viling tu du des. Pur Agnes brod him his ekstra strong kofi gast tu plis him. Bat, vi fergot Vasjas strong oposishen tu evriting vot vos elektrik.

"Vot is det boks ... der?" ask him traing tu rich him from his blesed vilcher.

"Det is de teip. Ju no, for storing jor vois," encr I, not ekspekting eni revolushen.

"O svit Ala! Ju tenk I am sam kain of bladi pikel, det ju kan slais saitveis and chok in solti viniger for a hefen jer?" jal hi, biting vit his enormes voking stik. I menagt tu sev de teip, bad maikrofon lain vos gan. Vi bot sturm for sefti of holovei, in vich gedert de ernoit meids. Left alon hi vos svering and benging eraund. I remember mai maikrofon. I van tu open de dor, bad Agnes stap mi.

"I hev jor maikrofon! I tuk him befor as heroikel deparcher."

"O tenkju so mach. I tod I lost him."

After auer of negociashen, vich kost as bod plenty of nervs, hi bring his juzuali ofer of pis. Tu as vos given stolen

needed almost three weeks to put him in a good mood to play. Finally, we were ready and he willing to do this. Poor Agnes brought him his extra strong coffee just to please him. But we forgot Vasja's strong opposition to everything that was electric.

"What is that box ... there?" he asked, trying to reach it from his blessed wheelchair.

"That is the tape. You know, for storing your voice," I answered, not expecting any revolution.

"Oh, sweet Allah! You think I am some kind of bloody pickle that you can slice sideways and choke in salty vinegar for half a year," he yelled, beating with his enormous walking stick.

I managed to save the tape, but the microphone line was gone. We both stormed for the safety of the hallway, in which gathered the annoyed maids. Left alone he was swearing and banging around. I remembered my microphone. I wanted to open the door, but Agnes stopped me.

"I have your microphone. I took it before our heroic departure."

"Oh, thank you so much. I thought I'd lost it."

After an hour of negotiation, which cost us both plenty of nerves, he brought his usual offer of peace. To us was given stolen frut from kafeteria. It vos oredi let, bat vi disaidet tu tep him nau. Ven vi finishet, ol ader residenc vos oredi sliping. I promis tu bring de storet Vasja mjusik sam ader dei. Vasja justu sei hi vos onli fortin ven his fjucher als kucher kranbelt. Van hevi vinter, de sno blisard after sno blisard strak his eria. Rods der vos gast klint vos sun blakt vit dip sno benks. Meni taims dos deis, horsis stak tu dei belis in de sno. Taet, anebel tu muv hevi lod, dei stap. Noing det volfs ar not veri far, dei shavelet sno tu fri dem. Vet, hevi sveting, frising an kold tinber tu de nekst sno benk vos tumach for his fader. His helt, oredi erodet from konstant drinking, koleps. Short befor Kasan, hi develop namonia and sun after hi dai. De femili fol apart. His mader tuk tu jang kidc and muv klos tu de fektori. His older sister vos meid bai rich lend oner, vich tuk Vasja als kerich dreiver for his doter.

Anas nobel frends laik a jang Vasili. Hi vos chip interteiner vit his balalaika. Bisaid det hi vos a gud dreiver, an vich ju kud kauntet et eni taim. Ven dei tuket long

fruit from the cafeteria. It was already late, but we decided to tape him now. When we finished, all other residents were already sleeping. I promised to bring the stored Vasja music some other day.

Vasja used to say he was only fourteen when his future as a teamster crumbled. One heavy winter, snow blizzard after snow blizzard struck his area. Roads that were just cleaned were soon blanketed with deep snowbanks. Many times those days the horses stuck to their bellies in the snow. Tired, unable to move their heavy load, they stopped. Knowing that wolves weren't very far off, they shoveled snow to free them. Wet,

heavily sweating, freezing on cold timber to the next snow bank was too much for his father. His health, already eroded from constant drinking, collapsed. Shortly before Kasan he developed pneumonia and soon after he died. The family fell apart. His mother took the two young kids and moved close to the factory. His older sister was a maid to a rich land owner, who took Vasja as carriage driver for his daughter.

Anna's noble friends liked young Vasili. He was a cheap entertainer with his balalaika. Besides, he was a good driver, on whom you could count at any time. When they took a long distanc raid tu nekst taun dei toket ebaud streng vorld, vorld det vos so bjutifol det pur Vasja kud hardli emegin. For instanc, vorm ailends an vich living neket pipel. Der is never kold, and dei dont soet ever de sno. Dei toket ebaut kantris det hev mach mor fektoris als Kasan. Pipel der hev fest trens det kud bring ju tu eni ples in de hri. Dei toket ebaut pur det van tu hev dei on haus, skul, fridem of spich, vot ever det min. Tu meni taims a laut diskashen vos entflemt in betvin his pasinger.

"Rashia is chenching mai pipel. Auer zar shud du samting nau ven hi kud, befor dos vet horsis ran lus and kil evrivan," justo jal Anas fader. Mosli of dem diden beliv him, or diden ker. Mosli de taim de badel of shanpein endet det diskashen. Et frst, Vasja diden andestand a vort from det. Vots min a fridem of spich? Hu de hel van tu hev his on haus? For instanc, vot ken hi du vit his on horsis? Dei nidet barli tu bi strong, bat hi hev nan. So hu van tu bi ... fri?

Sun an his traveling hi diskaver les forchinet. Dei gedert bisaid de rods, belo de briges. In auskrts of sitis ver de

⦿⦿⦿⦿⦿⦿⦿⦿⦿⦿⦿⦿⦿⦿⦿⦿⦿⦿⦿⦿⦿⦿⦿⦿⦿⦿⦿⦿⦿⦿⦿⦿⦿

distance ride to the next down they would talk about a strange world, a world that was so beautiful that poor Vasja could hardly imagine it. For instance, warm islands on which lived naked people. There it's never cold and they don't ever see snow. They talked about countries that have many more factories than Kasan. People there have fast trains that could take you any place in a hurry. They talked about the poor who wanted to have their own house, school, freedom of speech, whatever that meant. Too many times a loud discussion flared between his passengers.

"Russia is changing, my people.

Our czar should do something now when he can, before those wet horses run loose and kill everyone," Anna's father used to yell. Most of them didn't believe him, or didn't care. Most of the time a bottle of champagne ended the discussion. At first, Vasja didn't understand a word of it. What does freedom of speech mean? Who the hell wants to have his own house? For instance, what can he do with his own horses? They need barley to be strong, but he had none. So who wants to be ... free?

Soon, as he travelled, he discovered the less fortunate. They gathered beside the roads, below the bridges. In the outskirts of the cities,

⦿⦿⦿⦿⦿⦿⦿⦿⦿⦿⦿⦿⦿⦿⦿⦿⦿⦿⦿⦿⦿⦿⦿⦿⦿⦿⦿⦿⦿⦿⦿⦿⦿

hanger and kolera vos kiling tugedar. Hi njuet det no hjumen bin kud teket sacha biting. Hi disaidet tu liv. Onli for fju jers, inaf tu si de vorld. Seving evri peni hi gast berli menagt tu eskep. Vorld det ol dos rich gais beskraibet als bjutifol vos dol ... pur ... and brutal. Hi kuden go hom, and dei dont vanet him der.

Remembering his emigreshe vek olveis mai on ekspirianc. Dos deis hi remembert onli long deis an de si. Hi kudent remember, iven vit mai help, vich rut he vos akcheli travel.

Hmmm. In betvin his and main kaming in des kantri diden chench mach. Dos deis ju kud dai an ship from kolera, des deis ju daing veiding an jor trn. Dei teket taim tu openet jor fail. Hau ken klerk det hes ol sekjuriti in de vorld andestan jor nervis tok besaid his desk? Vot is a dei ... jer ... or iven dasent jers for des prson? Nating. Hi never vos alon, vit aut eni fjucher, not vante in de kantri ver hi veiding an des lital stemp det min so mach. Jes, sam of as daing veiding an visas, promises det tuket hef mens laif tu kam tru. Vi njuet hau isi prei vi ar for ol korts, lojers,

@@

hunger and cholera were killing together. He knew that no human being could take such a beating. He decided to leave. Only for a few years, enough to see the world. Saving every penny, he just barely managed to escape. The world that all those rich guys described as beautiful was dull ... poor ... and brutal. He couldn't go home, and they didn't want him there.

Remembering his immigration always awakened my own experience. Those days he remembered only the long days on the sea. He couldn't remember, even with my help, which route he actually travelled.

Hmmm. In between his and my coming to this country, not much changed. Those days you could die on ship from cholera, these days you'd die waiting for your turn. They take time to open your file. How can a clerk who has all the security in the world understand your nervous talk beside his desk? What is a day ... a year ... or even a dozen years to this person? Nothing. He has never been alone, without any future, not wanted in the country where he was waiting for this little stamp that means so much. Yes, some of us die waiting for visas and promises that take half a man's life to come true. We know what easy prey we are for courts, lawyers,

@@

inshurances. Brnet so meni taim vi dont trast noubadi eni mor. Vi simstu henging an litel tings det never lai tu as, det hev a plesent luk, vois, and vi gardet det vit auer laivs. Vasja never meri. Dei vos tu or tri svithart, bad nating dip inaf. Vork. Seving. Det ol vot hi njuet. Sardenli hi vos tu olt and tu lesi tu chench eniting. Samtaim I tenk hi si in mi his san, meibi gast him self. Hu rili nos?

During det samer I vork an paiplain, muving from ples tu ples. It pest olmost tri mants ven I kam tu visit him. Hi vanet olveis tu no vot I vork, ver. Hi lavet ven I teling him mai problems an vork. Preheps hi rili diden andestand mai vork, bat hi shor vos a gud lisener. I van tu sho him mai kolekshen of his mjusik his on vois. De strong Agnes vanet tu sei mi samting, bat I diden stap tu lisen. Probebli sam gok det goin eraund for sam deis nau, and shi faineli hrt him.

In Vasjas rum vos sam ader old gai.

"Ver is mai Vasja?" ask I pel skeri Agnes.

"Vel, ..." start she, luking for vorts. "He is gon. I min hi dai gast lets vik," she sei.

ⓢⓢⓢⓢⓢⓢⓢⓢⓢⓢⓢⓢⓢⓢⓢⓢⓢⓢⓢⓢⓢⓢⓢⓢⓢⓢⓢⓢⓢⓢ

insurance. Burned so many times, we don't trust anybody any more. We seem to hang onto the little things that never lie to us, that have a pleasant look, voice, and we guard that with our lives.

Vasja never married. There were two or three sweethearts, but nothing deep enough. Work. Saving. That was all that he knew. Suddenly he was too old and too lazy to change anything. Sometimes I think he saw in me his son, maybe just himself. Who really knows?

During that summer I worked on the pipeline, moving from place to place. Almost three months had passed when I came to visit him. He always wanted to know what I worked at and where. He loved it when I told him my problems at work. Perhaps he really didn't understand my work, but he sure was a good listener. I wanted to show him my collection of his music in his own voice. Strong Agnes wanted to say something to me, but I didn't stop to listen. Probably some joke that was going around for days now and she'd finally heard it.

In Vasja's room was some other old guy.

"Where is my Vasja?" I asked pale, scared Agnes.

"Well ...," she started, looking for words. "He is gone. I mean he died just last week," she said.

ⓢⓢⓢⓢⓢⓢⓢⓢⓢⓢⓢⓢⓢⓢⓢⓢⓢⓢⓢⓢⓢⓢⓢⓢⓢⓢⓢⓢⓢⓢ

Marijan Megla

"Demet ... " I trnet hom. Preheps I diden van tu krai der. Vi ol akspektet det hi bi no mor long, and nau ven es hepen I kud not beliv.

Gud strong Agnes, olveis peshent farm grl, menagt tu stap mi. She tek mi for mai hend laik hr kid and dregt tu de lital storich rum. An dasti teibel vos siting a beg of "stolen" frut, ofer for pis. Besait de beg vos his belavet balalaika.

"Hi liv det tu ju," sed de Agnes, vaiping hr ais.

I tuk de balalaika hom, drink hol badel of dem votka, and lisen tu his mjusik an teip.

"Dammit ..." I turned home. Perhaps I didn't want to cry there. We all expected that he wouldn't last much longer, but now that it had happened I could not believe it.

Good strong Agnes, always the patient farm girl, managed to stop me. She took me by my hand like her kid and dragged me to the little storage room. On a dusty table was sitting a bag of "stolen" fruit, an offering of peace. Beside the bag was his beloved balalaika.

"He left that to you," said Agnes, wiping her eyes.

I took the balalaika home, drank a whole bottle of damn vodka, and listened to his music on the tape.

Vajolin

Old Aldo stap for sekend befor hi ringt de bel of des vumens hostel. It vos kold vinter dei and sanset vos erli in de dei. Skai skrepers in Edmonton daun taun, gast kapel blok evei, vere fol in lait. For him vos olveis fascineting des invisibal border, det divaidet det siti. An van sait is de prosperiti, hop — and an ader sait, anforchinet. His laif vos laik det bloks of old hausis klos tu det lain. Hi vos so klos tu sekses, bat bed lak stap him. Ven evr hi stend hir, befor dos hevi hostel dors, hi rmember his vaif and doter. Dei dai jers ego. His dotar misforchin brod him tu des dor, and hi praktikli never left.

Sister Ana vos opening de dor. Shi is mach mor janger den him, and olveis so konsrn abaut him. Aldo vos lital let, and shi vos vorit. Tenks lord hi chench endlis his vait shrt.

"O-o-o. Sinjor Aldo! End I tot ju hev fergoten," chaklt she, opening de dor vaid tu liv korpulent men insait.

Old Aldo stopped for a second before he rang the bell of the women's hostel. It was a cold winter day and the sunset was early. The skyscrapers in Edmonton's downtown, just a couple of blocks away, were full of lights. He was always fascinated with this invisible border that divided the city. On one side is prosperity, hope — and on the other, the unfortunate. His life was like the blocks of old houses close to that line. He was so close to success, but bad luck stopped him. Whenever he stands here, before those heavy hostel doors, he remembers his wife and daughter. They died years ago. His daughter's misfortune had brought him to this door, and he practically never left.

Sister Anna was opening the door. She is much younger than him, and always so concerned about him. Aldo was a little late and she was worried. Thank the lord he'd at least changed into his white shirt.

"Ohhhh. Signor Aldo! And I thought you had forgotten," she chuckled, opening the door wide to let the corpulent man inside.

"Sister Ana, hir is de lital samting for ju," sed Aldo giving hr van chip ros, meking litel nik.

"O sinjor Aldo, tenkju. It is veri nais of ju," sed de nan, teking from him his big vinter gaket. "Dei veiding oredi."

Aldo tun his mandolina and step intu fol kafeteria. Vel non odor of chip prfjum mikst vit fud of a dei veidet for him. De smel chencht bai evri steps. Samtaim hi kud deskaver veri plesent indivigual, samtaim a tres of damp andervers. Fresh pjuk of akoholikerin, or strong stank of filti klos. For him vos det lital kafeteria laik a peshcher, fol of diferent flauers. Sam of dem viselt an hin, or giving him dei hends. Aders kud not kontrol dei hends, taching him his legs, giv a slep an his bam or bek. Dei giving him de kis, taching his mandolina, korekt his kolor of a shrt. Dei pul him an dei nis, korektet his herstail. Konplening over les atenchen. Dei are his maders, gelos vaivs, doters, grendoters. Him self is probebli for dem old prvers men, laver, lost dedi or brader.

⊚⊚⊚⊚⊚⊚⊚⊚⊚⊚⊚⊚⊚⊚⊚⊚⊚⊚⊚⊚⊚⊚⊚⊚⊚⊚⊚⊚⊚⊚⊚⊚⊚⊚⊚⊚

"Sister Anna, here is a little something for you," said Aldo, giving her one cheap rose, making a slight genuflection.

"Oh, Signor Aldo, thank you. That's very nice of you," said the nun, taking his big winter jacket from him. "They're waiting already."

Aldo tuned his mandolin and stepped into the full cafeteria. The well-known odour of cheap perfume mixed with the food of the day awaited him. The smell changed with every step. Sometimes he would discover a very pleasant individual, sometimes a trace of damp underwear. Fresh puke of an alcoholic or strong stink of filthy clothes. To him, this little cafeteria was like a pasture full of different flowers. Some of them whistled at him, or gave him their hands. Others couldn't control their hands, touching his legs, giving him a slap on his bum or back. They gave him a kiss, touched his mandolin, commented on his shirt colour. They pulled him to his knees and corrected his hairstyle. Complained over his lack of attention. They are his mothers, jealous wives, daughters, granddaughters. To them he is probably an old perverse man, a lover, a lost daddy or brother.

Hi stap in midel of a rum. Evrivan is kvaet. Letst naivs and forks slo daun ven hi start tu plei his feveret lav song, "O Mari". Meni of his grls singing sailend vit. Long taim ego ven hi gast start tu plei for dos grls, det destrb him. Tu dei hi faundet det les efenziv. Hi iven engoin tu lisen vot des pur sols meking from his plein Italian. Sam of dem desfigeret his vorts so bedli det hi lef an de vei hom. Meni singing nais, olmos prfekt.

Ven de melodi progreset, and his strong tenor rich evri korner of des haus, meni of dem kvaet daun not iven iting. Aldo never faund aut vot dei akcheli tenking in des moments. Preheps dei drim from old deis. Long abendet svithart, frst lav. Fju vere rich long taim ego and kud engoet long travels. Van older ledi visit de Itali. Aldo never faund aut if dei kud emegin vit help of his mjusik, vorm nero strits, kraudet markets, fisher bots kaming hevi lodet in port. Blaind strit senger, de aroma of ekxpreso mikset vit solti er of a si. Smel of fresh kukt pasta, parmesan, risoto, tometo. Hmm, "O Mari, O Mari".

He stopped in the middle of the room. Everyone was quiet. The last knives and forks slowed down as he started to play his favourite love song, "Oh Marie". Many of his girls sang along quietly. A long time ago when he'd just started to play for those girls, that disturbed him. Today he finds it less offensive. He even enjoys listening to what these poor souls could make of his plain Italian. Some of them disfigured his words so badly that he'd laugh on the way home. Many sang nicely, almost perfect.

When the melody progressed, and his strong rich tenor reached every corner of the house, many of them quieted down, not even eating. Aldo never found out what they were actually thinking in those moments. Perhaps they dreamed of the old days. A long abandoned sweetheart, first love. A few were rich a long time ago and could enjoy long trips. One older lady had visited Italy. Aldo never found if they could imagine from his music warm narrow streets, crowded markets, fishing boats coming heavily-loaded into port. Blind street singers, the aroma of espresso mixed with the salty sea air. Smell of fresh cooked pasta, parmesan, rizoto, tomatoes. Hmmm, "Oh Marie, Oh Marie".

Det melodi bring him so meni memoris bek. Hi justo sing det serenada tu his lavli Maria.

Tja. Dei vere jang. Jers of peshent lav, kises in dark entrences of old hausis. Et sims det iven a big voren aut stons an nero strits vere fol of romantik. Itali is bildet for peshent lavers. If ju in Itali dont fol in lav samting is rong vit ju. Dei taun vos smol, vit aut eni indastri, or prosperiti. Shor, dei vos hils, greibs, restorans, bat it vos not inaf tu bring de femili ab.

Dei merit and sun after his doter Graciela vos boren. Marija vos never veri strong grl and rekavering after aksepshenali hart brt fel hr hard. Preheps ader klaima, beter fud kud du mirikals. Dei muv tu Germani, Svicerland, bek and fort kros de borders of Europa vorking bot als sisonal kuk and veitres. Graciela vos ten ven dei eraivt in Canada. Sun dei muvet in lital old haus. It vos olmos laik a mirikal. Dei bot hevet gop, and Graciela vos hepi chaild. Hu kud prodiktet det sun after Marija bi det?

Ven "Torna a Sorento" kam elong, meni of dos broken

⊚⊚⊚⊚⊚⊚⊚⊚⊚⊚⊚⊚⊚⊚⊚⊚⊚⊚⊚⊚⊚⊚⊚⊚⊚⊚⊚⊚⊚⊚⊚⊚⊚⊚⊚⊚⊚⊚⊚

That melody brought back so many memories. He used to sing that serenade to his lovely Maria.

Tcha. They were young. Years of passionate love, kisses in dark entrances of old houses. It seemed that even the big worn stones of the narrow streets were full of romance. Italy was built for passionate lovers. If you are in Italy and don't fall in love something is wrong with you. Their town was small, without any industry or prosperity. Sure, there were hills, grapes, restaurants, but it wasn't enough to bring up a family.

They married and soon after his daughter Graziella was born. Maria was never a very strong girl and recovering after an especially difficult birth was hard for her. Perhaps a different climate and better food could do miracles. They moved to Germany, to Switzerland, back and forth across the borders of Europe working as seasonal cook and waitress. Graziella was ten when they arrived in Canada. Soon they moved into a little old house. It was almost like a miracle. They both had a job and Graziella was a happy child. Who could predict that soon after Maria would be dead?

When "Torna a Sorrento" came along, many of those broken

⊚⊚⊚⊚⊚⊚⊚⊚⊚⊚⊚⊚⊚⊚⊚⊚⊚⊚⊚⊚⊚⊚⊚⊚⊚⊚⊚⊚⊚⊚⊚⊚⊚⊚⊚⊚⊚⊚⊚

Marijan Megla

personaliti draet dei ais. Meibi is de vei hau de melodi sloli vorking hr vei tu prsons hart. Aut an de strit, dei are taf grls. Koping vit kold, rehen, sno blisards. Iven pims and hanger kud not brok dem. Hir, dei simstu releks for a short vail. Vumen sols is teket aut aut det grob kaver of drai skin. Dos pur ledis simstu tekinet ol dei of panishment for des van auer of hepinis. It is not his gud mjusik. Aldo is old inaf tu no det hi sing vit hart and not vit trot. Bad vot ever his musikal kritik kol his singing, dos grls laiket. It meks dem speshel. Preheps dei nidet tu tenk det romans is stil not det. Meibi det lital speshal kip dem an muving vit dei problems.

For his Marija hi vos never singing. No taim. Hi putet his haus befor his femili. It bi olveis taim ven vi go older, for sacha ting laik mjusik, lefing, a ivning in restorans. De laif hes his on voch, never konsidering jor vishes. If ju menagt tu heve fan, fain. If not, its fain tu. If he hes de chens vans egen liv vit his Marija and Graciela, fan, mjusik bi an frst ples. Aldo remember det moning ven tragedi strak

people dried their eyes. Maybe it was the way the melody would slowly work its way into a person's heart. Out on the street they are tough girls. Coping with cold, rain, snow blizzards. Even pimps and hunger couldn't break them. Here, they seemed to relax for a short while. Women's souls are taken out from under the rough cover of dry skin. Those poor ladies seem to have taken a whole day of punishment for this one hour of happiness. It wasn't his good music. Aldo is old enough to know that he sings with his heart and not with his throat. But whatever the music critics call his singing, those girls liked it. It made them special. Perhaps they needed to think that romance is still not dead. Maybe that little bit of feeling special would keep them moving on with their problems.

He never sang for his Maria. No time. He put his house before his family. There would always be time when we're older for such things as music, laughing, an evening in a restaurant. But life has its own watch, never considering your wishes. If you manage to have fun, fine. If not, that's fine too. If he had the chance to live once again with his Maria and Graziella, fun and music would have first place. Aldo remembered that morning when tragedy struck.

him. Nating, apsolutli nating indiketet an anhepenis. Preheps a masiv shok is de bigest kiler in eni kain of exident.

Hi vos veking ab ol femili laik juzuli. She meid de brekvest, and order vot hu bi veriing for klos. Dei brod de Graciela tu skul, goket over hr fani behevju als kaming tinager. Marija vos rili hepi des moning. Shi kis him gud bai, ven hi drop hr af not far from hr fektori. Ven Aldo rich his kontrakshen sait she vos det. Shi vos strakt from ankaming trak. Det an ples of exident. A jang draiver diden iven remember duing samting rong, ven hi faineli slip aut his bus.

It tuk him mor den a jer tu respektet de tot det she dai. Hi nju hr ol his laif, she vos pleing vit him singing, Marija vos part of his bodi. Deis bi goin bai and hi hardli etnoleg dem. Graciela vos in bed eg, left alon. His neibar vornet him meni taim. "Voch an Graciela, ju van tu lus des chaid tu?"

His laif vos tumach demicht tu rekognais sambadi als trobel. Vit sikstin she smok dop, drinkt laik oshen and ste meni taims

---

Nothing, absolutely nothing, pointed toward unhappiness. Perhaps massive shock is the biggest killer in any kind of accident.

He woke up the whole family as usual. She made the breakfast and ordered what who would be wearing for clothes. They took Graziella to school, joked over her funny behaviour as a pre-teenager. Maria was really happy that morning. She kissed him good-bye when he dropped her off not far from her factory. When Aldo reached his construction site she was dead. She was struck by an oncoming truck. Dead at the scene of the accident. The young driver didn't even remember doing anything wrong when he'd finally slept off his booze.

It took him more than a year to respect the thought that she'd died. He'd known her all his life, she played while he sang, Maria was part of his body. Days would go by and he'd hardly notice them. Graziella was at a bad age to be left alone. His neighbours warned him many times. "Watch out for Graziella. Do you want to lose that child too?"

His life was too damaged to recognize somebody else's troubles. At sixteen she was smoking dope, drinking like the ocean, and she often stayed over de nait bai hr frens. A jer after she kvit de skul, and pipel so hr seling hr badi. Tu jers after sister Ana kam an his dor. Graciela vos in des hostel. Skini, broken, hef drank. She krai an his sholder for long taim. Aldo hes his doter bek. Bat der vos preis tu pej. Hi vos kolt tu de doktor, vich polaitli eksplen him det Graciela is veri sik. Et frst hi diden andestand, hau kud bi sambadi laik his doter bi so sik. Shi is gast lital andernersht, nid de pasta, a gud sup. Bat vot ever hi kuket nating helped. Sister Ana ekxplen him den van dei, ven frst sedbeks ekors, det his dotar hes fetal venerik desis. Neks kapel jers dei separetet onli ven she vos in hospital. He chir hr ab, bring de flauer, interteinet laik a klaun. Vans dei vochet femili album. An lital old pikcher shi deskavere him vit de mandolin. Hi laik tu sing, bat hi vos never det big in pleing.

"I diden no ju plei de mandolin. Kud ju plei for mi, jor lital princes?" ask shi, so pel and skini.

Hau kud enibadi sei no tu de grl det onli mirikal kip a laiv. Des dei Aldo vos shoping for a gud mandolina. Hi vochet

---

overnight with her friends. A year later she quit school and people saw her selling her body. Two years later Sister Anna came to his door. Graziella was in this hostel. Skinny, broken, half drunk. She cried on his shoulder for a long time.

Aldo had his daughter back. But there was a price to pay. He was called to the doctor, who politely explained to him that Graziella was very sick. At first he didn't understand how somebody like his daughter could be so sick. She was just a little undernourished, needed pasta and a good bowl of soup. But whatever he cooked, nothing helped. Sister Anna explained to him one day, when the first setback occurred, that his daughter had a fatal venereal disease. In the next couple of years they were only separated when she was in hospital. He cheered her up, brought flowers, entertained like a clown. Once they looked through a family album. In a little old picture she discovered him with a mandolin. He liked to sing, but he was never that big on playing.

"I didn't know you played mandolin. Could you play for me, your little princess?" she asked, so pale and skinny.

How could anybody say no to a girl that only a miracle could keep alive. That day Aldo went shopping for a good mandolin. He checked

hau she is bildet, from vich vud. Laik det samting metar. His doter dont se nating eni mor. So sed hi trai piket ab sam of his noleg an des fregail instrument. Meni taim svoloing de tirs in his singing. In tri deis hi menagt tu plei "O Sole Mio". Befor Graciela dai hi lernt dasent of old songs. For meni det lost so mach in sacha short taim det bi de end. Hi vos tu old tu muv bek, tu jang tu retaer, tu lesi tu start a nju laif. For mants an de taim hi bi raning eraund de siti, sliping an de grev sait of his femili.

It tuket Sister Ana long taim tu faund de krich tu tok tu him. For kvait sam taim she so him vandering eraund. Shi vorit ebaut him. Men in des eg mas hev sam vil, risen tu vek ab in de moning if hi van tu bi hepi. Bat vot ken she du for him? Vorking hart in hostel kichen she srvt de mils, lisening det kvaking of dos vumens. Prepering lital program for krismos, she deskaver det dos hart ledis lak a mjusik. Tacet, letc kol de Aldo tu plei hir. After long tok vit hr hi egri tu trai.

Aldo tuk samtaim melodis an rekvest, fiksing his pingvin taj in taim ven vimen disaidet vich melodi dei vanet tu hir.

⊚⊚⊚⊚⊚⊚⊚⊚⊚⊚⊚⊚⊚⊚⊚⊚⊚⊚⊚⊚⊚⊚⊚⊚⊚⊚⊚⊚⊚⊚⊚⊚⊚⊚⊚⊚

how it was built, and from what kind of wood. As if something like that mattered. His daughter didn't say anything any more. So sad, he tried to recover some of his knowledge of this fragile instrument. Many times he swallowed tears in his singing. In three days he managed to play "O Solo Mio." Before Graziella died he learned a dozen old songs. For many who lose so much in such a short time, that would be the end. He was too old to move back, too young to retire, too lazy to start a new life. For months at a time he would be running around the city, sleeping on the graves of his family.

It took Sister Anna a long to find the courage to talk to him. For quite some time she saw him wandering around. She worried about him. A man of his age must have some will, a reason to wake up in the morning if he wants to be happy. But what could she do for him? Working hard in the hostel kitchen, she served the meals and listened to the quacking of those women. Preparing a little program for Christmas, she discovered that those hard ladies liked music. That's it, let's call Aldo to play here. After a long talk with her he agreed to try.

Aldo sometimes played melodies by request, fixing his penguin tie while the women decided which melody they wanted to hear.

⊚⊚⊚⊚⊚⊚⊚⊚⊚⊚⊚⊚⊚⊚⊚⊚⊚⊚⊚⊚⊚⊚⊚⊚⊚⊚⊚⊚⊚⊚⊚⊚⊚⊚⊚

Des ivning he song "Mama". Mosli of ledis finishet dei mil bai nau. Sun ol rum bi fol of smok. Vort "Mama" mins lats tu evri vumen. Sam of dem are maders dei diden soet dei kidc for long taim bikos dei dont ker for dem. Preheps sam of dos hart ledis diden menagt tu bi a gud mader. Na vot ever hepen hi is shor det sols endlis vans traet tu bi best maders. Sun or leter evrivan go evei from maders. It is normal behevju. Tu frgot dos det giv as a brd, skriming from pein, is sed. Puting dem an de strits is kraim.

De saper pest fest. Dei teking dei begs, dei smel, dei problems vans egen vit dem. Tumoro for sapar dei bi hir egen, tu lisen de mjusik and Aldo. Dei problems bi pusht an de sait vans egen.

Sister Ana and Aldo hes a kvaet sapar. Dei ched laik tu old merit sols deskavering kaming problems, signis. Dei grls a gon and andlis for nau dei danet vot dei kud. Sun old Aldo bi voking hom vit his mandolina belo his hend. Voching his grls vandering kros de strits, keching bojs, goining de hobos for a badel of chip vain. Going tu his hom

This evening he sang "Mama". Most of the ladies had finished their meals. Soon the whole room was full of smoke. The word "Mama" means lots to every woman. Some of them are mothers who haven't seen their kids for a long time because they don't care for them. Perhaps some of those hard ladies didn't manage to be a good mother. But whatever happened he was sure that these souls at least tried to be the best mothers. Sooner or later everyone goes away from their mother. It is normal behaviour. To forget those who gave us birth, screaming with pain, is sad. Putting them on the streets is a crime.

The supper passed quickly. They took their bags, their smells, their problems away with them once again. Tomorrow they will be here again for supper, to listen to the music and Aldo. Their problems will be pushed aside once again.

Sister Anna and Aldo had a quiet supper. They chatted like two old married souls discovering problems and sickness to come. Their girls are gone and at least for now they've done what they can. Soon old Aldo will be walking home with his mandolin under his arm. Watching his girls wandering across the streets, catching boys, joining the hobos for a bottle of cheap wine. Going to his home

gast a kapel bloks from daun taun hi stap for a moment tu
vev gudbei tu old strit ledi det olveis pinch his bam. "Nau
go and bi nais grl tu nait."

‍◎◎◎◎◎◎◎◎◎◎◎◎◎◎◎◎◎◎◎◎◎◎◎◎◎◎◎◎◎◎◎◎◎◎◎◎◎◎

just a couple of blocks from
downtown he'll stop for a moment
to wave good-bye to the old street
lady who always pinches his bum.
"Now go and be a nice girl
tonight."

◎◎◎◎◎◎◎◎◎◎◎◎◎◎◎◎◎◎◎◎◎◎◎◎◎◎◎◎◎◎◎◎◎◎◎◎◎

Of ol de pipel in Canada, preri foks klem tu bi mos frenlies. From ol preri pipel, Saskachevans soposto bi mos frenlies of ol. So, ven mai bas staped van erli fol dei in an largest taun saud ist of Regaina, I hev no risen tu mistrast de sain. "VOLKOM TU WEYBURN"

Vit aut eni fir for mai vel biing and pisfol egsistanc, I step aut in vorm ivning. I vos so shor det I am volkom hir, det I ignor mai pur onkel Emilko, vich vos in bek of mai main. "San," sed hi, "noubadi, vichvan dont van tu lus evriting vot hi on, kud bi tu frenli dos deis."

Vot he nju, de taim are chencht. Pipel are frenli dos deis, espesheli Seskechevans. I put de big smail an mai fes and grited laudli and chirfoli evri hjumen bin det hepen tu kam mai vei. Bad insted tu erning de seim kaind of recognishen in retrn, I enkonteret de redar dautfol luks of de pasant. O vel, hu nos, meibi til nau i had onli mit risent imigrants. Evri

---

Of all the people in Canada, prairie folks claim to be the friendliest. Of all prairie people, Saskatchewanians are supposed to be the friendliest of all. So, when my bus stopped one early fall day in a large town southeast of Regina, I had no reason to mistrust the sign. "Welcome to Weyburn."

Without any fear for my well-being and peaceful existence, I stepped out into the warm evening. I was so sure that I was welcome here that I ignored my poor Uncle Emil, who was in the back of my mind. "Son," he said, "nobody who doesn't want to lose everything he owns could be too friendly these days."

What did he know? Times are changed. People are friendly these days, especially Saskatchewanians. I put a big smile on my face and greeted loudly and cheerfully every human being that happened to come my way. But instead of earning some kind of recognition in return, I encountered rather doubtful looks from passers-by. Oh well, who knows, maybe up to now I had only met recent immigrants. Every hjumen bin nid sam taim tu ekonplish des level of frendlinis. Iven vi in Alberta, det samhau godet de sekend ples, dont displai auer smail at ol taims.

De motels in det i ran intu vos nice and kvajet. Bat if I van bring sam of des mani hom tu mai femili, I mas faund samting chiper. Maj rafnek saleri, vich said 80 has sin onli inflation, vos gast tu smol. So I disaidet tu ceri mai hevi lagich tu de old taun hotel, in de senter of des noisi taun, hoping for a beter dil.

A hjuch, frenli grl, pushing trti, ancver mai ringing on te bell. Prais vos ve daun, and iven mai onkel Emilko in bek of mai main diden no vot tu sei. Et simstu det I for frstaim toking tu truli netiv seskachevan. A preis vos egrit apon and she gev mi a form tu fil in. As she leined forvert tu voch mi sain in she sertenli lost no taim advertaising de hotel and hr magestik busem. I juzuali engoet sacha kvaet plezer of a laif, bad destaim vos de bed vot okupait mai main. After trtin auer an bas, mai hed nid sam releksing.

"Vi hev latc of partis hir, lac of gud luking grls are hir tu, ha ha ha. Ja, ja, vi are veri frenli komjuniti."

human being needs some time to accomplish this level of friendliness. Even we in Alberta, that somehow got second place, don't display our smiles at all times.

The motels I ran into were nice and quiet. But if I wanted to bring some of this money home to my family, I had to find something cheaper. My roughneck salary, which since 1980 has seen only inflation, was just too small. So I decided to carry my heavy luggage to the old town hotel, in the centre of this noisy town, hoping for a better deal.

A huge friendly girl, pushing thirty, answered my ring on the bell. The price was way down, and even my Uncle Emil in the back of my mind didn't know what to say. It seemed to be that for the first time I was talking to a truly native Saskatchewanian. A price was agreed upon and she gave me a form to fill in. As she leaned forward to watch me sign in she certainly lost no time advertising the hotel and her majestic bosom. I usually enjoyed such quiet pleasures of life, but this time it was bed that occupied my mind. After thirteen hours on the bus, my head needed some relaxing.

"We have lots of parties here, lots of good looking girls are here too, ha-ha-ha. Yeah, yeah, we are a very friendly community."

"Vel, je. Vi si vot hepen," I sed fil slaitli si sik from stering an des tu king sais baluns befor mai nos. I diden si de rest of det ah so lavli clerk. Hau ever iv her havenli posterior vos de seim sais as de bolges henging over mai hed, shi mast hav a gud per of legs tu ceri her femininiti.

"Forener, ei," shi gigelt.

"Jes madem, I kam from gulash kantri," I ancered in mai ist erupeen dajalekt.

"Des taun is femos for his partis. Ju si," eksplening vividli, hjuch fimel. "Vi partiing evri dei, evri nait."

"Tenkju mem, tenkju. Vi si," I seid, and boing laik a lital Japanish, I muved tuvords de dark stip sters and, hopfoli, tuvords sam bedli nidet praivasi.

Te afternun vent bai fest. After gud snus, I vok kros de mein strit in de taun and hev a bir in a dark bar in main hotel. Iven den det dei are most frenliest pipel in kanada, it is gud to mek sam freinds, gast in kes.

Mai hjuch svit fimel vos charming droping from taim tu taim hevi bar goks. Lokal men det diden chencht dei vorking

---

"Well, yeah. We'll see what happens," I said, feeling slightly seasick from staring at those two king-sized balloons before my nose. I couldn't see the rest of that oh-so-lovely clerk. However, if her heavenly posterior was the same size as the bulges hanging over my head, she must have a good pair of legs to carry her femininity.

"Foreigner, eh," she giggled.

"Yes madam, I come from goulash country," I answered in my East European dialect.

"This town is famous for its parties, you'll see," the huge female explained vividly. "We're partying every day, every night."

"Thank you ma'am, thank you. We'll see," I said, and bowing like a little Japanese, I moved towards the dark steep stairs and, hopefully, towards some badly needed privacy.

The afternoon went by fast. After a good snooze, I walked across the main street in the town and had a beer in the dark bar in my hotel. Even though they are the friendliest people in Canada, it is good to make some friends, just in case.

My huge sweet female was charming, from time to time dropping heavy bar jokes. Local men who didn't change their work klos lef laudli. Bisaid mi I hardli soet eni forener hir. Shor, dei ol kud bi brev men det after long dasti dei loking dem in dei lital chenbers, peshentli veiding an nju dei. Inposibel, der soposto bi tvelv regs vorking eraund des taun and no van vinci tini taini drank rafnek? Streng, inposibel. Mai kveshchen "Ver der de gais from regs vere haiding?" vos kold encert. "Dos pusis, sliping mosli de taim, ignoring as grls, and partis," sed hjuch fimel. Sun after, noing hau hart gop veidet for mi tumoro, I hit de bed.

I got as far as puling de cavers over mai self ven a feroshes reket caming from de bar belou jolted mi aut of maj bed. Svit gesus, vot is det ... an erdkvik, or ver dei tering de bilding apart? Scriming, I ran aut of mai chip rum. I vos olredi in de dimli lait of holovei, ven I remember mai denchurs in de glas on mai nait teibel. "Go get dem boi! Ju no hau mach dos ting cost," I vos teling tu mai self in penik. Mai neiber from ader rum, caming from de pablik vashrum, stoped bai mai dor. Hi vos a jang men mai eges, vich fes haidet behain tu big ai begs.

⊚⊚⊚⊚⊚⊚⊚⊚⊚⊚⊚⊚⊚⊚⊚⊚⊚⊚⊚⊚⊚⊚⊚⊚⊚⊚⊚⊚⊚⊚⊚⊚⊚⊚⊚⊚⊚⊚

clothes laughed loudly. Besides me, I hardly saw any foreigners here. Sure, they all could be brave men that after a long dusty day locked themselves in their little chambers, patiently awaiting a new day. Impossible, there's supposed to be twelve rigs working around this town and not one teeny tiny drunk roughneck? Strange, impossible. My question, "Where are the guys from the rigs hiding?" was coldly answered. "Those pussies, sleeping most of the time, ignoring us girls and the parties," said the huge female. Soon after, knowing how hard a job awaited me tomorrow, I hit the bed.

I got as far as pulling the covers over myself when a ferocious racket coming from the bar below jolted me out of my bed. Sweet Jesus, what is that ... an earthquake, or were they tearing the building apart? Screaming, I ran out of my cheap room. I was already in the dimly-lit hallway when I remembered my dentures in the glass on my night table. "Go get them boy! You know how much those things cost," I was telling myself in a panic. My neighbour from the other room, coming from the public washroom, stopped by my door. He was a young man my age, whose face was hidden by two big bags under his eyes.

⊚⊚⊚⊚⊚⊚⊚⊚⊚⊚⊚⊚⊚⊚⊚⊚⊚⊚⊚⊚⊚⊚⊚⊚⊚⊚⊚⊚⊚⊚⊚⊚⊚⊚⊚⊚⊚

Marijan Megla

"It is ol part of a nait laif! Dej are shoing as onli hau freindli dei are, dencing de hol nait. Bisaid, ju are invaidet!" des broken indivigual vos jaling sarkastikli in mai ir.

"Ju min ... des ... vil bi ol nait so?" I asked, shokt, laik I vold hev bin at de njus of de det of a lavet van, or at a doktor dijagnosis of a siries ilnis.

"I am sori, det is a laif hir ebauts," de taered felo sed and disapired in his dark rom, like sam karakter in Hichkok muvis.

"Ha, ha, ha," hir I lefing mai fet onkel Emilko. "Diden I tel ju? Diden I? Der is olveis a kech samver. Frenli? Fu. Nau ju hevet jor frenlinis."

I spendet det hol nait evek in a sheking, skviking, tapdencing bed. Laik in an noisi lucifer expres, hedet for de holokost. Sloli ekcepting de torcher I veidet for a nju dei. In de bek of mai main, auer hjuch onkel Emilko vos enjoing his profesi. "Tek pipel det olveis smail siriosli, det is de devels sols tolking aut of der bodis." Iven det I hev not ap tu nau had pruv det det vas rili so, it vos astonishing hau mach des aplaed.

𖠫𖠫𖠫𖠫𖠫𖠫𖠫𖠫𖠫𖠫𖠫𖠫𖠫𖠫𖠫𖠫𖠫𖠫𖠫𖠫𖠫𖠫𖠫𖠫𖠫𖠫𖠫𖠫𖠫

"It is all part of the night life! They are only showing us how friendly they are here, dancing the whole night. Besides, you are invited!" the broken individual was yelling sarcastically in my ear.

"You mean ... this ... will be so all night?" I asked, shocked, like I would have been at the news of the death of a loved one, or at a doctor's diagnosis of a serious illness.

"I am sorry, that is life hereabouts," the tired fellow said and disappeared in his dark room, like some character in Hitchcock movies.

"Ha, ha, ha," I heard my fat Uncle Emil laughing. "Didn't I tell you? Didn't I? There is always a catch somewhere. Friendly? Phoo. Now you have your friendliness."

I spent that whole night awake in a shaking, squeaking, tapdancing bed. It was like a noisy Lucifer express, headed for a holocaust. Slowly accepting the torture, I waited for a new day. In the back of my mind, our huge Uncle Emil was enjoying his prophesy. "Take people who always smile seriously, that is the devil's soul talking out of their bodies." Even though I hadn't up to now had proof that that was really so, it was astonishing how much this applied.

Stambling along de vols laik a sovaiver, siking eshoranc of a felo saferer hu hed shered sach an inkredibel nait vit mi, I voked tuvord de restorant. I vos so taet det onli de laud and vulger joking of de king sais fimel provented mi from colepsing in laud snoring. Shi simed tu bi incredibel mobail in a per of jins several saises smoler den she akchuali nidet. I vandering if she is sam kain of beonik kricher det dont nid de slip, or eni kain of rest.

For deis hed pest sait the blesed ivning on maj eraivel in dis taun of torcher. I hed never slept mor den tri auers a nait. For deis of konstant nois on de job and in de hotel. And frenli pipel organais van parti after anader. I voking eraund in a daze from lek of slip and cold not remember vhat i had bin duing during dos days. As hjuch seksi fimel preper van parti after ader. Evri singel ivning she faund de vei and risen tu ekurich as tu partiing. Droming an as dor, iven jaling in big vashrum an end of a holovei, ver vi frikventli snoring after egsosting bajologikal nids, lefing laudli ven vi refjus.

❦❦❦❦❦❦❦❦❦❦❦❦❦❦❦❦❦❦❦❦❦❦❦❦❦❦❦❦❦❦❦❦❦❦❦❦❦❦

Stumbling along the walls like a survivor, seeking assurance of a fellow sufferer who had shared such an incredible night with me, I walked toward the restaurant. I was so tired that only the loud and vulgar joking the king-size female prevented me from collapsing into loud snoring. She seemed to be incredibly mobile in a pair of jeans several sizes smaller than she actually needed. I was wondering if she was some kind of bionic creature that doesn't need sleep, or any kind of rest.

Four days had passed since the blessed evening of my arrival in this town of torture. I had never slept more than three hours a night. Four days of constant noise on the job and in the hotel. And friendly people organized one party after another. I was walking around in a daze from lack of sleep and could not remember what I had been doing during those days. Our huge sexy female prepared one party after another. Every single evening she found ways and reasons to encourage us to party. Drumming on our doors, even yelling into the big washroom at the end of the hallway, where we were frequently snoring after exhausting biological needs, laughing loudly when we refused.

"Pusis! Dei dont meket de men eni mor laik dei justu!"

Gelosli I voch ol dos Seskechevan mens, det pesing tru de laif never slip a minit, living an endlos partis, never mising no fans. I kveshchenet mai self, hau mach mor dei ekchili hev from laif, als vi normal slipi felos from rest of a Canada.

Tu mai big sopreis, I cot mai self toking tu a strenger in de miror ... anshevt, vit big poteto eis. I did not rialais for a long taim det I vos actuali toking tu mai self. Mai blesed vaif, ... kud shi onesli nju hau hevi is tu kolekt dos dolars des I bring hom? Kud she emegin hau mach I vanet tu slip nau? Iven mai onkel Emilko heving bai nau his naitmers in mai main. Hi sver an holi krucefiks, tu si his monster fet vaif, det let him long taim befor in des laif alon. Brrrr, vot a drims. Pur onkel Emilko.

Den from long holovei, a skrimi vois of vel non hjuch fimel, sloli fladet evri dark rum on de flor. Her pich vois vos so inposebel det dors a involunterli opening. Taet rafneks, motormens, derikmans, laudli promising tu atend tu des nju parti, if she kvaet a lital daun. She interdjus evribadi vit her

⁂

"Pussies! They don't make men like they used to any more!"

Jealously, I watched all those Saskatchewan men, who passed through life never sleeping a minute, living on endless parties, never missing any fun. I questioned myself, how much more did they have out of life than we normal sleepy fellows from the rest of Canada.

To my big surprise, I caught myself talking to a stranger in the mirror ... unshaved, with big potato eyes. I did not realize for a long time that I was actually talking to myself. My blessed wife, ... could she honestly know how hard it is to collect those dollars I bring home? Could she imagine how much I wanted to sleep now? Even my Uncle Emil was by now having nightmares in my mind. He swore on his holy crucifix to see his monster fat wife that left him alone in this life a long time ago. Brrrr, what dreams. Poor Uncle Emil.

Then from along the hallway the screaming voice of the well-known huge female slowly flooded every dark room on the floor. The pitch of her voice was so impossible that doors were involuntarily opening. Tired roughnecks, motormen, derrickmen, loudly promised to attend this new party if she'd quiet down a little. She introduced everybody to her gerlfrens, most laikli kolekchen of nonmerit hevi set fimel monsters. Dei gigelet, faind evribadi so hendsam and sloli muving tu mai rum dor. I prsonli pushing endlis tri handert paund and onli de vumen vit bigeste emagination kud kol mi seksi, in mai best taim. I opening de dor. Mai gud neibar stend in his dor oredi, faiting vit dasent soft hends det kondakt badi serch an him.

"Ouuuuuuuu! Grls det is van from Evropa. Gud bildet shasi, lital hevi an de grab," sed she, seing mai sogi beli and anshevt fes, det resenbelt de shnauc of a english buldog, gast kam from de long vok. "I tenk hi kam from est Evropa .... eeiii," tok a drank bajonik vumen.

Vit mai lest bit of energi, I ran aut intu de strit, lisening laud gigeling of overfetet taun bjutis behain mi. I van no seks, no romans, I give dem if dei tenk I am a feg. I van tu slip ... slippppppp. Raning aut in vorm nait I luking for sambadi vich kud help mi. I spatet a polisman crusing araund in des Sodoma and Gomora daun taun. Histerikli I stap de kar, kleming for it laik a drauning men for pis of log.

⊚⊚⊚⊚⊚⊚⊚⊚⊚⊚⊚⊚⊚⊚⊚⊚⊚⊚⊚⊚⊚⊚⊚⊚⊚⊚⊚⊚⊚⊚⊚⊚⊚⊚⊚⊚⊚

girlfriends, most likely a collection of unmarried heavy-set female monsters. They giggled, found everybody so handsome and slowly moved to my room door. I personally push at least three hundred pounds and only women with the biggest imagination could call me sexy, in my best time. I opened the door. My good neighbour was standing in his door already, fighting with a dozen soft hands that conducted a body search on him.

"Ouuuuuu! Girls, that is one from Europe. Good build on the chassis, a little heavy on the grub," she said, seeing my saggy belly and unshaved face that resembled the schnoz of an English bulldog, just come from a long walk. "I think he comes from East Europe ... eeiii," said a drunk bionic woman.

With my last bit of energy, I ran out into the street, listening to the loud giggling of the overfed town beauties behind me. I want no sex, no romance, I could give a damn if they think I am a fag. I want to sleep. Sleeeeeeeep. Running out into the warm night I looked for somebody who could help me. I spotted a policeman cruising around in the Sodom and Gomorrah downtown. Hysterically I stopped the car, clambering for it like a drowning man for a piece of log.

⊚⊚⊚⊚⊚⊚⊚⊚⊚⊚⊚⊚⊚⊚⊚⊚⊚⊚⊚⊚⊚⊚⊚⊚⊚⊚⊚⊚⊚⊚⊚⊚⊚⊚⊚⊚⊚

"Ofiser, if ju are gud crishchen, pleas bring mi samver ver I can slip. I van onli tu slip. Vans a vik ... vans," visperet I in desper. "I deservet. Preheps I dont andestan Saskachevan vei of frendlinis. Sev mi, o plis! Pliiis!"

His sopreist fes did not show if hi shuld lef or ignor mi. Gast in kes, hi hed de ched vit his bos. Den hi kaindli invaidet mi tu slip in gel, if I vanet tu. Det vos de onli ples det hi nju, det hi kud ofer mi for mai bedli nidet slip. I egri, and tu gel vi vent. Hi gev mi a special cel reserved for vumen onli, and I grabed de chens. It vos 12 oklok in de nait, and if I vanet sam rest I beter hri. Kiping mai deli prei short, I faineli faundet soft ples an des hard bet.

"O lord, tenkju. Slip endles." Bad, at de moment I vos crusing de lain intu dip slip, an enormas raket vok mi ab egen. Opening and klosing de slemer gast vudent endet.

"Let mi aut, du ju her mi? Let mi aut ... emidiatli." A totali drank vumen vos shauting, pauding on hr cell dor at de ader end of de coridor. It vos vel non vois of as hotel fimel, pekicht in blu des taim.

⊙⊙⊙⊙⊙⊙⊙⊙⊙⊙⊙⊙⊙⊙⊙⊙⊙⊙⊙⊙⊙⊙⊙⊙⊙⊙⊙⊙⊙⊙⊙⊙⊙⊙⊙

"Officer, if you are a good Christian, please bring me somewhere where I can sleep. I want only to sleep. Once a week ... once," I whispered in despair. "I deserve it. Perhaps I don't understand the Saskatchewan way of friendliness. Save me, oh please! Please!"

His surprised face didn't show if he should laugh or ignore me. Just in case, he had a chat with his boss. Then he kindly invited me to sleep in jail, if I wanted to. That was the only place that he knew that he could offer me for my badly needed sleep. I agreed, and to jail we went. He gave me a special cell reserved for women only, and I grabbed the chance. It was 12 o'clock in the night, and if I wanted some rest I'd better hurry. Keeping my daily prayer short, I finally found a soft place on that hard bed.

"Oh Lord, thank you. Sleep at last." But at the moment I was crossing the line into deep sleep, an enormous racket woke me up again. Opening and closing the slammer wouldn't end.

"Let me out, do you hear me? Let me out ... immediately." A totally drunk woman was shouting, pounding on her cell door at the other end of the corridor. It was the well-known voice of our hotel female, packaged in blue this time.

⊙⊙⊙⊙⊙⊙⊙⊙⊙⊙⊙⊙⊙⊙⊙⊙⊙⊙⊙⊙⊙⊙⊙⊙⊙⊙⊙⊙⊙⊙⊙⊙⊙⊙⊙

Vajolin

I veited a bet and traed tu sorvaiv dis bladi eksploshen, bat mai gel meit gast diden vanet tu stap her drank brawling. I ganped aut of mai bed, held on tu dor of mai svit alkatras and jaled daun de holovei.

"Wil ju bi kvaet daun der?"

"Hu ar ju? God demet ..." mambelt de drank seks sinbol of as daun taun hotel.

"Geki de liver riper! If ju dont belivet, kip shauting. Bad dont bi sopreist if ju vek ab in St Piters kort. In gesus kindem," sed I in most rafeste vois ever produst in mai blesed trot.

I never faund aut if she vos skert or gast tu drank, bad she never sed van vort des nait. After a vail, she fel tu laud snoring. As I vos veiding for slip tu retrn, I luked on de vols of mai cel on vich mesiges vere vriten. "Meri vos hir an 25. 8. Guliet is a bich. Trpen is an ashol. I never drink in mai laif eni mor, Shirli."

Vot shud I putet on de vol? Nau det I vos member of det sosaeti, iven it vos onli for sliping prpises. "Marijan, let 85?" Or shud I jus mai kriminal neim? "Geki de liver-riper, staped in for a nait." Far daun de holovei, a frenli polismen

⊚⊚⊚⊚⊚⊚⊚⊚⊚⊚⊚⊚⊚⊚⊚⊚⊚⊚⊚⊚⊚⊚⊚⊚⊚⊚⊚⊚⊚⊚⊚⊚⊚⊚⊚

I waited a bit and tried to survive this bloody explosion, but my jail-mate just didn't want to stop her drunk brawling. I jumped out of my bed, held onto the door of my sweet Alcatraz and yelled down the hallway.

"Will you be quiet down there?"

"Who are you, goddamit ..." mumbled the drunk sex symbol of our downtown hotel.

"Jackie the Liver Ripper! If you don't believe it, keep shouting. But don't be surprised if you wake up in St. Peter's court. In Jesus' kingdom," I said in the roughest voice ever produced in my blessed throat.

I never found out if she was scared or just too drunk, but she never said one more word that night. After a while, she fell to loud snoring. As I was waiting for sleep to return, I looked at the walls of my cell, on which messages were written. "Marie was here on 25/8. Juliet is a bitch. Turpen is an asshole. I'll never drink in my life any more, Shirley."

What should I put on the wall? Now I was a member of that society, even if only for sleeping purposes. "Marijan, late '85?" Or should I use my criminal name? "Jackie the Liver Ripper, stopped in for a night." Far down the hallway, a friendly policeman

⊚⊚⊚⊚⊚⊚⊚⊚⊚⊚⊚⊚⊚⊚⊚⊚⊚⊚⊚⊚⊚⊚⊚⊚⊚⊚⊚⊚⊚⊚⊚⊚⊚⊚⊚

kveshenet de totali taet gai hu roled de car. It vos mai safering neiber, from taun hotel, det olveis kip mai desapiring moral haj. In dos short for deis vi gron from totali strenger tu gud frends. I vandering if hi is ingert and hau hi ever kam tu des plesher.

"Hu vos a dreiver?" ask de polisman.

"I vos not," ancer de pur gai.

"Vos sambadi vit ju draiving?" ask de polismen.

"Not rili. Thet min, not det ju no him," mameling de over taet man.

"So ju ver de draiver? Or, sambadi als vos de draiver, vich left after aksident."

"Not mi, hi is stil in mai hed."

"A ju hev sam gost letli, in jor hed?"

"No! I never hev eni gost! Not bisaid mi, not in mai hed!"

"So, hu vos a draiver?"

"Not mi."

"De gost?"

"Not him."

◎◎

questioned the totally tired guy who had rolled the car. It was my suffering neighbour, from the town hotel, who always kept my despairing morale high. In those short four days we'd grown from total strangers to good friends. I wondered if he was injured and how he had come to this pleasure.

"Who was the driver?" asked the policeman.

"I was not," answered the poor guy.

"Was somebody with you driving?" asked the policeman.

"Not really. That means, not that you'd know him," mumbled the overtired man.

"So you were the driver? Or, somebody else was the driver, who left after the accident."

"Not me, he is still in my head."

"Have you had some ghosts lately, in your head?"

"No! I never have any ghosts! Not beside me, not in my head!"

"So, who was the driver?"

"Not me."

"The ghost?"

"Not him."

◎◎◎

"Ju?"

"No!"

In bek of mai hed I hr mai onkels laud snoring. Befor hi kud rekaver and bader mai konchans, I dos of. Bisaid I nju pridi vel vot hi kud sei tu mi. "Shem ... shem. Ju no det ju frst in femili tu bi in de gel? Shem. Pur jor fader, ju put de dark klaud over his laif."

Erli in de nekst moning, I drank cofi vit de simpatetik ofiser, after vi pest stinki cel of "Hotel drakula". Pur neiber, faineli edmitet heving bin draiven de roled kar. His gost simst tu bi klirt aut, and vos markt als not egsistet. Ven hi rekognais mi his ais produs tirs of hepinis.

"Vot ju du hir?" ask a broken indivigual.

"I kam for gud, bedli nidet slip."

"Nekstaim ju tek mi vit ju," sed pur gai foling in laut snoring. As frenli gardian of pis kud hardli belivet vich torcheres laif vi akcheli liv in his taun. "No gais, I ken not belivet. Vi kud bi so bed pipel? Vi a non tu bi a frenliest foks in Canada," sed hi sheking his hed over as misforchin.

***

"You?"

"No!"

In the back of my head I heard my uncle's loud snoring. Before he could recover and bother my conscience, I dozed off. Besides, I knew pretty well what he'd say to me. "Shame ... shame. You know that you're the first in the family to be in jail? Shame. Your poor father, you put a dark cloud over his life."

Early the next morning I drank coffee with the sympathetic officer after we passed the stinky cell of "Hotel Dracula". My poor neighbour finally admitted having been driving the rolled car. His ghost, it seemed, was cleared out and marked as non-existent. When he recognized me his eyes produced tears of happiness.

"What are you doing here?" asked the broken individual.

"I came for a good, badly needed sleep."

"Next time you take me with you," said the poor guy, falling into loud snoring. Our friendly guardian of the peace could hardly believe what a torturous life we actually lived in this town. "No guys, I can not believe it. How could we be such bad people. We are known to be the friendliest folks in Canada," he said, shaking his head over our misfortune.

Vi bot kvit det monig. It vos inposibel tu vork an de reg if ju never kud kech inaf slip. Raiding hom tu Edmonton, hi tel mi vai hi hepili merit men vos kot vit streng vumen. "Let des nait, a grup of egsostet rafneks kam an mai dor. Dei promis mi if I draiv hr hom, dei staped de parti for tu nait. It vos olmos inposibel tu sei no, voching dos jang broken gais pliding ais. I egri. De bois vere so hepi det dei putet tugeder tri handert dolar for mai kost. Bad ... I vos tu taet, and she tu drank, tu seksefoli endet as grnei. So, I lost mai nju kar, an van sharp kurv."

"Ju shor hev jor sher of lak, in des frenli kaunti," tok I teping him an de bek.

"De bigeste trobel is stil tu kam ... mai vaif. Brrrrr. Ju kan isier skruet porki pain als teling her de rili trut."

Mai onkel Emilko vos protesting over mai klos tais vit des felo saferer. Meni of travelers not noing de risen for as tuking tugeder, konplening tu bas dreiver over noisi snoring and anplesent sait. "Homosekshul shud bi ferbiten de seim bas," laudli protesting a konsern gentlemen in konservativ

---

We both quit that morning. It was impossible to work on the rig if you never could catch enough sleep. Riding home to Edmonton, he told me why he, a happily married man, was caught with strange women.

"Late that night a group of exhausted roughnecks came to my door. They promised me if I'd drive her home they'd stop the party for tonight. It was almost impossible to say no, watching those young broken guys' pleading eyes. I agreed. The boys were so happy that they put together three hundred dollars for my costs. But ... I was too tired, and she too drunk, to successfully end our journey. So, I lost my new car on a sharp curve."

"You sure had your share of luck in this friendly country," I said, tapping him on the back.

"The biggest trouble is still to come ... my wife. Brrrrr. You could easier screw a porcupine than tell her the real truth."

My Uncle Emil was protesting over my close ties with this fellow sufferer. Many of the travellers not knowing the reason for our tucking together complained to the bus driver over the noisy snoring and unpleasant sight. "Homosexuals should be forbidden on the same bus," loudly protested a concerned gentleman in conservative

klosing, fiksing his hevi tai. I diden ker. I faundet a fren, det vit mi sher de seim horobel ekspirienc. As tu sopreist vumen kud vek as ab in frenli Edmonton, meni auers evei from Weyburn.

clothing, fixing his heavy tie. I
didn't care. I found a friend, who'd
shared with me the same horrible
experience. Our two surprised
women could wake us up in
friendly Edmonton, many hours
away from Weyburn.

Lio vos nervesli veiding, det des denc begin. In ol dos jers det hi livet in des juvel hom, he never vos so enkches not tu mis de denc. Skvising his long voking stik, he vochet de old pipel det oredi gedert in de dencing rum. In his sheki hends, overgroen vit strong vens and her, hi keriet a tri rosis. Nais pekicht in his rum, dei luking oredi bed from raf handeling, and meiger skvis in overkraudet elevator.

Hoping det old gais gedert in korner ver hi hedet never ask him ebaut dos flauers, he vas hepi tu rich de emti cher. Tu meni efert hi putet in des denc ivning and nau hi van tu hev pis. Bjutifol ... no koments from old bojs thet onli shoing interest for opening de bar. Sun, onli his selten just gut parfjum an his speshel rob givet ab his presentc.

An sopreist of strong Agnes de nursing eid, det nju him for jers nau, hi chenchet his blesed anderver an his on vish. Put his nju vait shrt and best penc, gelosli sevt for his visit tu auer lord.

◉◉

Leo was nervously waiting for the dance to begin. In all the years he had lived in this old folks' home, he never was so anxious that he would miss a dance. Squeezing his long walking stick, he watched the old people who had already gathered in the dance room. In his shaky hands, overgrown with strong veins and hair, he carried three roses. Nicely packaged in his room, they were already looking bad from rough handling and the major squeeze in the overcrowded elevator.

Hoping that the old guys gathered in the corner where he hid would never ask about those flowers, he was happy to reach the empty chair. He had put too much effort into this dance evening and now he wanted to have peace. Beautiful ... no comments from the old boys who only showed interest in the opening of the bar. Soon, only his seldom used jute perfume and his special suit would give up his presence.

To the surprise of strong Agnes the nursing aid, who knew him for years now, he'd changed his blessed underwear at his own wish. Put on his new white shirt and the best pants, jealously saved for his visit to our Lord.

◉◉

After shi put him his blek pingvin tai, hi vos voching him self in miror for a long taim. Desperatli koming his tin grei her tu vorts big pink bol det start tu apir an tope of his hed. Hu nju juzuli Lio laif stail vere shokt. Ol nurses an de flor lefet et him, komplimenting him olovei tu de entrenc of de elevator.

"Vot a nais flauer ju hev der Lio. ... O luket are dei pridi!" chakelet der staping him an de long flor.

"Mmmmmmmmm, Lio ju mai svithart. Vot hepen tu ju? ... A ju in de trobel, hmmm?"

"Nou," sed hi, vishing det dei liv him alon. "Ju vumen. Ju gast mek mi kresi! 'Lio, vot is det? Lio vot hepen?'" trai he emitetet des jang grls, gledli akcepting de sefti of elevetor.

Lio vos a old reilroder, det engoi a vok eraund de bilding iven an most miserabel dei. If noubadi kem along, he teket an his on, kosing meiger srch partis koming de kvaet neiberhud. Ven sambadi of volunters tuk him for a vok hi bi toking dei irs fol, vit scinen from his jang deis. Lio beskreib snoi vinters, kold blisard. Rehen, fladet rivers

After she put him in his black penguin tie, he watched himself in the mirror for a long time. Desperately combing his thin grey hair towards the big pink bald spot that had started to appear on top of his head. Those who knew Leo's usual lifestyle were shocked. All the nurses on the floor laughed at him, complimenting him all the way to the entrance of the elevator.

"What nice flowers you have there, Leo. ... Oh, look, aren't they pretty!" they chuckled, stopping him on the long floor.

"Mmmmm, Leo, you're my sweetheart. What happened to you? ... Are you in trouble, hmmmmm?"

"No," said he, wishing they would leave him alone. "You women. You just make me crazy! 'Leo, what is that? Leo, what happened?'" He tried to imitate the young girls, gladly accepting the safety of the elevator.

Leo was an old railroader who enjoyed a walk around the building even on the most miserable day. If nobody came along, he'd take it on his own, causing major search parties to comb the quiet neighbourhood. When one of the volunteers took him for a walk he'd talk their ears full with scenes from his young days. Leo described snowy winters, cold blizzards. Rain, flooded rivers

det samtaim tuket vuden reilrod briges, demicht reilrod. Vild laif det kam veri klos tu him ven hi dos in, taet from hevi vork, teking longer kofi brek.

Lio lav tu tok, and samhau hi menagt tu tel his laif over and over vit aut meking his lisener bort. Samtaim hi edet a nju tels, or koncentret an personaliti det vos put an de sait ab tu nau. Nju svitharts apirt, and vos fergoten vit seim spid.

"Vi kam hir from ist. An sekend dei hir in Alberta mai fader dai. Gast hir bisaid as belavet St. Albert chrch. Hi vos a strong gai, never sik, and noubadi akspektet det. Ja, ja, so fest det gos samtaim," tokin hi visibel hepi tu rich de emti benk in de park.

Hi remein der for a minit or so. Den pruving him self and tu his konpenien det hi kud stil duet, hi prosju tu vok.

"Mi and mai mader sevet hard tu meket inaf for a farm. It vos hr and mai vish. Bad vit gops eraund de taun, vi gast kuden menagt. I vos 23, short after de frst vor vor and I tuket gop an de reilrod. Dei konplening over mai boni bodi. Ha ha ha. Mai formen vos konsrn det I kud not keri

ⓔⓔⓔⓔⓔⓔⓔⓔⓔⓔⓔⓔⓔⓔⓔⓔⓔⓔⓔⓔⓔⓔⓔⓔⓔⓔⓔⓔⓔⓔⓔⓔⓔⓔⓔ

that sometimes took out the wooden railroad bridges, damaged the railroad. Wildlife that came very close to him when he was dozing, tired from the heavy work, taking a longer coffee break.

Leo loved to talk, and somehow he managed to tell his life over and over without making his listener bored. Sometimes he added a new tale, or concentrated on a personality that was put on the side up to now. New sweethearts appeared and were forgotten with the same speed.

"We came here from the east. On the second day here in Alberta my father died. Just here beside our beloved St. Albert church. He was a strong guy, never sick, and nobody expected it. Yeah, yeah, so fast they go sometimes," he said, visibly happy to reach an empty bench in the park.

He remained there for a minute or so. Then proving to himself and to his companion that he could still do it, he proceeded to walk.

"Me and my mother saved hard to make enough for a farm. It was her and my wish. But with jobs around the town, we just couldn't manage it. I was 23, shortly after the First World War, and I took a job on the railroad. They complained over my bony body. Ha-ha-ha. My foreman was concerned that I could not carry

ⓔⓔⓔⓔⓔⓔⓔⓔⓔⓔⓔⓔⓔⓔⓔⓔⓔⓔⓔⓔⓔⓔⓔⓔⓔⓔⓔⓔ

Vajolin

on vit sacha hard gop, bad I sho dem. Sun after dei god mi mai on strech, vich van I vochet," tok hi keching de bred an end of slaiseste hil.

"I vos alon, onli living sol an des strech of reilrod. Beliv mi. Meni taim I hed big trobels, bad dei nju I finishet ol. An mai part of a reil rod never hepen eni aksident, in mai taim. If I am praud? Shor, its min det I am a gud reilroder," finishet hi his long stori ven dei richet dors of de old pipel hom. Noing det frst emti cher is not far, hi jusuli egsist tu open de hevi dor for his kanpani.

De rest of a dei, hi spendet fiding de brds dei kam kloser tu kafeterija balkoni. His sekend fevert vos a hom meid cigarets, dei kud chok iven komjuniti insineretor, and dei driming. Kecht in snus, he mek shor det prson liv vit inpreshen det hi vos gast dip tenking. Hi vos not chusi in fainding a kvaet ples. Samtaim vos det his rum, or emti koridor of his flor, or hiden korners spredet kros det big bilding.

Lio vos boren in lital taun in Qvibek. His mader vos french, and fader kam from de steits. Hontet vit drims of

⊚⊚⊚⊚⊚⊚⊚⊚⊚⊚⊚⊚⊚⊚⊚⊚⊚⊚⊚⊚⊚⊚⊚⊚⊚⊚⊚⊚⊚⊚⊚⊚⊚⊚⊚⊚

on with such a hard job, but I showed them. Soon afterward they got me my own stretch, which I looked after," he said, catching his breath at the end of a slight hill.

"I was alone, the only living soul on this stretch of railroad. Believe me. Many times I had big troubles, but they knew I finished it all. On my part of the railroad there never was any accident in my time. Am I proud? Sure, it means that I am a good railroader," finishing his long story when they reached the doors of the old people's home. Knowing that the first empty chair is not far, he'd usually insist on opening the heavy door for his company.

The rest of the day he spent feeding the birds that came close to the cafeteria balcony. His second favourite was home-made cigarettes that could choke even the community incinerator, and daydreaming. Caught in a snooze, he'd make sure that that person left with the impression that he was just deeply thinking. He was not choosy about finding a quiet place. Sometimes it was in his room, or the empty corridor of his floor, or hidden corners spread across the big building.

Leo was born in a little town in Quebec. His mother was French and his father came from the States. Haunted with dreams of

⊚⊚⊚⊚⊚⊚⊚⊚⊚⊚⊚⊚⊚⊚⊚⊚⊚⊚⊚⊚⊚⊚⊚⊚⊚⊚⊚⊚⊚⊚⊚⊚⊚⊚⊚⊚

vait kold vildernis in vest of a Canada, hi tuket his femili in Manitoba. Lio remembert onli de dukebords, and redheri german neiber, det hi bit samtaim an de vei hom from skul. For dukebords hi hes onli best rememberings. "Boj dei du evriting in der on jard. Groing evri vegetebel alon. Dei dont go mach in stor. Dei kuk gud, and dei are gud neibar," justu tel he. Old men remember de indians and dei fait for dei raits. Dei vos gud traper, and dei dont bader as stetlers mach.

In his tels ebaut his laif, he remember ol pipel laik a gud sols. Inkredibal inaf, he never menchenet van neim of his enimi. Hi vos alon for mosli of his laif. In his album vos onli fju pikcher. Sam of dem vos pult aut an lital teibel, kompliting vit stein cirkels from de liking kofi mags and overfolt estri, an hepi kolaz.

Zaklin vos his svit vaif and rili, shi luk lak a engel, an dos fju pikcher stil hevili gardet in his old album. Dei bod vos oredi in dei trtis ven dei disaidet tu meri. Ten jers of merich diden brod eni children. An van trip tu Kalifornia,

᠍᠍᠍᠍᠍᠍᠍᠍᠍᠍᠍᠍᠍᠍᠍᠍᠍᠍᠍᠍᠍᠍᠍᠍᠍᠍᠍᠍᠍᠍᠍᠍᠍᠍᠍᠍᠍᠍

the white, cold wilderness in the west of Canada, he took his family to Manitoba. Leo remembered only the Doukhobors, and red-haired German neighbours, who he beat up sometimes on the way home from school. Of the Doukhobors he had only the best memories. "Boy, they'd do everything in their own yard. Growing every vegetable alone. They didn't go much to the store. They cooked good and they were good neighbours," he used to say. The old man remembered the Indians and their fight for their rights. "They were good trappers, and they didn't bother us settlers much."

In his tales about his life, he remembered all people as good souls. Incredibly enough, he never mentioned one name of an enemy. He was alone for most of his life. In his album were only a few pictures. Some of them were pulled out on a little table, completing with stained circles from leaking coffee mugs and an overflowing ashtray, a happy collage.

Jacqueline was his sweet wife and really, she looked like an angel in those few pictures still well protected in his old album. They both were already in their thirties when they decided to marry. Ten years of marriage didn't bring any children. On a trip to California,

᠍᠍᠍᠍᠍᠍᠍᠍᠍᠍᠍᠍᠍᠍᠍᠍᠍᠍᠍᠍᠍᠍᠍᠍᠍᠍᠍᠍᠍᠍᠍᠍᠍᠍᠍᠍

vich vos acheli Zaklins and his let hanimun, dei hev a terebel eksident. Not far of US border dei kresh vit a biger trak. Zaklin dai emidietli and Lio brok his legs, his langs koleps and onli vit mirekal hi sorvaiv. For rest of his laif he blem him self for des tragedi, iven det eksident vos kost from det drank traker. His rekavering vos slo and sam inguri ste vit him for rest of laif. De farm vos solt after his mader dai. For old Lio, hevi farm chors vos gast tu mach. Sun after hi vos rekomendet in des old pipel hom. Sevir artraitis diden mech vit his bechler laif in de siti.

Sait dem peset meni jers. Evrivan vos mor hevier tu kros, a lital mor tu remember. Pikcher of jang jers go blurijer, hi diden ker for mils, vich kain of shu hi ver. Ais ste de ais, onli de ekspirienc, koshen from desapoitment, ist biger and mek him apir slolier. Rifleks giving evei, end ar haidet vit overdosis of prkoshens.

Kaming van dei from his vok, hi vos rekuporeting in his feveret spat bisaid de vindo. Spredet bred krums an de kold vindi balkoni atrakt sam speros, and blek kro. Dei faitet for

which was actually Jacqueline's and his late honeymoon, they had a terrible accident. Not far from the U.S. border they crashed with a bigger truck. Jacqueline died immediately and Leo broke his legs, his lungs collapsed and only with a miracle did he survive. For the rest of his life he blamed himself for this tragedy, even if the accident was caused by that drunk trucker. His recovery was slow and some injuries stayed with him for the rest of his life. The farm was sold after his mother died. For old Leo, heavy farm chores were just too much. Soon after, he was recommended to this old people's home. Severe arthritis didn't match with his bachelor life in the city.

Since then, many years passed, every one of them heavier to bear, a little more to remember. Pictures of the young years went blurrier, he didn't care for meals, what kind of shoes he wore. Eyes are still eyes, only the experience, cushioned from disappointment, is bigger and makes him appear slower. Reflexes are giving away, and are hidden with overdoses of precaution.

Coming one day from his walk, he was recuperating in his favourite spot beside the window. Bread crumbs spread on the cold windy balcony attracted some sparrows and a black crow. They fought for

evri bait, piking aut fresh sno evri lital krum. Den de strong Agnes kam tu gok vit him and tel him det he hes a visit.

He nju det vest of Manitoba border hi hes onli a femili of his vaif Zaklin and dei vuden kam tu visit him. Voching his brds he trai tu ignor hr, bad she vuden bek ab vit des streng aidijas.

"Lisen Agnes, liv mi alon," sed hi.

"Mister Lio, det is not nais of ju. Det ledi hir van tu tok vit ju," tok de stabern nursing eid.

"So, I dont vanet eni ledis. Mai taim vit dos sentimental krichers are over. Tenkju lord," sed hi krosing him self, risking pik an des ledi.

A older vumen his eg stend bisaid de Agnes. Eshemt, shi trai tu haid hr nervesnis, roling de henkerchivs in hr pel lital hends. Shi is not iven so bed luking. O kaman, des tu chiken shud no det he is not interestet in sam kain of releshen ship. Dont dei si det? Vimen, nating bad trobel.

"I am Meri," sed de older ledi.

"And I am king Liopold," brasht de old Lio bek.

every bite, picking from the fresh snow every little crumb. Then strong Agnes came to joke with him and tell him that he had a visitor.

He knew that west of the Manitoba border he had only the family of his wife Jacqueline, and they wouldn't come to visit him. Watching his birds, he tried to ignore her, but she wouldn't back off with these strange ideas.

"Listen Agnes, leave me alone," he said.

"Mr. Leo, that is not nice of you. This lady here wants to talk with you," said the stubborn nursing aid.

"So, I don't want any ladies. My time with those sentimental creatures is over. Thank you Lord," he said, crossing himself and risking a peek at this lady.

An older woman his age stood beside Agnes. Ashamed, she tried to hide her nervousness, rolling a handkerchief in her pale little hands. She is not even so bad looking. Oh come on, these two chickens should know that he is not interested in some kind of relationship. Don't they see that? Women, nothing but trouble.

"I am Marie," said the older lady.

"And I am King Leopold," old Leo brushed back.

"Mister Lio, dont ju tok tu des pur vumen laik det," tok laudli de fetfol Agnes, panping sam kurich in des pur vumen, stending bisaid hr.

Lio kuden eskep, and for shor diden hev a nervs tu tok vit des so-so plesent prson. Meri? Hau an erd he shud no, hu is des Meri? Grebing tu his big prs, hi tuket van of his big stinki cigaret. Sun dei bi inaf smok tu kil de hors. Preheps, dei tu hjumen kricher det destroi his fri taim, bi desapiring aut of his laif. Bad ... in sted tu ran for a kaver, dei ledis sedaun besaid him, kofing and draing diskret dei ais.

"Lio, I am Meri. Doter of Pelatjes... jor neibers in Manitoba. Dont ju remember mi?" sed de older ledi, luking for sam inshuranc from Agnes.

"Ja Lio, tenk lital an jor jang eg, ju old hang. Diden ju hev sam grl daun in Manitoba? Remember?" tok old fetfol Agnes, going laik a nesti flai an his nervs.

"I never hev a grl. I am sori mai vaif dai in jang eg, bad heving a grl, no," sed de Lio bek, olmos sker of sam kain of konplikation det kud kam from noing sam grl.

ⓢⓢⓢⓢⓢⓢⓢⓢⓢⓢⓢⓢⓢⓢⓢⓢⓢⓢⓢⓢⓢⓢⓢⓢⓢⓢⓢⓢⓢⓢⓢⓢⓢⓢⓢⓢ

"Mr. Leo, don't you talk to this poor woman like that," faithful Agnes said loudly, pumping some courage into the poor woman standing beside her.

Leo couldn't escape, and for sure didn't have the nerve to talk with this so-so pleasant person. Marie? How on earth should he know? Who is this Marie? Grabbing his big purse, he took out one of his big stinky cigarettes. Soon there would be enough smoke to kill a horse. Perhaps these two human creatures who were destroying his free time would disappear out of his life. But .. instead of running for cover, these ladies sat down beside him, coughing and discreetly drying their eyes.

"Leo, I am Marie. Daughter of Pelletiers ... your neighbours in Manitoba. Don't you remember me?" said the older lady, looking for some assurance from Agnes.

"Yeah Leo, think a little about your young age, you old hunk. Didn't you have some girl down in Manitoba? Remember?" said old faithful Agnes, going like a nasty fly at his nerves.

"I never had a girl. I am sorry my wife died at a young age, but having a girl, no," Leo replied, almost scared of some kind of complication that could come from knowing some girl.

ⓖⓖⓖⓖⓖⓖⓖⓖⓖⓖⓖⓖⓖⓖⓖⓖⓖⓖⓖⓖⓖⓖⓖⓖⓖⓖⓖⓖⓖⓖⓖⓖⓖⓖⓖⓖ

Marijan Megla

"Lio ju mas remember samting. I am de doter from Palatjes," sed old vumen lusing de fet in hr spich.

"So vat? I nju sam Pelatjes bek in Manitoba. Dei hev meni doters," tok laut de old gai. "Is samting rong vit det?"

"No Lio, nating is rong," lefing sed de Agnes, pinching de older ledi.

"Vel, I vos Mari Pelatje, jor frst svithart," tok older ledi, going red in chiks. "Endlis, ju sed so tu mi ven jor femili stap tu sei gudbai tu as."

"Dem. Ju sed ju de Pelatjes doter Meri?" Old Lio kiling rest of cigaret. "I tenk I mas go nau, tu hev a nep," mamelt he in his chin, desperatli luking for svift deparcher. Hi nju de Meri vel. Sardenli ol dos memoris sverm in his brein and hi diden nju hau shud hi reakt. Vot shud he sed tu her.

De best ting bi an emidiat deparcher. Voking fest vot hi kud, he trnet bek tvais onli tu si lefing Agnes vispering samting in Meris ir.

"Demet, after olmos siksti jers, nau she kam bek? Vot for? Dei plening samting, samting bed. Dos vumen nating

***

"Leo, you must remember something. I am the daughter of the Pelletiers," said the old woman, losing faith in her speech.

"So what? I knew some Pelletiers back in Manitoba. They had many daughters," said the old guy. "Is something wrong with that?"

"No Leo, nothing is wrong," Agnes laughed, pinching the older lady.

"Well, I was Marie Pelletier, your first sweetheart," said the older lady, going red in the cheeks. "At least, you said so to me when your family stopped to say good-bye to us."

"Damn. You said you're the Pelletier's daughter Marie?" Old Leo killed the rest of his cigarette. "I think I must go now, to have a nap," he mumbled into his chin, desperate for a quick departure. He knew Marie well. Suddenly all those memories swarmed in his brain, and he didn't know how he should react. What he should say to her.

The best thing would be an immediate departure. Walking as fast as he could, he turned back twice, only to see the laughing Agnes whispering something in Marie's ear.

"Dammit, after almost sixty years, now she comes back? What for? They're planning something, something bad. Women are nothing

bad trobel... Sori Zaklin, I diden min ju," tod hi voking tu his rum. Sev ples, evei of ol dos streng pipel det van tu preheps meri him, or samting als det hi dont andestan and dont nidet. Riching his roking cher hi pustet for a long taim.

Dei vos kolt and de hevi dark klauds muvet kros de skai. Vinter is gast bihain de korner, is des his letct? If not, hau meni mor? In his eg hi rili dont ker eni mor.

Hmmm. Meri, ... shi is de grl det he vans mor den lav. Jes, it vos de krismos ven hi so hr for frst taim. Dei gast badet de farm a mail daun de rod.

Ja, ja. Hmmmm. Siksti jers pest, from des gud old taim. Vit evri pesing auer mor and mor memoris srfes. Shi vos so skini den, bad so svit in hr long flaueri dres. Gast a jang grl redi tu fol in lav at eni taim. Igor tu denc, hev a fan. Des ivning he fol in lav vit hr. Dei voch ichader ol ivning, never lost van vort. Lio vanet tu denc vit hr, bad his perenc never sho im eniting inportant in laif. Pushing his frst denc an nekst ... nekst ... nekst taim, he never akcheli menagt tu

but trouble... Sorry Jacqueline, I didn't mean you," he thought, walking to his room. A safe place, away from all those strange people who perhaps want to marry him, or something else that he doesn't understand and doesn't need. Reaching his rocking chair, he pushed it for a long time.

The day was cold and the heavy dark clouds moved across the sky. Winter is just around the corner, is this his last? If not, how many more? At his age he really doesn't care any more.

Hmmmmmm. Marie. She is the girl that he once more than loved. Yes, it was Christmas when he saw her for the first time.

They'd just bought the farm a mile down the road.

Yeah, yeah. Hmmmmm. Sixty years passed since that good old time. With every passing hour more and more memories surfaced. She was so skinny then, but so sweet in her long flowery dress. Just a young girl ready to fall in love at any time. Eager to dance, have fun. That evening he fell in love with her. They watched each other all evening, never lost one word. Leo wanted to dance with her, but his parents never showed him anything important in life. Pushing his first dance to the next ... next ... next time, he never actually managed to

denc vit hr. Dei ais komenting hepenings in de dencing hol. Hi nju emidietli hu she dont laiket, and hu is hr feveret.

Vel, at vas klir, dei are boren for ichader and dei sit sait bai sait ven de taun fotografer vos teking pikcher from ol taun sols. Let des nait ven dei drov hom in de dip fresh sno, hi soet hr vans egen. She vos vit rest of hr sisters siting an biger sled. Dei tim of gud horsis pes his femili old Besi at long hil. Ven his mader and hi vevet, his fader gelosli luket hau der lait desapiring in darknis. Hmm. Hau gast van ivning kud chench entaerli his hol laif. De rest of a vinter hi luk for sam kain of risen tu visit de Pelatjes farm gast daun de rod. Ven ever his perenc ran intu de taun, his ais stak tu hr vindo. She vos der, bjutifol and kvaet.

It vos bed vinter and dei lostet meni of stak. For his fader det vos risen inaf tu bring his old anbishen for vest. In spring his perenc disaidet tu muv vest, tu Alberta. "Der is inaf chip lend tu hev a big farm," justu sed his fader. "Inaf fud for stak, vi bi never egen lusing as kaus." Dei ol stap bai

@@

dance with her. Their eyes commented on happenings in the dance hall. He knew immediately who she didn't like and who were her favourites.

Well, at last it was clear, they were born for each other and they sat side by side when the town photographer was taking pictures of all the town souls. Late this night when they drove home in the deep fresh snow he saw her once again. She was with the rest of her sisters sitting on a bigger sled. Their team of good horses passed his family's old Bessie on a long hill. While his mother and he waved, his father jealously watched their light disappearing in the darkness.

Hmmm. How just one evening could entirely change his whole life. The rest of the winter he looked for some reason to visit the Pelletier's farm just down the road. Whenever his parents ran into town, his eyes stuck to her window. She was there, beautiful and quiet.

It was a bad winter and they lost many of their stock. For his father that was enough reason to bring back his old ambition for the west. In the spring his parents decided to move west, to Alberta. "There is enough cheap land to have a big farm," his father used to say. "Enough food for stock, we'll never again be losing our cows." They all stopped by the

@@

Pelatjes. It vos his mader aidija. Never befor she egsistet an hr vish so hard. Des taim she vane de vor. Fader never left de vegen, chuing nervosli an his gelosi tu mister Pelatje.

Voching hr ais fol of tirs Lio promis him self tu kis hr, laik ol dos gentelmens du in big siti pepers. Vel ven dei vos bek an de kerich hi remember hr kis. Ven his pernc vos trning tu horsis hi vevt tu hr.

"Meri, o mai svit Meri. I lav ju," mamelet he, overkam vit sednis, ven Agnes vek him ab for saper.

"O Lio ju old devel, a ju in lav?" goking old fetfol nurs.

"O vat, ju vimen gast tenket ebaut lav. Ju si," prosju de old Lio filosofikali, "vi men a in des point veri diferent."

"Ha ... ha ... ha. Preheps, bad I teling ju Lio, lav is mai feveret bisnis. Nating is beter als a men, det mek sam trobel in de bet," goking, haging de old gai, vich gladli tuket hr belo de arm and start tu lef.

After diner hi smok his cigaret, voching de jang vumen noisi klining de olmos emti kafeteria. In ader korner of a lital vorm hol, in vich hepili flotet de smel of a pest

———

Pelletiers. It was his mother's idea. Never before had she insisted so hard on her wish. This time she won the war. Father never left the wagon, chewing nervously on his jealousy of Mr. Pelletier.

Watching her eyes full of tears Leo promised himself to kiss her like all those gentlemen in the big city papers. Well, when they were back in the carriage, he remembered her kiss. When his parents were turned to the horses he waved to her.

"Marie, oh my sweet Marie. I love you," he mumbled, overcome with sadness, when Agnes woke him up for supper.

"Oh Leo, you old devil, are you in love?" joked the old faithful nurse.

"Oh what, you women just think about love. You'll see," continued old Leo philosophically, "we men on this point are very different."

"Ha ... ha ... ha. Perhaps, but I'm telling you Leo, love is my favourite business. Nothing is better than a man that makes some trouble in bed," joking, hugging the old guy, who gladly took her below the arm and started to laugh.

After dinner he smoked his cigarette, watching the young women noisily cleaning the almost empty cafeteria. In another corner of a little warm hall, in which happily floated the smell of a past

Marijan Megla

saper, sitet de Meri. Gesus, she is sed and van tu tok vit him, bad vot shud he tel hr? Vot is left after siksti jers? Demet, in sted tu go slip he breking his dem brein an samting so aninportent laik lav. It is gast bed taim tu start vit des egen. Bisaid, vot bi Zaklin sei tu him? No. Hi gast kan not duet. Kiling his cigaret, hi desapir in his rum. Kofing laudli hi preper him for slip, and onli after gut hot ti, hi dos in.

If she kud she bi kraing. Det aidija det he kud remember hr after so meni jers vos bed and she bi peing for det. She vos krset vit bed lak in hr laif, det lets is not iven so bed.

Long taim ego she vos laving de Lio. He njuet, bad he diden ask hr for denc. Vot ever she traet tu help him in his kurich, nating vos vorking aut. He kud sho ab after de jer or so, bad ... nating. He kud raid de leter, du samting. De vorld brok for hr in pisis and Erl, det she meri after faif jers of veiding an Lio, tuket des als his adventich. For him she vos olveis old spinstres, det he hes tu meri tu fri her from gosoping. Der vos never mach lav or eni gud vorts. After tri kidc and muving from van tu ader taun she hes inaf from him.

@@

supper, sat Marie. Jesus, she is sad and wants to talk to him, but what should he tell her? What is left after sixty years? Dammit, instead of going to sleep he's breaking his damn brain on something as unimportant as love. It is just a bad time to start with this again. Besides, what would Jacqueline say to him? No. He just cannot do it. Killing his cigarette, he disappeared into his room. Coughing loudly he prepared himself for sleep, and only after a good hot tea he dozed off.

If she could she'd be crying. The idea that he would remember her after so many years was bad and she was paying for it. She was so cursed with bad luck in her life that this last is not even so bad.

A long time ago she loved Leo. He knew it, but he didn't ask her for a dance. Whatever she tried to help him with his courage, nothing worked out. He could have showed up after a year or so, but ... nothing. He could write a letter, do something. The world broke in pieces for her, and Earl, who she married after five years of waiting for Leo, took this to his advantage. For him she was always an old spinster who he had to marry to save her from gossip. There was never much love or any good words. After three kids and moving from one town to another she'd had enough of him.

Dei faif jer old san dai, beteling vit hai fiver. Shi vos vorking, suporting femili and his drinking. Dei brod dei san oredi an simenteri ven Erl sho ab. Ven tu older grls tel him vot hepen in des taim hi simpli desapir. Sait den shi hrt onli van njus ebaut him. Erl vos kecht from polis for sam mord det hi or sam of his foni frens danet.

So alon vit tu grls she muv vest. It vos not isi bad dei menagt tu hev frst taim en stedi apartment. Nau de grls a gon dei on vei and selten visit hr. Dei raid de leter, baing a krismos present det she never jus enivei, bad dei dont visit. Et frst she vos visiting hr doters evri jer, bad vit taim it vos tu stresfol for her. Van kold dei she slip keriing de groseris and brok hr lek and for mants she vos kept in hospital. Ven dei giv hr faineli promishen tu go she mas hev a ples in old pipel hom. It vos nju ekspirienc, bad tu fel an hr doters beg she diden vanet. Sun after hr kidnis giv evei and shi vos akcheli hepi tu bi hir.

"Misis Meri... Misis Meri. Dei ol sliping oredi," sed de nait nurs. "A ju filing vel? Brrrr, autsaid is snoing. After ol vi mei hev a vait krismos."

Their five-year-old son died battling a high fever. She was working, supporting the family and his drinking. They'd already taken their son to the cemetery when Earl showed up. When the two older girls told him what had happened in this time he simply disappeared. Since then she heard only one bit of news about him. Earl was caught by police for some murder that he or some of his phoney friends did.

So, alone with two girls, she moved west. It was not easy, but they managed for the first time to have a steady apartment. Now the girls are gone their own way and seldom visit her. They write letters, buy a Christmas present that she never uses anyway, but they don't visit. At first she visited her daughters every year, but with time it was too stressful for her. One cold day she slipped carrying the groceries and broke her leg and for months she was kept in hospital. When they finally gave her permission to go, she had to find a place in an old people's home. It was a new experience, but she didn't want to fall begging on her daughters. Soon after, her kidneys gave out and she was actually happy to be there.

"Mrs. Marie... Mrs. Marie. They're all sleeping already," said the night nurse. "Are you feeling well? Brr, it's snowing outside. We may have a white Christmas after all."

Marijan Megla

"O jes. I am sori,... I fol tu slip. Ju no in old eg, is onli det vot is left. Driming," sed de old vumen voking sloli vit de jang nurs tu vords hr rum.

After de nurs help hr tu de bet, Meri kuden slip for a vail. Snoing ... det sailend chenching of de necher. In hr laif she vos engoin de sno fol onli laik a lital grl. Leter in laif det sno brodet onli hediks. Hau tu bai shus for kidc, vorm klos, vot tu bai krismos if ju dont hev a daim tu spend. It is interesting det krismos she filt for frst taim egen sev. Is det bikos shi faundet de Lio? Hmm, he dont iven ker ebaut hr.

She remember det ivning shi van tu visit hr nju gofren. Voking in des flor, she samhau mis de namber of a rum and endet in konplitli streng rum. An de teibel vos det pikchers, and shi spotet de Lio and her self. De seim old pikcher det shi so meni taim voch. Et frst she kuden belivet, bad ven she faineli sed det tu old fetfol Agnes dei cheket vans egen. After det she njuet for shor det she faund de Lio.

It vos tri dei befor krismos. Hol juvel hom glenct vit nju shain. An evri flor vos a krismos tri, and kuk van tu inpres

⊚⊚⊚⊚⊚⊚⊚⊚⊚⊚⊚⊚⊚⊚⊚⊚⊚⊚⊚⊚⊚⊚⊚⊚⊚⊚⊚⊚⊚⊚⊚⊚⊚⊚⊚⊚⊚

"Oh yes. I am sorry,... I fell asleep. You know in this old age it's all that's left, dreaming," said the old woman, walking slowly with the young nurse towards her room.

After the nurse helped her to bed, Marie couldn't sleep for a while. Snowing ... that silent changing of nature. In her life she only enjoyed the snowfall as a little girl. Later in life the snow only brought headaches. How to buy shoes for the kids, warm clothes, what to buy for Christmas if you don't have a dime to spend? It is interesting that this Christmas she felt safe again for the first time. Is that because she found Leo? Hmmm, he doesn't even care about her.

She remembered the evening that she wanted to visit her new girlfriend. Walking on this floor she somehow missed the room number and ended in a completely strange room. On the table were those pictures, and she spotted Leo and herself. The same old picture that she'd looked at so many times. At first she couldn't believe it, but when she finally mentioned it to old faithful Agnes they checked once again. After that she knew for sure she'd found Leo.

It was three days before Christmas. The whole old folks' home gleamed with new shine. On every floor was a Christmas tree, and cook wanted to impress

⊚⊚⊚⊚⊚⊚⊚⊚⊚⊚⊚⊚⊚⊚⊚⊚⊚⊚⊚⊚⊚⊚⊚⊚⊚⊚⊚⊚⊚⊚⊚⊚⊚⊚⊚⊚

evribadi vit his fantastik dishes. Hmm, krismos vans egen. Iven de fon kols of her bot doters kud meked des krismos hepier. Krismos hes in hr laif teking mining of lonlinis, anferfilt drims. Hepinis? Hmmmm. Des hepen tu enibadi als, bad not tu her.

She diden fil tu gud des ivning after lanch. It vos denc daun in de beisment, bad she prefer bi left alon. Dos jang volunters mek hr skeri and dei denc so fest. Lio? No. Hi nju det she vos filing bed bad hi never sho ab tu ask hr "Hau ju duing?" She dont akspekt mach, a sinpel kart for krismas bi inaf for hr. Hi kud kam endlis and sei Meri Krismas Meri. Luking an kvaet neiberhud vich hausis glenct in shain of kolorfol bolbs shi dos in.

"Misis Meri... Misis Meri. A ju going for denc?" asking de Agnes, noking an hr dor. "It bi rili nais if ju kud go."

"I tenk I ste hir. In mai rum."

"Misis Meri, I tenk ju rong des taim. Lio is oredi der. In his best shrt, penc. He iven chench his blesed anderver. Dont put him nau daun," sed de Agnes voking aut from de rum.

⊙⊙⊙⊙⊙⊙⊙⊙⊙⊙⊙⊙⊙⊙⊙⊙⊙⊙⊙⊙⊙⊙⊙⊙⊙⊙⊙⊙⊙⊙⊙⊙

everybody with his fantastic dishes. Hmmm, Christmas once again. Even the phone calls from both her daughters couldn't make this Christmas happier. Christmas had taken the meaning in her life of loneliness and unfulfilled dreams. Happiness? Hmmm. That happens to anybody else, but not to her.

She didn't feel too good this evening after lunch. There was the dance down in the basement but she preferred to be left alone. Those young volunteers made her scared, and they danced so fast. Leo? No. He knew that she was feeling bad but he never showed up to ask "How are you doing?" She didn't expect much, a simple card for Christmas would be enough for her. He could at least come and say Merry Christmas Marie. Looking onto the quiet neighbourhood whose houses gleamed in the shine of coloured bulbs, she dozed off.

"Mrs. Marie... Mrs. Marie. Are you going to the dance?" asked Agnes, knocking on her door. "It'll be really nice if you could go."

"I think I'll stay here. In my room."

"Mrs. Marie, I think you're wrong this time. Leo is already there. In his best shirt and pants. He even changed his blessed underwear. Don't put him down now," Agnes said, walking out of the room.

⊙⊙⊙⊙⊙⊙⊙⊙⊙⊙⊙⊙⊙⊙⊙⊙⊙⊙⊙⊙⊙⊙⊙⊙⊙⊙⊙⊙⊙⊙⊙⊙⊙

"Meri krismos Meri!" shaut she from de dor.

Meri kam let tu de denc. Ol aders or dencing or singing. Anshor vot tu du, shi veidet for a moment an de entrenc dor of a hjuch hol. De Lio vos siting in de mens korner. He dos in holding an dos tri rosis det olmost slipt aut aut his hend. His best shrt vos skvosht and pingvin aut a level. She kroset de hol and vos hepi tu si emti cher, if hr fit shud koleps.

"Kan I hev des volc Lio?" ask she skeri.

Hi open his ais. Sopreist, he olmost drop de flauers. Den hi stud ab, vit hr help.

"Srtenli Meri. Gast giv mi taim tu fiks mai self," sed hi giving hr hr roses.

ⓔⓔⓔⓔⓔⓔⓔⓔⓔⓔⓔⓔⓔⓔⓔⓔⓔⓔⓔⓔⓔⓔⓔⓔⓔⓔⓔⓔⓔⓔⓔⓔⓔⓔⓔⓔⓔ

"Merry Christmas Marie," she shouted from the door.

Marie came late to the dance. All the others were dancing or singing. Unsure what to do, she waited for a moment at the entrance of the huge hall. Leo was sitting in the men's corner. He was dozing, holding onto those three roses that almost slipped out of his hand. His best shirt was squashed and the penguin tie off-level. She crossed the hall and was happy to see an empty chair, in case her feet collapsed.

"Can I have this waltz, Leo?" she asked, frightened.

He opened his eyes. Surprised, he almost dropped the flowers.

Then he stood up, with her help.

"Certainly Marie. Just give me time to fix myself," he said, giving her her roses.

ⓔⓔⓔⓔⓔⓔⓔⓔⓔⓔⓔⓔⓔⓔⓔⓔⓔⓔⓔⓔⓔⓔⓔⓔⓔⓔⓔⓔⓔⓔⓔⓔⓔⓔⓔ

Vajolin

Sick of the same old bedtime reading? Looking for a challenge? Well, look no further. Slipstream Books publishes on the edge: the far boundaries of form and of content.

If you liked *VAJOLIN*, try these other fine Slipstream books:

My Tongue All Thumbs by Gerry Dotto

ISBN: 1-895836-47-6 **$17.95**

Talented and seriously weird, Gerry Dotto is both artist and writer, and the mixture of visual impact and idiosyncratic content makes *My Tongue All thumbs* unique, funny, thoughtful and very strange. Dotto's gonzo combination of poetry and graphic art has reached audiences in Canada, the US, Europe and the Orient through touring exhibitions, multi-media shows, and periodicals. Now available in this classy edition with two colours throughout.

The Edmonton Queen: not a riverboat story by Darrin Hagen

ISBN: 1-895836-46-8 **$15.95**

Darrin Hagen's meteoric and award-winning career has crossed over intotheatre, music, media and film, but this is where he began: as one of Edmonton's most notorious drag queens. His autobiographical one-queen show was a sold-out hit of the Edmonton Fringe Theatre Festival, winning Best New Fringe Play at the Stirling Awards. Now the tell-all script has been expanded to a book-length expose of the life and times of a decade of drag. First printing sold out.

Neurotic Erotica by Timothy J. Anderson

ISBN: 1-895836-18-2 **$15.95**

Is poetry necessarily an expression of personal truth? Or can it be a series of fictions and fantasies in search of a greater truth? In this provocative examination of human sexual behaviour, Timothy J. Anderson invites readers to share a dialogue about what is normal and what is neurotic in the ways humans express their sexuality. Anderson is an award-winning playwright, an actor who has worked in national and international productions including *Phantom of the Opera*, a classical and opera singer, a composer, a librettist, and a published short story writer. Foreword by Dr. Robyn Mott. Cover art by internationally renowned Polaroid artist Evergon. Cover design by Gerry Dotto.

Or try these other books from our parent imprint, River Books:

Coppernob by George Wing   1-895836-20-4 $15.95

Relationship intrigue among the expat community of Ramakhan in the aftermath of World War II. Author George Wing travelled, lived and taught in the places he writes about in his novel, including this award-winning novel.

Fruitbodies by Mary Woodbury   1-895836-17-4 $15.95

Brilliant, emotive writing about older women and work, creativity and sexuality. Aired on CBC radio, the work proviked more requests for copies than any other piece in the history of the programme! Now in book form, with illustrations by Kendra McCleskey.

Leaving Marks by Candas Jane Dorsey   1-895836-00-X $10.95

A love affair/with words. The poet marks the sensual progress of a love affair—and remarks on the process of writing about love—with a lyric eroticism which is both intense and original. Cover and interior photographs by Sima Khorrami.

Llamas in the Snow by Cullene Bryant   1-895836-04-2 $12.95

Short stories by a United Church minister, single mother and former hospital chaplain about human ssues: spiritual health, relationships in crisis, and the confrontation between life and death. First printing sold out.

Order from your favourite bookstore through The Literary Press Group/General Publishing (via Coteau catalogue) in Canada, or mail order from anywhere in the world directly from **Slipstream Books, 214-21 10405 Jasper Avenue, Edmonton, AB Canada, T5J 3S2.** Canadians add 7% GST, US residents pay in US dollars. Add $3 each for shipping. Write or e-mail us at tesseract@istream.com for a complete list of over 40 Books Collective titles from our four imprints.